HOW THE
Gifted
Brain Learns

Use what talent you possess:
the woods would be very silent
if no birds sang
except those that sang best.

— Henry Van Dyke

HOW THE
Gifted
Brain Learns

David A. Sousa

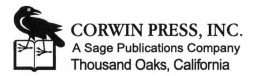
CORWIN PRESS, INC.
A Sage Publications Company
Thousand Oaks, California

For information:

Corwin Press, Inc.
A Sage Publications Company
2455 Teller Road
Thousand Oaks, California 91320
www.corwinpress.com

Sage Publications Ltd.
6 Bonhill Street
London EC2A 4PU
United Kingdom

Sage Publications India Pvt. Ltd.
M-32 Market
Greater Kailash I
New Delhi 110 048 India

Printed in the United States of America

Library of Congress Cataloging-in-Publication Data

Sousa, David A.
  How the gifted brain learns / David A. Sousa.
    p. cm.
  Includes bibliographical references (p.) and index.
  ISBN 0-7619-3828-1 (pbk. :alk. paper)—ISBN 0-7619-3829-X (cloth : alk. paper)
    1. Gifted children—Education—United States. 2. Gifted children—United
States—Identification. 3. Brain—Localization of functions. I. Title.

LC3993.9 .S68 2002

                              2002031375

This book is printed on acid-free paper.

02 03 04 05 06 07 6 5 4 3 2 1

Acquiring Editor: Kylee Liegl
Cover Designer: Tracy E. Miller

Contents

LIST OF APPLICATIONS

About the Author

David A. Sousa, Ed.D., is an international educational consultant. He has made presentations at national conventions of educational organizations and has conducted workshops on brain research and science education in hundreds of school districts and at several colleges and universities across the United States, Canada, Europe, and Asia.

Dr. Sousa has a bachelor's degree in chemistry from Massachusetts State College at Bridgewater, a master of arts in teaching degree in science from Harvard University, and a doctorate from Rutgers University. His teaching experience covers all levels. He has taught junior and senior high school science, served as a K–12 director of science, and was Supervisor of Instruction for the West Orange, New Jersey, schools. He then became superintendent of the New Providence, New Jersey, public schools. He has been an adjunct professor of education at Seton Hall University, and a visiting lecturer at Rutgers University. He was president of the National Staff Development Council in 1992.

Dr. Sousa has edited science books and published numerous articles in leading educational journals on staff development, science education, and brain research. He is listed in *Who's Who in the East* and *Who's Who in American Education* and has received awards from professional associations and school districts for his commitment and contributions to research, staff development, and science education.

He has been interviewed on the NBC *Today* show and on National Public Radio about his work with schools using brain research. He makes his home in Florida.

**CORWIN
PRESS**

The Corwin Press logo—a raven striding across an open book—represents the happy union of courage and learning. We are a professional-level publisher of books and journals for K-12 educators, and we are committed to creating and providing resources that embody these qualities. Corwin's motto is "Success for All Learners."

Introduction

This book was inevitable. My first book, *How the Brain Learns* (Second Edition), was intended to explore the nature of teaching and learning for the majority of mainstream students. The second book, *How the Special Needs Brain Learns*, was written to help parents and educators understand what we are discovering about students who have learning difficulties. This book is designed to examine the needs of gifted and talented students, to uncover what—if anything—we are learning about the gifted brain, and to suggest strategies and programs that can help our best and brightest students achieve their full potential.

Classroom teachers, education specialists, school and district administrators, college instructors, and parents should all find items of interest in *How the Gifted Brain Learns*. Although many books have been written about the gifted, this book focuses primarily on insights to be gained about the gifted brain from the current explosion of research in neuroscience. It also reviews research information about the gifted learner for prospective and current teachers and administrators so that they may consider alternative instructional approaches.

WHAT DO WE MEAN BY *GIFTED AND TALENTED*? ■

Many terms are used to describe the student who demonstrates exceptional talent, and sometimes these terms themselves become a challenge to understand. *Gifted* is the most commonly used word, but it has hundreds of definitions, from legal to jargon. *Talented* usually describes an individual with a performance skill that has been refined through practice, such as music or dance. *Precocious* and *prodigy* are most commonly used to describe young children who display a high level of skill in a particular endeavor at a very early age.

In earlier times, *genius* was widely used, but it is now limited to the phenomenally gifted. *Superior* has recently come into vogue. Being a comparative term, it tempts one to ask superior to whom or to what, and to what degree. The vagueness of the term limits its usefulness in helping educators design an educational program for an individual student. *Exceptional* is an appropriate term when referring to a gifted child as being different from the regular school population, although it is also used to describe children with learning difficulties.

During the 1970s, the combined term *gifted and talented* came into common use. Although *gifted* and *talented* are often used interchangeably, Gagne (1985) differentiated between the two terms. For Gagne, *giftedness* is above-average aptitude (as measured by IQ tests) in creative and intellectual abilities, and *talent* is above-average performance in an area of human activity, such as music, mathematics, or literature.

In recent years, most researchers have moved away from defining *giftedness* solely in terms of IQ tests and have broadened its usage to include the characteristics of giftedness, such as creativity and motivation. Some definitions also consider the person's contributions to culture and society. People from diverse cultural and ethnic backgrounds may display their gifts and talents in ways that are recognized and valued by their own culture, but these individuals may not be recognized or valued by other cultures. A review of the literature on the characteristics of gifted and talented children from across different ethnic groups found some common indicators (e.g., problem-solving ability, intense interest, and motivation) but also found that each ethnicity had distinct and unique behavioral attributes (Frasier and Passow, 1994). As a result, one of the greater concerns in the field of gifted education is the realization that gifted children from diverse cultural backgrounds, or who have some type of learning disability, will not be recognized as gifted in our schools.

Given the various interpretations of the terminology used to describe students of high ability, I had to decide on a working definition that would be meaningful for all readers. For the purposes of this book, then, I use the term *gifted* to be an inclusive one in that it comprises high intellectual ability in academic areas as well as high levels of ability in areas of performance, such as music, theater, and dance. My simple definition is that a gifted person demonstrates (or

> **For the purposes of this book, a gifted person is defined as one who demonstrates an exceptionally high level of performance in one or more areas of human endeavor.**

has the potential for demonstrating) an exceptionally high level of performance in one or more areas of human endeavor. Not all readers may agree with this definition, and some may object that using it as an inclusive term de-emphasizes the importance of talent. That is certainly not my intent, which I think will become clear as one reads the book. However, to avoid any misinterpretation, and because the combined term is so widespread, many references to *gifted and talented* will be found in the text.

Myths and Realities About Giftedness

Myths abound about the nature of giftedness, largely because public schools have not really had the resources to fully and accurately identify the gifted and to understand their needs. A prevailing notion for many years in public education has been that these students can take care of themselves and learn a great deal on their own. Consequently, schools have concentrated on providing a broad curriculum for mainstream students and then devoting a significant portion of remaining resources to students with learning difficulties. Little has been left over to identify or support the gifted, despite federal and state mandates to do so.

We are slowly gaining a greater understanding of the idiosyncracies of gifted children and the implications for parenting and teaching them. But to be successful at this, we must dispel the myths and look to credible research about the realities of being gifted and talented. The following list (Winner, 1996; Gentry and Kettle, 1998) summarizes some myths and realities regarding gifted children. Several of the topics are discussed in greater detail throughout the book.

Myth #1: Little is really known about how we learn. So how can we know about the gifted brain?	**Reality:** Research is providing a deeper understanding of how the human brain learns, including insights into the phenomenally gifted brain. See Chapters 1 and 2.
Myth #2: Academically gifted students have general intellectual power that makes them gifted in all areas.	**Reality:** Giftedness tends to be specific to a given domain of learning. Children can be gifted in one area and learning disabled in another. See Chapter 8.
Myth #3: *Gifted* refers just to academic ability, but *talented* refers to high ability in music and the arts.	**Reality:** There is no justification for this distinction. The domains of excellence are merely different, and in many cases the words can be used interchangeably. See Chapter 2.

Myth #4: Gifted students have lower self-esteem than nongifted students.

Reality: The majority of studies indicate that gifted students have a somewhat higher level of self-esteem than nongifted. However, they are at risk for isolation and loneliness, and they can become arrogant. See Chapters 2 and 7.

Myth #5: Giftedness in any domain requires a high IQ.

Reality: There is little evidence that giftedness in music or art requires an exceptional IQ. Moreover, IQ tests measure a narrow range of ability. See Chapters 2 and 6.

Myth #6: Acceleration options, such as grade skipping, early entrance, and early exit, tend to be harmful for gifted students.

Reality: Although it is important to consider the social and psychological adjustment of every student, there is little evidence that acceleration options are in any way detrimental. See Chapter 3.

Myth #7: Cooperative learning in heterogeneous groups provides academic benefits to gifted students and can be effectively substituted for specialized programs for academically talented students.

Reality: Recent studies show that gifted students receive greater academic benefit from being grouped with other gifted students, and that cooperative learning is not an effective replacement for specialized programs for academically talented students, such as new courses or acceleration options. See Chapter 3.

Myth #8: Giftedness is inborn, or giftedness is entirely the result of hard work.

Reality: True giftedness results from both genetic predispositions *and* hard work. See Chapter 2.

Myth #9: Creativity tests are effective means of identifying artistically gifted and talented students.

Reality: Creativity tests measure problem-solving and divergent thinking skills, but have not proved valid in predicting the success of students with high abilities in the visual arts. See Chapters 2, 6, and 9.

Myth #10: Pushy parents who drive their children to overachieve create gifted children.

Reality: Gifted children are usually pushing their parents, who are trying to accommodate and nurture them. However, some parents do try to live vicariously through their children and lose sight of the child's emotional well-being. See Chapters 3 and 7.

Myth #11: Early reading and writing skills should keep pace with each other.

Reality: Although this is a commonly held belief, there is no relationship between reading and writing skills in the development of young talented children. See Chapters 4 and 8.

Myth #12: All children are gifted, and there is no special group of children that needs enriched or accelerated education.

Reality: Although all children have strengths and weaknesses, some have extreme strengths in one or more areas. Extreme giftedness creates a special education need the same way that a learning disability does. See Chapters 3 and 8.

Myth #13: Highly gifted children go on to become eminent and creative adults.

Reality: Many gifted children, even prodigies, do not become eminent in adulthood, and many eminent adults were not prodigies. See Chapters 3, 5, 6, and 8.

GIFTED AND TALENTED PROGRAMS IN TODAY'S SCHOOLS ■

Because some parents and educators believe that truly gifted children will remain gifted and fulfill their educational needs on their own, schools have historically done little to identify and encourage the gifted. As a result, potentially gifted students have gone through school without their gifts ever being recognized. This has been a long-standing problem as history will attest. Sir Isaac Newton was considered a poor student in grammar school; he left at age 14, was sent back at 19 because he read so much, and graduated at Cambridge without any distinction whatsoever. The poet Shelley was expelled from Oxford; James Whistler and Edgar Allen Poe were both expelled from West Point. Charles Darwin dropped out of medical school, and Edward Gibbon, the noted British historian, considered his education a waste of time.

Gregor Mendel, founder of the science of genetics, flunked his teacher's examination four times in a row and finally gave up trying. Thomas Edison's mother withdrew him from school after 3 months in the 1st grade because his teacher said he was "unable to perform." Winston Churchill ended up last in his class at the Harrow School. Albert Einstein found grammar school boring. It was his uncle, showing the boy tricks with numbers, who stimulated his interest in mathematics. For a long time and in many places, traditional academic programs have often been poorly suited to humans of extraordinary potential. One is left to wonder how many Edisons did not survive their educational experiences.

> **Our society has not given the same attention to the education of the gifted as it has given to other special groups.**

Our society has not given the same attention to the education of the gifted as it has given to other special groups. For example, we spend millions every year for the mentally handicapped. But, too often, children of superior intellect spend their time in a commonplace school, assimilating a curricular diet far below their potential. Thus, gifted children pose one of our greatest present-day problems, beginning in the home and ultimately becoming a concern of the school. Teachers at all grade levels bear the responsibility to recognize and plan for the needs of the gifted.

Currently, the process of identifying gifted students and the programs designed to address their needs vary greatly by grade level and school district. Gifted students who are not identified and served by these programs are not likely to ever have their needs fully met while in school. The loss of such potential is a serious blow to society as well as to the student and teacher. The student never feels fulfilled, loses self-esteem, and lacks direction. The teacher, meanwhile, is faced with student boredom, underachievement, and a litany of discipline problems that could have been avoided. One purpose of this book is to examine the current state of programs for the gifted and to suggest what we might do to make them better serve the gifts and talents of all students.

Programs in Elementary and Middle Schools

Identification and Teacher Bias

Identification of gifted students begins in elementary school. Students who get high scores (usually the 95th percentile or greater) on standardized achievement tests are referred by teachers as potential candidates for the gifted program. Acceptance into the program is typically made on the basis of several factors, but teacher recommendations tend to carry a lot of weight during final selections. Much debate has occurred about whether classroom teachers are qualified to identify gifted students. Some researchers argue that teacher biases related to differences in performance between male and female students, and other stereotypic beliefs, undermine the reliability and objectivity of their judgments.

A recent study to test the nature of teacher bias found that gender stereotypes and other biases still exist (Powell and Siegle, 2000). For example, classroom teachers rated males who were avid readers higher than similar females. Even males who were not interested in reading were rated higher than non-interested females. Introverted, absent-minded females were nominated with less confidence than males who also had these characteristics.

> **A recent study found that gender stereotypes and other biases still exist in teachers.**

The study also found that students who were interested in topics unusual for their age, such as airplane design and flying, were more likely to be nominated than students interested in dinosaurs, a topic of interest for most elementary students. Meanwhile, gifted and talented specialists tended to rate students higher than did classroom teachers because, as the researchers suggested, these specialists tend to focus more on student strengths. Classroom teachers, on the other hand, often have to diagnose and prescribe and this, according to the researchers, may cause them to be more sensitive to student weaknesses. In any event, a major implication of this study is that classroom teachers probably need more training to recognize any stereotypical beliefs they may hold about the nature of gifted and talented students.

The Pull-Out Format

Elementary and middle school programs for gifted students usually follow a pull-out format in which these students meet once or twice a week to engage in problem-based learning activities or other similar experiences. Rarely is there any planned scope or sequence to the curricular activities, and little or nothing is shared when the students return to their regular classes. Research studies reveal that gifted students gain little to modest benefit from these types of classes, and that they would probably gain the same benefits if they carried out these activities in their regular classes. Undoubtedly, the pull-out format results in missed opportunities for gifted students as well as for the remaining students in the class. This book suggests some other ways to configure programs and design curriculum for gifted students at these grade levels that can result in greater achievement.

Programs in High Schools

The common belief in high schools is that honors and advanced placement-type courses are sufficient to meet the needs of gifted and talented students. Some schools also offer mentoring programs or have dual enrollment agreements with local colleges. A recent study from the National Research Center on the Gifted and Talented (NRC/GT) reported on the nature of programs for gifted high school students. Surveys were mailed to nearly 8,000 randomly selected high schools in all 50 states. Of that sample, 546 high schools responded. The following are some of the survey's findings:

- Nearly 66 percent of the respondents said they had a gifted education program at their high school and 34 percent reported that no such program existed. However, the surveys revealed that there was a great deal of overlap between what was offered in the schools claiming they *did not* have a gifted program and in the schools claiming they *did* have one. Apparently, there was a lack of understanding about what kind of program constituted gifted education at the high school level.
- About 50 percent of the schools reported having opportunities beyond academic courses for gifted students, e.g., internships/mentorships, early college programs, independent study, and academic clubs or competitions.
- Nearly all respondents offered advanced placement courses; the most common were English, calculus AB, biology, and US history.
- Approximately 50 percent of the schools had a consultant or coordinator associated with these programs, some serving only in a part-time capacity.

More attention needs to be given to clarifying what constitutes a comprehensive and effective gifted program at the high school level and to what other steps high schools can take to ensure a broad and rich variety of educational experiences for their most gifted students.

■ ORGANIZATION OF THIS BOOK

Basic brain structures and their functions are the main topics in Chapter 1. This information serves as a useful resource for identifying brain regions that are referenced in other chapters. Learning, the stages and types of memory, and retention are also reviewed.

Chapter 2 looks at various conceptual schemes (e.g., psychological, socio-emotional) that attempt to define the nature of intelligence and giftedness. Of particular interest is the discussion over the long-standing debate about whether nature (i.e., genetic programming) or nurture (i.e., environment and upbringing) has greater impact on talent development. Gender differences in cognitive styles are discussed along with some differences in brain structure and brain chemistry.

In Chapter 3, we examine specific suggestions for designing curricular and instructional strategies that are more likely to challenge the gifted brain. Because many teachers are faced with addressing the needs of gifted students within the context of the inclusive classroom, this chapter focuses on the concept of differentiated curriculum. Also discussed are acceleration, curriculum compacting, grouping formats, and other techniques that have been successful in developing the talents of gifted students.

Chapters 4, 5, and 6 deal with attempts to understand the nature of giftedness in three specific areas: language, mathematics, and music, respectively. As scientific evidence accumulated over the last few decades suggesting that the human brain is hard-wired for language, mathematics, and music, research resources were directed toward investigating the cerebral nature of these activities. Consequently, we include these areas because they currently have the largest base of research studies among all the school disciplines. Furthermore, there is little evidence at this time to indicate that the brain is specifically wired for science, economics, or history. According to current thinking, it is more likely that high ability in these areas results from high ability in one or more of the hard-wired areas (e.g., mathematics for science, and language for history) coupled with intense personal interest in, say, scientific phenomena or historical events.

Chapter 7 investigates the various symptoms, causes, and types of underachievement in gifted students. A somewhat overlooked area of gifted education, this chapter presents ways of identifying these students and suggests strategies for reversing underachievement. Particular attention is paid to the growing number of underachieving minority students and to ways for addressing their needs.

Although the notion that a person can be both gifted and learning disabled may seem strange, Chapter 8 examines the twice-exceptional student. Some of the more common combinations of giftedness and learning disabilities are discussed—gifted children with attention-deficit hyperactivity disorder, for example—as well as rare phenomena, such as savant syndrome.

Finally, Chapter 9 suggests some ways of identifying gifted children and setting up a learning environment where gifted students, along with their classmates, can excel in the inclusive classroom. The effectiveness of current programs to aid gifted students in elementary and secondary schools is also discussed.

Other Features of the Book

At the end of most chapters, a section called **Applications** includes activities reflecting my interpretation of how research might translate into effective classroom strategies. Obviously, some of the strategies are appropriate for all learners; however, the suggestions have been written specifically to address the needs of gifted students. Even though this book does not present every strategy for teaching gifted students, those that best match the research information in the corresponding chapters are mentioned. Readers are invited to critically review my suggestions and rationale to determine if these ideas have any value for their work.

The book will help answer the following questions:

- How different are the brains of gifted students?
- What kinds of strategies are particularly effective for students with specific gifts?
- What progress is brain research making in discovering the nature of intelligence and giftedness?
- Will brain research help us identify potentially gifted students sooner and more accurately?
- Are schools adequately challenging gifted students today? If not, what can we do about it?
- How can improving programs for the gifted and talented benefit other students?
- What insights are we gaining about students who are gifted in language, mathematics, and music?
- What can we do to identify and help gifted students who are underachievers?
- How can we identify students who are both gifted and learning disabled, and how can we help them?

Some of the information and suggestions you will find here came from advocacy organizations including the National Association for Gifted Children and the National Research Center on the Gifted and Talented (see **Resources**). Where possible, I have sought out original medical research reports, which are noted in the **References**. A few of the strategies are derived or adapted from the second edition of my book, *How the Brain Learns* (2001).

> As we gain a greater understanding of the human brain, we may discover ways to identify gifted students sooner and more accurately.

As we gain a greater understanding of the human brain, we may discover ways to identify gifted students more quickly and more accurately. This means that schools can begin to provide for student needs earlier and with greater effectiveness. Sometimes, these students are attempting to learn in environments that are designed to help but instead inadvertently frustrate their efforts. By looking for ways to differentiate the curriculum and by changing some of our instructional approaches, we may be able to move gifted students to exceptional levels of performance. My hope is that this book will encourage all school professionals and parents to learn more about how the brain learns so that they can work together for the benefit of all students.

A WORD ABOUT ELITISM ■

Some parents, educators, and politicians object to any special programs for gifted children on the grounds of elitism. This word has acquired the negative connotations of snobbishness, selectivity, and unfair special attention at a time, critics say, when we should be emphasizing egalitarianism. The reality is that gifted students are elite in the sense that they possess skills to a higher degree than most people in their class. The same is true for professional athletes, musical soloists, inventors, or physicians. Parents and schools must provide children with equal opportunity, not equal treatment. Treating all students as though they learned exactly the same way is folly. Therefore, schools have a responsibility to challenge gifted students to their fullest potential while, at the same time, challenging those who cry elitism to rethink the true meaning of the word and the real purpose of education.

1

Brain Structure and Learning

No other known entity in the universe is as complicated and as fascinating as the human brain. This three-pound mass of hundreds of billions of nerve cells is intricately organized to control our feelings, behavior, and thoughts. It collects and sorts information, learns complex skills, masters spoken language, stores the memories of a lifetime, and contains the secret of ourselves. For centuries, scientists have been attempting to understand exactly how the brain grows and develops into this amazing organ.

Until recently, their efforts where thwarted by the reality that the brain could be examined only in autopsy. Microscopic and macroscopic sections of brain tissue gave clues about structure but not function. Today, however, brain imaging technologies have given neuroscientists powerful new tools to look at brain structure *and* function in living persons. Computerized tomography (CT scans, also called CAT scans), positron-emission tomography (PET scans), and magnetic resonance imaging (MRI) are especially helpful in deciphering the complex cerebral processes involved in language acquisition and reading.

In addition to the imaging techniques, advanced systems monitor and record the electrical signals (electroencephalography, or EEG) as well as the magnetic fields (magneto-encephalography, or MEG) that are produced when electrical impulses travel within the neurons. These recordings are valuable in localizing the source of signals originating in brain regions as small as one cubic millimeter of cerebral cortex and in timing any changes to the nearest thousandth of a second.

Imaging techniques offer different views of brain structure and function. Already, more advanced imaging technologies are providing innovative ways of studying the brain. Table 1.1 and Table 1.2 show the major imaging technologies and other techniques that allow us to examine the inner workings of the human brain (Beatty, 2001).

Table 1.1 Imaging Technologies for Examining Brain Structure and Function	
Name	**How It Works**
Computerized Tomography (CT)	First introduced in 1973, CT is an enhancement of X-rays that reconstructs an image of a horizontal slice of tissue. A large number of X-ray beams pass through the tissue at a variety of angles, and the amount of radiation absorbed is measured. This allows a computer to determine the density of tissue at each point and produce the image. CT scans show *structure*.
Positron Emission Tomography (PET)	Introduced in the early 1980s, this technology indicates brain *function* and tells us what the brain is doing rather than how it looks. To accomplish this, the patient is injected with glucose containing a radioactive nucleus that emits positrons. More active portions of the brain will metabolize more glucose and thereby concentrate more radioactivity than the less active areas. The radioactivity is detected by the scanner and an image is produced by a computer.
Magnetic Resonance Imaging (MRI)	Like CT, MRI provides images of *structure*; but, unlike CT, it does not use X-rays. MRI is non-invasive and is safe to use repeatedly on the same patient. The procedure uses a strong magnetic field and radio frequency energy to generate signals from atoms (usually hydrogen) within tissue. Images are compiled that have a much greater resolution than CT and that can be taken from any angle.
functional Magnetic Resonance Imaging (fMRI)	By detecting the minute changes in the magnetic properties of blood hemoglobin and oxygen, the fMRI can measure *function* as well as *structure*. Active neurons need more blood and so generate a signal in an fMRI scan. Unlike the PET, it is non-invasive and is thus used to measure brain function in healthy subjects.

Table 1.2 Other Technologies for Examining Brain Structure and Function	
Name	How It Works
Electroencephalography (EEG)	This technique dates back to the 1920s and involves measuring the electrical activity of neurons by attaching electrodes to the scalp. Because it is very difficult to determine which part of the brain is generating the signals, EEG is used mainly for examining general brain activity as in the sleep-wake cycle and during epileptic seizures.
Magnetoencephalography (MEG)	In a fashion similar to EEG, MEG measures the small magnetic fields generated by the electrical activity in neurons, but it can be more useful in localizing the source of the signals.
Brain Lesion Analysis	This procedure involves examining human brain tissue for lesions and determining whether a deficiency can be associated with the lesion. Researchers can also intentionally introduce lesions in the brains of laboratory animals and interpret the resulting behavioral changes.

BASIC BRAIN STRUCTURES ■

To understand the complexity of the human brain, we will first look at the major parts of the outside of the brain (Figure 1.1). Three major structures are visible: the cerebral hemispheres, the cerebellum, and the brain stem.

The Cerebral Hemispheres

The cerebral hemispheres comprise the largest part of the brain (about 85 percent by weight), called the *cerebrum*, and their surface is highly convoluted. The ridges of these convolutions are called *gyri* (singular is *gyrus*). This convoluted surface is covered with a laminated sheet of six layers of cells approximately two millimeters (about one-tenth of an inch) in thickness. The convolutions allow a great deal more of this laminated sheet (called the *cerebral cortex*) to be packed into the confines of the human skull. Although the minor wrinkles are unique in each brain, several major folds are common to all brains. In the largest part of the brain is a set of four lobes, each of which specializes in performing certain functions.

Four Cerebral Lobes

Frontal Lobe. Often referred to as the executive control center, the frontal lobe contains almost 50 percent of the volume of each cerebral hemisphere. It controls movement through a narrow strip across the top of the hemispheres called the *motor cortex*. The area at the very front of this lobe (i.e., just behind the forehead) is called the *prefrontal cortex*, which is believed to be the site of our personality, curiosity, decision making, and reflecting on the consequences of our actions. Curbing the excesses of our emotions is another of the prefrontal cortex's important functions. Because emotions drive attention, the efficiency of this area is linked to the limbic centers.

Most of the working memory is located in the frontal lobe, so this is the area where focus occurs. The frontal lobe, however, matures slowly. MRI studies of postadolescents reveal that the frontal lobe continues to mature into early adulthood. Thus, the emotional regulation capability of the frontal lobe is not fully operational during adolescence (Sowell, Thompson, Holmes, Jernigan, and Toga,

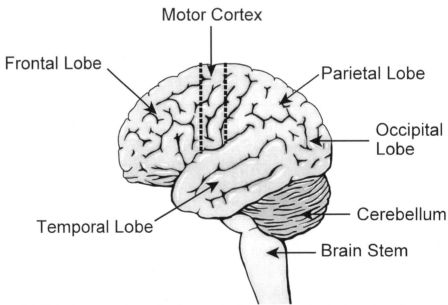

Figure 1.1 This diagram shows the four major lobes of the brain (cerebrum) as well as the motor cortex, the brain stem, and the cerebellum.

1999). This is one reason why adolescents are more likely than adults to submit to their emotions and resort to high-risk behavior.

Temporal Lobe. The temporal lobe is the speech center. It is involved in the interpretation of sound, speech (primarily on the left side), and some aspects of long-term and visual memory.

Occipital Lobe. Visual processing is the main function of the occipital lobe.

Parietal Lobe. The parietal lobe is primarily concerned with attending to stimuli, sensory integration, and orientation.

The Cerebellum

The cerebellum (Latin for "little brain") coordinates every movement. Because the cerebellum monitors impulses from nerve endings in the muscles, it is important in the learning, performance, and timing of complex motor tasks including speaking. The cerebellum may also store the memory of rote movements, such as touch-typing and tying a shoelace. A person whose cerebellum is damaged cannot coordinate movement, has difficulty with speech, and may display the symptoms of autism.

The Brain Stem

The oldest and deepest area of the brain, often referred to as the reptilian brain, the brain stem resembles the entire brain of a reptile. Here is where vital body functions (e.g., respiration, body temperature, blood pressure, and digestion) are monitored and controlled. The brain stem also houses the reticular activating system (RAS), which plays an active role in sleep, waking, and attention.

Next, we will look at the inside of the brain and at some of its major structures (see Figure 1.2). These include the limbic area and the cerebrum.

The Limbic Area

Above the brain stem lies the limbic area, most of whose structures are duplicated in each hemisphere of the brain. This area regulates fear conditioning and other aspects of emotional memory. Some parts of the limbic area process and interpret specific sensory information, but the three parts of the limbic area important to learning and memory are the following:

Thalamus. This structure is the brain's switching station. All incoming sensory information (except smell) goes first to the thalamus for preliminary

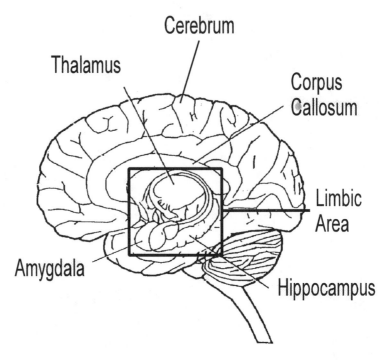

Figure 1.2 A cross section of the human brain.

processing and integration. From here it is directed to other parts of the brain for additional processing.

Hippocampus. Derived from the Greek word for a sea monster resembling a seahorse, because of its shape, the hippocampus hugs the inside of the temporal lobe. It plays a major role in consolidating learning and in converting information from working memory via electronic signals to the long-term storage regions, a process that may take from days to months. This brain area constantly checks information relayed to working memory and compares it to stored experiences. This process is essential for the creation of meaning.

Amygdala. Attached to the end of the hippocampus, the amygdala (Greek for "almond") plays an important role in emotional behavior, especially the fear response. It regulates those interactions that are necessary for the organism's survival, such as whether to fight or flee, to eat or not eat, and when to mate. Because of its proximity to the hippocampus and its activity on PET scans, researchers believe that the amygdala encodes an emotional message, if one is present, whenever an experience is destined for long-term storage. Apparently, these memories can even be established unconsciously (LeDoux, 2002). This explains why we tend to remember vividly the best and the worst things that happen to us.

The Cerebrum

The cerebrum encompasses the four lobes of the brain. For some still unexplained reason, the nerves from the left side of the body cross over to the right hemisphere, and those from the right side of the body cross over to the left hemisphere. The two hemispheres are connected by a thick cable, called the *corpus callosum*, composed of over 250 million nerve fibers. The hemispheres use this bridge to communicate with each other and to coordinate activities.

Brain Cells

The activities of the brain are carried out by signals traveling along brain cells. The brain is composed of a trillion cells of at least two known types: nerve cells and their support cells. Nerve cells are called *neurons* and represent about one tenth of the total number of cells—roughly 100 billion. Most of the cells are support cells, called *glial* (Greek for "glue") cells, that hold the neurons together and act as filters to keep harmful substances out of the neurons.

With few exceptions, all of the neurons in the human brain are produced before birth from a small number of precursor cells. During gestation, neurons are multiplying at an astonishing rate, reaching about 250,000 per minute at peak production (Restak, 2001). Neurons are the functioning core for the brain and the entire nervous system. They come in different sizes, but it takes about 30,000 brain neurons to fit on the head of a pin. Unlike other cells, the neuron (Figure 1.3) has

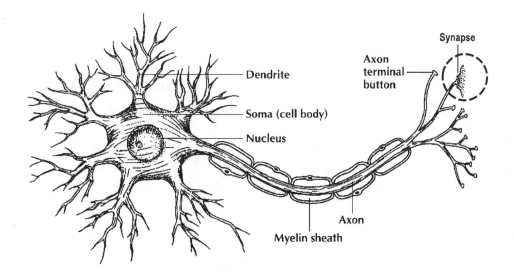

Figure 1.3 Neurons transmit impulses along an axon and across the synapse (in dotted circle) to the dendrites of a neighboring cell.

tens of thousands of branches or *dendrites* (from Greek for "tree") emerging from its center. The dendrites receive electrical impulses from other neurons and transmit them along a long fiber, called the *axon* (Greek for "axis"). Each neuron has a cell body (called the *soma*) and only one axon. Some axons are only a few millimeters in length and affect just nearby neurons. Other axons stretch over to the other side of the brain and influence neurons a considerable distance away.

Neurons have no direct contact with each other. Between each dendrite and axon is a small gap of about a millionth of an inch called a *synapse* (from Greek for "to join together"). This system allows for maximum flexibility. Because the neurons are not physically tied to each other, neuron-to-neuron interactions can form, reform, and dissolve from one moment to the next. This flexibility accounts for the brain's *plasticity* and explains why learning occurs during our entire lifetime.

Signals generated within neurons are electrical, but communication between neurons is chemical. A typical neuron collects signals from others through the dendrites. The neuron sends out spikes of electrical activity (impulses) through the axon to the synapse where the activity releases chemicals stored in sacs (called *synaptic vesicles*) at the end of the axon. The chemicals, called *neurotransmitters*, travel across the *synaptic gap* to a *receptor site* and either excite or inhibit the neighboring neuron (see Figure 1.4). Nearly 100 different neurotransmitters have been discovered so far. Some of the more common neurotransmitters are dopamine, glutamate, acetylcholine, epinephrine, and serotonin. Some neurotransmitters, such as glutamate, are found everywhere in the brain but others, like dopamine, are restricted to certain regions.

Electrical transmission can be exceedingly slow in brain cells. During early brain development, a layer called the *myelin* (related to the Greek word for marrow) *sheath* surrounds each axon. As the amount of electrical activity through a neuron increases, more myelin is produced, so the thickness of the sheath increases—a process called *myelination*. MRI scans confirm that myelination is carried out at a staggering rate during childhood (Blanton, Levitt, Thompson, Narr,

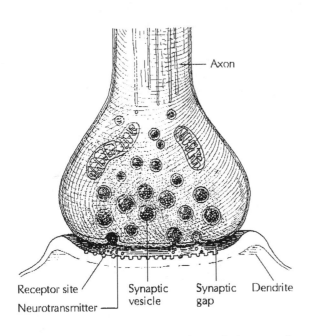

Figure 1.4 The neural impulse is carried across the synapse by chemicals called neurotransmitters that lie within the synaptic vesicles.

Axon

Receptor site

Neurotransmitter

Synaptic vesicle

Synaptic gap

Dendrite

Capetillo-Cunliffe, Nobel, Singerman, McCracken, and Toga, 2001). The sheath insulates the axon from other cells and increases the speed of impulse transmission. The impulse travels along the neurons through an electrochemical process and can move the entire length of a 6-foot adult in two tenths of a second. A neuron can transmit between 250 and 2,500 impulses per second.

The presence or absence of myelin around neurons may be the main determinant of their fate during early brain development. Newborns have many more neurons than they need, and after the first 3 years or so after birth, the brain begins to eliminate those neurons that have little myelination, thus indicating little use. This pruning process—called *apoptosis*—ensures that the remaining neural networks can function more efficiently.

Brain Size and Intelligence

The idea that a relationship exists between brain or head size and intelligence has long been the subject of controversy. Popular in the 19th century, the concept seemed to make sense: the more brain, the more intelligence. Although early 20th-century biologists ridiculed the idea, modern brain imaging studies show a small positive correlation between brain volume and intelligence. A more specific study was carried out by Paul Thompson and his colleagues (Thompson, et al., 2001). Using MRI, they scanned the brains of 20 pairs of identical and fraternal twins. The researchers gave the subjects intelligence tests and found that intelligence as measured by these tests was significantly linked with the amount of brain matter in the frontal lobes.

> **Recent studies show a link between intelligence and the size of some regions of the brain.**

Thompson was surprised by this result, finding it hard to believe that something as simple as frontal lobe brain volume could affect something as complex as intelligence. Nonetheless, it could be that the larger the brain cell mass, the greater the number of cell-to-cell connections. What still remains a mystery is whether the larger cell volume was the cause of higher intelligence or the other way around—people with strong motivation might use their brains more and thus develop a higher density of neurons. The researchers cautioned, however, that because this study involved collective data, the size of brain volume in the frontal lobes cannot be used to measure the intelligence of an individual.

■ LEARNING AND MEMORY

Learning is the process by which we *acquire* new knowledge and skills; memory is the process by which we *retain* knowledge and skills for the future. At the cellular level, learning occurs when the synapses make physical and chemical changes so that the influence of one neuron on another also changes. Investigations into the neural mechanisms required for different types of learning are revealing more about the interactions between learning new information, memory, and changes in brain structure. Just as muscles improve with exercise, the brain seems to improve with use.

> **Learning does not always result in long-term retention.**

Although learning does not increase the number of brain cells, it does increase their size, their branches, and their ability to form more complex networks.

Learning and memory also occur in different ways. Learning involves the brain, the nervous system, and the environment as well as the process by which their interplay acquires information and skills. Whether this learning becomes a memory is something else. Sometimes, we need information for just a short period of time, like the telephone number for a pizza delivery, and then the information decays after a few seconds. Thus, learning does not always result in long-term retention.

Neural Efficiency

The brain goes through physical and chemical changes when it stores new information as the result of learning. For instance, a set of neurons "learns" to fire together. Repeated firings make successive firings easier and, eventually, automatic under certain conditions. Thus, a memory is formed. Storing the memory gives rise to new neural pathways and strengthens existing pathways. Over time, these small networks of memories begin to form larger associations. Hence, every time we learn something, our long-term storage areas undergo anatomical changes that, together with our unique genetic makeup, constitute the expression of our individuality.

As the repetition of stimuli causes neural circuits to become more associated and efficient, the threshold for forming new circuits lowers. Consequently, subsequent learning may form strong neural circuits with less repetition, thereby increasing the speed of learning. This process describes *neural efficiency*. If an important aspect of intelligence is speed of learning, then it is likely that individuals born with a predisposition for developing neural circuitry rapidly are destined to be gifted in some way. Further, this trait is likely to appear during the early years in a child's development when neuron circuit building is at its peak. And so, the child genius appears.

Genetic composition is likely to be a strong determinant in an individual's predisposition for neural efficiency. But there is substantial evidence that environmental influences can also provide opportunities for improving the speed with which new learning takes place (Buckner, Kelley,

> **If an important aspect of intelligence is speed of learning, then it is likely that individuals born with a predisposition for developing neural circuitry rapidly are destined to be gifted in some way.**

and Petersen, 1999). One teaching strategy that is particularly successful in this area is rehearsal, which is discussed later in this chapter.

STAGES AND TYPES OF MEMORY ■

Trying to explain the components and mechanisms associated with human memory has confounded scientists for centuries. However, during the last 20 years, most researchers have adopted a general memory model that distinguishes between *how long* something is stored (the stages of memory) from *what* is being stored (the types of memory)(see Figure 1.5).

1. Stages of Memory

The stages of memory deal with the temporal nature of memory. They describe the length of time a memory can be present to influence behavior or thought. Neuroscientists generally agree that there are three types of temporal memory: *immediate memory* and *working memory* for temporary interactions and *long-term memory* for permanent storage.

Immediate Memory

Immediate memory is the ability to hold on to items, from a few seconds up to about a minute, to accomplish a particular task. Repeating a short list of items or remembering a telephone number just long enough to dial it are examples of using immediate memory. The task is often completed subconsciously and the memory of it quickly fades. Thus, items that have been just in immediate memory

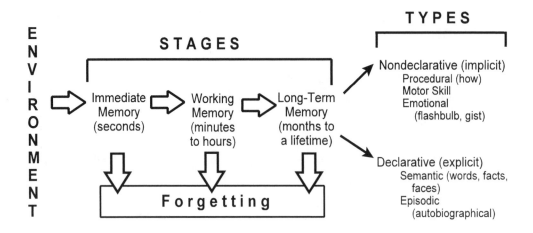

Figure 1.5 The stages and types of memory.

cannot be recalled. However, if you recite the list or dial the phone number repeatedly, there is a high probability that the information will move to the conscious processor—working memory.

Working Memory

Working memory is the ability to hold items long enough to consciously process and reflect on them and to carry out related activities during that processing, which can take from minutes to hours. If, for example, the route you normally drive from home to work were blocked by an accident, working memory and frontal lobe processing would be recruited to assess the situation and help determine an alternate route.

Studies of working memory indicate that it has a limited capacity of about six to seven verbal items for most people. This capacity (called the *phonologic loop*) is likely to be greater for highly talented individuals and less for those with learning problems. Working memory capacity seems to be closely related to the amount of attention one gives to situations requiring problem solving. Individuals with higher working memory capacity give more controlled attention to problem solving tasks and are less likely to be diverted by other distractions. Working memory also shows a strong connection to general intelligence, probably because working memory's connections within the frontal lobes keep the representation active for further processing (Engle, Laughlin, Tuholski, and Conway, 1999; Tuholski, Engle, and Baylis, 2001).

Another component of working memory is the *visuospatial sketchpad*, which holds visual and spatial information in a similar loop (Beatty, 2001). To date, only a few studies have sought to examine this facet of working memory. As might be expected, one EEG study found that high IQ individuals performed better than their lower IQ peers on tasks requiring the rehearsal of spatial information in working memory. One surprising finding, however, was that when the memory load of the task increased, areas in the rear of the brain were activated, but only in the high IQ subjects. The researchers speculated that a characteristic of high intelligence may be the ability of the frontal lobes to store and rehearse

> **A characteristic of high intelligence may be the ability of the frontal lobes to store and rehearse spatial information in working memory and in the posterior areas (occipital lobe) of the brain**.

spatial information in working memory and in the posterior areas (occipital lobe) of the brain (Van Rooy, Stough, Pipingas, Hocking, and Silberstein, 2001).

Long-Term Memory

Long-term memory is the ability to store information in a permanent form for months, years, and even for a lifetime. Storing occurs when the hippocampus encodes information and sends it to one or more long-term storage areas. The encoding process takes time and usually occurs during deep sleep, resulting in permanent physical changes and an increase in the efficiency of transmission in the synaptic areas associated with the memory. This physical embodiment of the memory is called an *engram*. Note that forgetting can occur in all stages of memory.

An important question is what factors increase the probability that information in working memory will be encoded into long-term storage sites for future recall? That is how can teachers help students to retain the learning objective for future use. This is an important matter because we cannot recall what we have not stored.

Information that has survival value is quickly stored. You don't want to have to learn every day that walking in front of a moving bus or touching a hot stove can injure you. As already mentioned, the amygdala ensures that emotional experiences also have a high likelihood of being permanently stored. But, in classrooms—where the survival and emotional elements may be minimal or absent—other factors need to come into play if the learner is ever to recall information. In this situation, it seems that permanent storage is most likely to occur when the learning makes sense and has meaning. *Sense* refers to whether the learner can understand the item on the basis of past experiences. On the other hand, *meaning* refers to whether the item is *relevant* to the learner. For what purpose should the learner remember it? Meaning, of course, is a personal thing and is greatly influenced by that person's prior experiences. The same item can have great meaning for one student and none for another. When a student asks "Why do I have to know this?" or "When will I ever use this?", it indicates that the student has not, for whatever reason, accepted this learning as relevant.

Whenever the learner's working memory decides that an item does not make sense or have meaning, the probability of it being stored is extremely low. If either sense or meaning is present, the probability of storage increases significantly (assuming, you remember, no survival or emotional component). If both sense *and* meaning are present, the likelihood of long-term storage is very high. For more on sense and meaning and how they affect retention, see Sousa (2001a).

Effect of Past Experiences on Memory

Past experiences always influence new learning. What we already know acts as a filter, helping us attend to those things that have meaning (i.e., relevancy) and discard those that don't. Meaning, therefore, has a great impact on whether information and skills will be learned and stored. If students have not found meaning by the end of a learning episode, there is little likelihood that much will be remembered.

Teachers spend about 90 percent of their planning time devising lessons so that students will *understand* the learning objective (i.e., make sense of it). But to convince a learner's brain to persist with that objective, teachers need to be more mindful of helping students establish *meaning*. We should remember that what was meaningful for us as children may not necessarily be meaningful for children today.

Curriculum Implications

If we expect students to find meaning, we need to be certain that the curriculum contains connections to *their* past experiences, not just ours. Further, the enormous size and the strict compartmentalization of secondary curriculum areas do little to help students find the time to make relevant connections between and among subjects. Helping students to link subject areas by integrating the curriculum increases meaning and retention, especially when students recognize a future use for the new learning.

Students who are gifted in acquiring information and skills often have an extensive knowledge base that allows them to make meaningful connections to new learning quickly. They are then ready to move on to other challenges.

> **Students gifted in acquiring information and skills have an extensive knowledge base that allows them to make meaningful connections to new learning quickly.**

Rehearsal

Attaching sense and meaning to new learning can occur only if the learner has adequate time to process and reprocess it. This continuing reprocessing is called *rehearsal* and is a critical component in the transference of information from working memory to long-term storage. Two major factors should be considered in evaluating rehearsal: the amount of time devoted to it, which determines whether there is both initial and secondary rehearsal, and the type of rehearsal carried out, which can be rote or elaborative.

Time for Initial and Secondary Rehearsal

Time is a critical component of rehearsal. Initial rehearsal occurs when the information first enters working memory. If the learner cannot attach sense or meaning, and if there is no time for further processing, the new information is likely to be lost. Providing sufficient time to go beyond initial processing to secondary rehearsal allows the learner to review the information, to make sense of it, to elaborate on the details, and to assign value and relevance, thus increasing significantly the chance of long-term storage.

Scanning studies of the brain indicate that the frontal lobe is very much involved during the rehearsal process and, ultimately, in long-term memory formation. This makes sense because working memory is also located in the frontal lobe. Several studies using fMRI scans of human subjects showed that, during longer rehearsals, the amount of activity in the frontal lobe determined whether items were stored or forgotten (Wagner, Schacter, Rotte, Koutstaal, Maril, Dale, Rosen, and Buckner, 1998; Buckner, et al., 1999).

Students carry out initial and secondary rehearsal at different rates of speed and in different ways, depending on the type of information in the new learning and on their learning styles. As the learning task changes, learners automatically shift to different patterns of rehearsal. An individual's neural efficiency will most likely play a role in this process as well.

Rote and Elaborative Rehearsal

Rote Rehearsal. This rehearsal is used when learners need to remember and store information exactly as it is entered into working memory. This involves a simple strategy necessary to learn information or a skill in a specific form or sequence. We employ rote rehearsal to remember a poem, the lyrics and melody of a song, multiplication tables, telephone numbers, and steps in a procedure.

Elaborative Rehearsal. By contrast, elaborative rehearsal is used when it is unnecessary to store information exactly as learned, and when it is important to associate new learnings with prior learnings to detect relationships. This is a complex thinking process, in which the learners reprocess the information several times to make connections to previous learnings and assign meaning. For example, students use rote rehearsal to memorize a poem, but elaborative rehearsal to interpret its message. Elaborative rehearsal is also likely to enhance neural efficiency as larger associative networks are being made. When students get very little time for, or training in, elaborative rehearsal, they resort more frequently to rote rehearsal. Consequently, they fail to make the associations or discover the relationships that only elaborative rehearsal can provide. Also, they continue to believe that the value of learning is merely the recalling of information as learned rather than the generating of new ideas, concepts, and solutions.

> **There is almost no long-term retention without rehearsal.**

When deciding how to use rehearsal in a lesson, teachers need to consider the time available as well as the type of rehearsal appropriate for the specific learning objective. Keep in mind that rehearsal only contributes to, but does not guarantee, information transfer into long-term storage. However, there is almost no long-term retention in the classroom *without* rehearsal.

2. Types of Memory

Some stimuli that are processed in the immediate and working memories are eventually transferred to long-term memory sites, where they actually change the structure of the neurons so they can last a lifetime. Although neuroscientists are not in total agreement as to all of the characteristics of long-term memory, there is considerable agreement on some of their types, and their description is important to understand before setting out to design learning activities accordingly. Long-term memory can be divided into two categories, *nondeclarative memory* and *declarative memory* (Figure 1.5).

Nondeclarative Memory

Nondeclarative memory (sometimes called *implicit* memory) exists in several different forms including procedural memory, motor skill memory, and emotional memory.

Procedural Memory. Procedural memory refers to remembering *how* to do something, like riding a bicycle, driving a car, swinging a tennis racket, and tying a shoelace. As practice of the skills continues, these memories become more efficient and can be performed with little conscious thought or recall. The brain process shifts from *reflective* to *reflexive*. For example, you may remember the first time you drove an automobile by yourself. No doubt you gave a lot of conscious attention to your speed, maneuvering the vehicle, putting your foot on the correct pedal, and observing surrounding traffic (reflective thought). However, as you continued to practice this routine, the skills were stored in procedural memory and became more automatic (reflexive activity). Now, it is possible to focus on abstract thoughts while taking that familiar and mundane drive between home and work, giving no conscious thought to the motor skills required to operate the automobile. Procedural memory drives the car while working memory plans your day.

Procedural memory helps us to learn things that don't require conscious attention and to habituate ourselves to the environment. Thus, we can become accustomed to the clothes we wear, the daily noisy traffic outside the school, a ticking clock in the den, or the sounds of construction. This adjustment to the environment allows the brain to screen out unimportant stimuli so it can focus on those that matter.

We also learn *perceptual skills*, such as reading, discriminating colors, and identifying tones in music, and *cognitive skills*, such as figuring out a *procedure* for solving a problem. Cognitive skills are different from cognitive concept building in that cognitive skills are performed automatically and rely on procedural memory rather than declarative memory. Acquiring perceptual and cognitive skills involves brain processes and memory sites that are different from those used in learning cognitive concepts. If they are learned differently, should they be taught differently?

Motor Skill Memory. Much of what we do during the course of a day involves the performance of skills. We go through the morning grooming and breakfast rituals, read the newspaper, get to work, and shake the hand of a new acquaintance. We do all of these tasks without realizing that we have learned them and without being aware that we are using our memory. Although learning a new skill involves conscious attention, skill performance later becomes unconscious and relies essentially on nondeclarative memory.

Emotional Memory. Emotions can positively or negatively affect the acquisition of new learning. Emotions associated with a learning become part of the nondeclarative memory system. These emotions can return and change how students *feel* about what they learned. This unconscious response can turn them toward or away from a similar learning experience.

A powerful emotional experience can cause an instantaneous and long-lasting memory of an event, called a *flashbulb memory*. An example is remembering where you were and what you were doing when the Challenger space shuttle exploded or during the terrorist attacks on New York City and Washington. Although these memories are not always accurate, they do attest to the brain's ability to record emotionally significant experiences. This ability most likely results from the stimulation of the amygdala and the release throughout the body of emotion-arousing substances, such as adrenaline.

Sometimes, an experience is stored merely as an emotional *gist* or summary of the event, that is, we remember whether we liked it or not. A year after seeing a movie, for example, we might be able to recall only bits of the storyline and perhaps its mood. Students often can remember whether they liked a particular topic, but cannot recall many details about it.

Declarative Memory

Declarative memory (also called *conscious* or *explicit* memory) describes the remembering of names, facts, music, and objects (e.g., where you live and the kind of car you own) and is processed by the hippocampus and cerebrum. Items in declarative memory are readily available through consciousness and thus can be expressed through language—that is, declared. Think for a moment about a person who is now important in your life. Try to recall that person's image, voice, and mannerisms. Then think of an important event you both attended, one with an emotional connection, such as a concert, wedding, or funeral. Once you have the context in mind, note how easily other components of the memory come together. This is declarative memory in its most common form—conscious and almost effortless recall. It should be noted, however, that the emotional memory you just recalled is a separate component that may be stored in declarative memory but kept as a declarative fact. The emotional memory is mediated by the amygdala and operates independently of conscious awareness (LeDoux, 2002).

Declarative memory can be further divided into episodic memory and semantic memory. *Episodic memory* refers to the memory of events in one's own life history. It helps a person identify the time and place when an event happened. *Semantic memory* is knowledge of facts and data that may not be related to any event. A veteran knowing that there was a Vietnam War in the 1970s is using semantic memory; remembering his experiences in that war—including emotional memories—is episodic memory.

It seems that procedural and declarative memories are stored differently. Studies of brain- damaged and amnesia victims show that they may still be perfectly capable of riding a bicycle (procedural) without remembering the word *bicycle* or when they learned to ride (declarative). Procedural and declarative memory seem to be stored in different regions of the brain, and declarative memory can be lost even though procedural is spared.

RETENTION ■

Retention is the process whereby long-term memory preserves a learning in such a way that the memory can be located, identified, and retrieved accurately in the future. This is an inexact process influenced by many factors, including the degree of student focus, the length and type of rehearsal that occurred, the critical attributes that may have been identified, the student's learning style, any learning disabilities, and, of course, the inescapable influence of prior learning. For all practical purposes, the capacity of the brain to store information is unlimited. That is, with about 100 billion neurons, each with thousands of dendrites, the number of potential neural pathways is incomprehensible. The healthy brain will never run out of space to store all that an individual learns in a lifetime.

> **Different parts of a memory are stored in various sites which reassemble when the memory is recalled.**

Memories are not stored as a whole in one place. Different parts of a memory are stored in various sites, and they reassemble when the memory is recalled. These virtual assembly sites are sometimes referred to as *convergence zones*. Researchers believe that long-term memory is a dynamic, interactive system that activates storage areas distributed across the brain to retrieve and reconstruct memories (Squire and Kandel, 1999; Schacter, 2001).

Effects of Emotions on Memory and Retention

Any input from a person's environment that stimulates the limbic area will get high priority for processing. Highest priority goes to any situation interpreted as posing a threat to the survival of the individual. For example, data related to a burning odor, a snarling dog, or someone threatening bodily injury are processed immediately. Upon receiving the stimuli, the brain stem sends a rush of adrenaline throughout the brain, shutting down all unnecessary activity and directing the brain's attention to the source of the stimulus.

Emotional data also take high priority. When an individual responds emotionally to a situation, the older limbic system (stimulated by the amygdala) takes a major role and the complex cerebral processes are suspended. We have all had experiences when anger or fear of the unknown quickly overcame our rational thoughts. The resulting overriding of conscious thought can be strong enough to cause a temporary inability to talk ("I was dumbfounded") or move ("I froze"). This fear response occurs because the hippocampus is susceptible to stress hormones, which can inhibit cognitive functioning and long-term memory.

Under certain conditions, however, emotions can enhance memory by causing the release of hormones that stimulate the amygdala to signal brain regions to strengthen memory. Strong emotions can shut down conscious processing during the event while enhancing our memory of it. Emotion is a powerful and misunderstood force in learning and memory.

Implications for Teaching

How the learner processes new information presented in school has a great impact on the quality of what is learned and is a major factor in determining whether and how it will be retained. Memories, of course, are more than just information. They represent fluctuating patterns of associations and connections across the brain, from which the individual extracts order and meaning. Teachers with a greater understanding of the types of memory and how they form can select strategies that are more likely to improve the retention and retrieval of learning.

A good portion of the teaching done in schools centers on delivering facts and information to build concepts that explain a body of knowledge. We teach numbers, arithmetic operations, ratios, and theorems to explain mathematics. We teach about atoms, momentum, gravity, and cells to explain science. We talk about countries and famous leaders and discuss their trials and battles to explain history, and so on. Students may hold on to this information in working memory (a temporary memory) just long enough to take a test, after which the knowledge readily decays and is lost. Retention, however, requires that the learner not only give conscious attention but also build conceptual frameworks that have sense and meaning for eventual consolidation into long-term storage networks.

2

What Is a Gifted Brain?

sking 50 people what is meant by giftedness is likely to produce 50 different definitions. Nonetheless, some common elements will emerge from most of the descriptions. These might include describing a person's aptitude in a specific subject area or a talent in the visual or performing arts, or in sports. Also mentioned might be creativity, inventiveness, or just plain "intelligent in everything." Descriptions of giftedness also vary from one culture to another. For example, in a culture with no formal schooling, a skilled hunter might be the gifted one. Gifted abilities are also more

> From one perspective, giftedness is what people in a society perceive to be higher or lower on some culturally embedded scale.

likely to emerge when the individual's talents coincide with what is valued by the culture. Chess prodigies, for example, appear in cultures where such talent is valued and nurtured. So it can be said that giftedness is what others in a society perceive to be higher or lower on some culturally embedded scale.

THEORIES OF INTELLIGENCE AND GIFTEDNESS ■

In the 1950s, researchers and psychologists described giftedness mainly in terms of intelligence: high IQ was the same as gifted. Creativity and motivation were soon added as other characteristics of gifted performers. Consequently, as the push in schools for special programs for gifted students got underway, IQ tests became the primary screening vehicle for program selection. But IQ tests had their own problems. They assessed analytical and verbal skills but failed to measure practical knowledge and creativity, components critical to problem solving and success in life. Furthermore, the predictive abilities of IQ tests deteriorated once situations or populations changed. For example, research studies found that IQ tests predicted leadership skills when the tests were given under low-stress conditions. Under high-stress conditions, however, IQ was negatively related to leadership. In other words, it predicted the opposite.

It eventually became apparent that IQ tests were not a satisfactory measure of giftedness and that people could be gifted in different ways (e.g., academic areas, sports, performing arts, or in business ventures). Very few people are gifted in all areas. Paradoxically, some people can be gifted in some aspects of learning while displaying learning disorders in others (see Chapter 8). Clearly, relying on only one quantitative criterion (the IQ score) and maybe two qualitative criteria (creativity and motivation) was not adequate in the process of describing the collective and varied characteristics of gifted (and talented) people.

Revising the Definition of Giftedness

In an effort to challenge the notion that *giftedness* meant demonstrating high performance in nearly all areas of intellectual and artistic pursuit, Joseph Renzulli (1978) proposed his own definition. He suggested that it resulted from the interaction of three traits: general or specific abilities that were above average, commitment to task, and creativity. Later, he distinguished two types of gifted performance (Renzulli, 1986):

- Schoolhouse giftedness, which is characterized by the ease of acquiring knowledge and taking tests as demonstrated through high grades and high test scores, and
- Creative-productive giftedness, which involves creating new products and ideas designed to have an impact on a specific audience or field.

Renzulli's work stimulated school districts to include more opportunities for creative expression in their programs for gifted students.

Multiple Intelligences

During the 1980s, psychologists unleashed new and different models to describe intelligence. Harvard researcher Howard Gardner (1983) published a significant book suggesting that intelligence is not a unitary concept, that humans possess at least seven intelligences (recently, he added an eighth), and that an individual is predisposed to developing each of the intelligences to different levels of competence (Table 2.1). For Gardner, the intelligences represented ways of processing information and of thinking. He also suggested that the intelligences are the product of the interaction between genetic predisposition and the environment, a sort of nature-nurture combination that is not a question of either–or, but both–and. He selected an intelligence if it met the following eight criteria:

- Potential isolation by brain damage
- Existence of idiots savants, prodigies, and other exceptional individuals
- An identifiable core operation or set of core operations
- A distinctive developmental history, along with a definable set of expert "end-state" performances
- An evolutionary history and evolutionary plausibility
- Support from experimental psychological tasks
- Support from psychometric findings
- Susceptibility to encoding in a symbol system

According to Gardner, the intelligences are not the same as thinking style, which tends to remain consistent and independent of the type of information being processed. Rather, individuals at any given time use those intelligences which will allow them to solve specific problems, generate new problems, or create products or services of value to their particular culture. As the information and tasks change, other intelligences are called into action. One of Gardner's legacies is the oft-quoted aphorism, "Ask not how smart is the child, but how is the child smart?" Nevertheless, in this schema, *giftedness* can be defined as a child being exceptionally competent in one or more of Gardner's intelligences.

Table 2.1 Howard Gardner's Eight Intelligences

- **Bodily/Kinesthetic** - The capacity to use one's body to solve a problem, make something, or put on a production.
- **Naturalist** - The ability to discriminate among living things and sensitivity to other features of the natural world.
- **Logical/Mathematical** - The ability to understand logical systems and to manipulate numbers and quantities.
- **Musical/Rhythmic** - The capacity to think in music and to hear, remember, recognize, and manipulate patterns.
- **Verbal/Linguistic** - The capacity to use one's language (and other languages) to express oneself and understand others.
- **Visual/Spatial** - The ability to represent the spatial world internally in one's mind.
- **Interpersonal** - The ability to understand other people.
- **Intrapersonal** - The capacity to understand oneself.

Using Multiple Intelligences Theory With the Gifted

In the past two decades, the multiple intelligences (MI) theory has been used to promote all sorts of curricular and instructional changes in school systems across North America. Several curricular programs are almost exclusively based on MI. In his writings, Gardner (1983) has suggested that traditional measures for identifying gifted students rely too heavily on IQ tests that focus on linguistic and logical/mathematical skills. Consequently, schools are increasingly resorting to MI as an alternative means of identifying gifted students. However, the problem with this approach is deciding how to develop instruments that can measure each of the intelligences with reliability and validity. Some new instruments, such as those developed, by Udall and Passe (1993), show internal consistency with some student groups but not with others.

A few critics (Delisle, 1996) of using MI theory to identify gifted students point out that MI's appeal is its simplicity, convenience, and egalitarian theme. It focuses toward developing every learner's intelligence rather than the exceptionalities of the gifted. Consequently, MI has spawned "talent developers," who disregard the emotional element as well as important concepts, such as compassion, self-knowledge, and respect for others.

Other critics (White and Breen, 1998) caution that although MI may be appropriate for accommodating those children who are multiply gifted, it does not help them decide what to do and when to do it. It is their ability to reason and evaluate that allows them to make these decisions, not MI. White and Breen also question whether MI are intelligences or maybe talents or abilities, and if they remain constant during one's lifetime. Even though they lament that the use of the common word *intelligences* to describe all the abilities conceals some of the important differences among them, they commend MI theory for raising educators' awareness to the multiple talents of gifted children. Just the same, they continue, some education programs based on MI look more like entertainment and serve only to dilute the teaching of fundamental skills.

> **Educators need to be wary of the fad-like nature of some of the MI programs and recognize that, without further research support, they cannot depend on MI as a panacea for gifted education.**

Although MI may be theoretically useful in identifying gifted and talented children, especially those from culturally diverse backgrounds, more empirical data are needed to help develop reliable measures for the identification process. Educators need to be wary of the fad-like nature of some of the MI programs and recognize that, without further research support, they cannot depend on MI as a panacea for gifted education.

Emotional Intelligence

No discussion of the different intelligences would be complete without mentioning Daniel Goleman's (1995) concept of emotional intelligence. His book summarized the breakthroughs in understanding the strong influence that emotions have as we grow and learn. Emotions interact with reason to determine how we view the world and to support or inhibit learning. According to Goleman, an individual who can use emotions effectively is likely to become a more successful and productive citizen.

Sternberg's Theories

The Triarchic Theory

Two years after Gardner's work appeared, Robert Sternberg (1985) at Yale proposed a theory that distinguishes three types of intelligence: analytical, creative, and practical. People with analytical intelligence (the analyzers) have abilities in analyzing, critiquing, and evaluating. Those who are creatively intelligent (the creators) are particularly good at discovering, inventing, and creating. By contrast, the practically intelligent (the

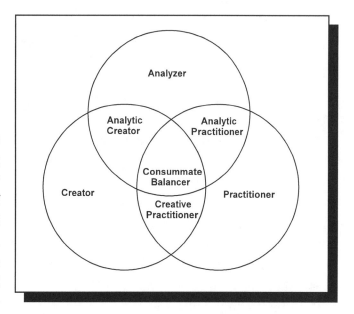

Figure 2.1 In Sternberg's model, the combinations of the three types of intelligence produce different patterns of giftedness.

practitioners) excel at applying, utilizing, and implementing. In this model, *intelligence* is defined by these three types of behavior, and *giftedness* results from the ability to perform the skills in one or more of these areas with exceptional accuracy and efficiency. According to Sternberg, various combinations of these three areas produce different patterns of giftedness (Figure 2.1). This concept was tested in several studies conducted by Sternberg and his colleagues. Students were assessed for their memory as well as their analytical, creative, and practical achievement. The results showed that those students who were taught in ways that best matched their achievement patterns outperformed those whose method of instruction was not a good fit for their pattern of abilities (Sternberg, Ferrari, Clinkenbeard, and Grigorenko, 1996; Sternberg, Griorenko, Jarvin, Clinkenbeard, Ferrari, and Torfi, 2000).

The Pentagonal Implicit Theory of Giftedness

More recently, Sternberg (1995) has introduced another theory that describes a gifted person as one who meets the following five criteria:

Excellence. The individual is superior in some dimension or set of dimensions relative to peers.

- Rarity. The individual possesses a skill or attribute that is rare among peers.
- Productivity. The individual must produce something in the area of giftedness.
- Demonstrability. The skill or aptitude of giftedness must be demonstrable through one or more valid assessments.
- Value. The individual shows superior performance in a dimension that is valued by that person's society.

Sternberg's theory helps provide a basis for understanding why we call some people gifted and others not. He cautions, however, that although this theory can be helpful in identifying gifted individuals, it should be used in conjunction with other generally accepted assessment measures.

Even with all these theories, the definition of *giftedness* remains elusive. Yet, most of us recognize a gifted or talented person when we see one in action. We might wonder whether the person was born with those abilities, or whether their skills are the result of hard work, or both. As the trend toward moving away from using IQ measures to understand gifted individuals gained momentum, the question remained: What characteristics of a person should be measured instead? The many research studies designed to address this question can be categorized in various ways. One useful method, suggested by Robinson and Clinkenbeard (1998), sorts the studies into those looking either for psychological characteristics or social and emotional characteristics.

■ PSYCHOLOGICAL CHARACTERISTICS OF GIFTEDNESS

Thinking About Problems and About Thinking

Most of the research on the psychological characteristics of giftedness has focused on cognition and metacognition. In these studies, researchers observed how students identified as gifted thought through a given problem or situation (cognition), and how they reflected on their thinking throughout the problem-solving experience (metacognition).

Cognitive Strategies

Not surprisingly, the studies showed that gifted students acquired information and solved problems faster, better, or at earlier stages than other students. Some studies showed that higher IQ individuals had more efficient memories, more information- processing strategies, larger and more elaborately organized knowledge bases, and a better ability to solve mathematical problems by employing their own symbolic encoding (Robinson and Clinkenbeard, 1998).

Sternberg has also investigated how different thinking styles in gifted students affect their academic performance (Grigorenko and Sternberg, 1997). The study found that there were no differences in thinking styles among groups of students at different ability levels, and that certain thinking styles contributed significantly to prediction of academic performance. For example, the style that involved analyzing, grading, or comparing things had the highest predictive value. Further, this contribution was independent of the type of instruction the students were given. One other finding of interest was that the gifted students performed best on assessment procedures that closely matched their thinking style. (This last finding corroborates the results of decades of earlier research on different types of student learning styles.)

Metacognitive Strategies

Research studies in metacognition (i.e., thinking about one's own thinking) have focused around three aspects:

- What do students know about thinking strategies?
- Can they use the strategies?
- Can they monitor their own cognitive processing?

Compared to other students, the studies showed that gifted students knew more about metacognitive strategies and could use them more easily in new contexts. However, a significant finding was that, contrary to popular beliefs, the gifted students did not use a wider variety of metacognitive strategies than other students, nor did they monitor their

> Gifted students may know more about metacognitive strategies but, surprisingly, do not use a wider variety of them. Nor do they monitor their strategies any more than other students.

strategies any more than the other students (Alexander and Schwanenflugel, 1995; Carr, Alexander, and Schwanenflugel, 1996). Several researchers in this area caution that motivation and creativity may influence the results of studies on metacognition.

Neuroscientists—or more specifically, cognitive neuroscientists—also think about thinking. In recent years, they have explored what differences in the structure and functions of the gifted brain may allow it to achieve remarkable levels of performance. These researchers use many tools in their investigations, such as advanced imaging techniques, EEG, and MEG, to reveal similarities and differences in the function of high-performing brains compared with the brains of students showing no signs of the same kinds of giftedness. Here are some of their findings.

The Cortex

Any attempt to examine giftedness through the lens of neuroscience needs to begin with an understanding of the complexity and functional diversity of the brain. Of particular importance is the cortex, considered the brain's most advanced structure. In the history of our species, the cortex was the most recent part of the human brain to evolve, eventually developing two abilities that seem unique to humans: spoken language and cognitive thought. The cortex, you will recall, is the six-layer covering of the cerebrum that is divided into two hemispheres, each consisting of the frontal, temporal, parietal, and occipital lobes. Although the neurons in the cortex are heavily interconnected, certain regions in each lobe and hemisphere are organized into units that perform specific functions.

The Cerebral Hemispheres

Since the work of Roger Sperry in the 1960s (Sousa, 2001a), neuroscientists have accepted the notion that the two cerebral hemispheres are not mirror images of each other. That is, they differ structurally, biochemically, and functionally. In most people, for example, the right frontal lobe protrudes over, and is wider than, the left frontal lobe. The left occipital lobe (at the back of the brain) protrudes over, and is wider than, the right occipital lobe. The neurotransmitter norepinephrine is more prevalent in the right hemisphere, while dopamine is more prevalent in the left hemisphere. Estrogen receptors are more prevalent in the right hemisphere than in the left hemisphere.

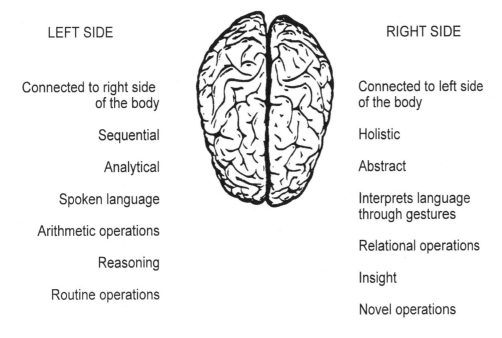

LEFT SIDE

Connected to right side
of the body

Sequential

Analytical

Spoken language

Arithmetic operations

Reasoning

Routine operations

RIGHT SIDE

Connected to left side
of the body

Holistic

Abstract

Interprets language
through gestures

Relational operations

Insight

Novel operations

Figure 2.2 The left and right hemispheres of the human brain are specialized and process information differently.

As for brain functions, more evidence is accumulating that the brain has a much greater degree of specialization than was previously thought. Even so, because of advancements in neuroimaging, the earlier idea that the brain is a set of modular units carrying out specific tasks is giving way to a new model, which holds that moving across the cortical surface results in a gradual transition from one cognitive function to another. Goldberg (2001) refers to this as the "gradiental" view of brain organization. This view does not necessarily discard the notion that specific areas of the brain perform specific functions. Rather, it uses recent evidence from neurological studies to suggest a pattern of organization whereby the boundaries between the specific areas are fluid, not fixed. The ability of certain areas of the brain to perform unique functions is known as *lateralization* or *specialization* (Sousa, 2001a). Brain imaging scans and other studies reveal remarkable consistency in the way the two hemispheres store and process information (Figure 2.2).

Specialization and Learning

The two hemispheres of the brain communicate with each other through a tight bundle of about 200 million nerve cells called the *corpus callosum* (see Figure 1.2). Researchers have been particularly interested in how the specialized functions of each hemisphere affect new learning, and the degree to which they communicate

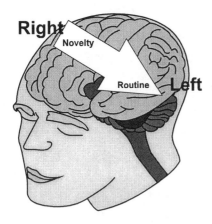

Figure 2.3 With repeated exposures, novel experiences become routine and their cortical processing areas shift from the right hemisphere to the left hemisphere.

with each other during that process. Early theories held that new learning occurs in the hemisphere mainly responsible for the functions associated with that learning. Thus, the left hemisphere would be largely involved in spoken language acquisition and sequential procedures, and the right side would support the learning of visual images and spatial relationships. These theories were based mainly on the results of tests done with patients who had damage to specific areas of the brain.

More recent research, however, lends credence to an alternative explanation. Goldberg (2001), for example, proposes that hemispheric specialization may center around the differences between novelty and routine. Closer examination of brain-damaged patients shows that those with severe right hemisphere problems experience difficulty in facing new learning situations, but can perform routine, practiced tasks (e.g., language) normally. Conversely, patients with severe left hemisphere damage can create new drawings and think abstractly, but have difficulty with routine operations.

Goldberg's notion gives us a different way of looking at how the brain learns. It suggests that upon encountering a novel situation for which the individual has no coping strategy, the right hemisphere is primarily involved and attempts to deal with the situation. With repeated exposure to similar situations, coping strategies eventually emerge and learning occurs because it results in a change of behavior. In time, and after sufficient repetition, the responses become routine and shift via the corpus callosum to the left hemisphere (Figure 2.3). The amount of time and the number of situational exposures needed to accomplish this right-to-left hemisphere transition vary widely from one person to the next. But it may be that one component of giftedness is the ability of that person's brain to make the transition in less time and with fewer exposures than average.

> It may be that one component of giftedness is the brain's ability to make the transition from novelty to routine in less time and with fewer exposures than average.

Studies using neuroimaging provide evidence to support Goldberg's theory. In one study, researchers used PET scans to measure the changes in brain flow patterns when subjects were asked to learn various types of information. Changes in blood flow levels indicate the degree of neural activation. When the information was novel, regions in the right temporal lobe were highly activated. After the information had been presented several times to the subjects, activity in the right temporal lobe decreased dramatically (Figure 2.4). In both instances, however, the level of activation in the left temporal lobe remained constant (Martin, Wiggs, and Weisberg, 1997).

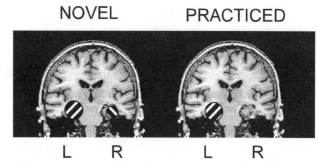

NOVEL   **PRACTICED**

L   R   L   R

Figure 2.4 A representation of PET scans showing the changes in regional blood flow for novel and practiced tasks. The highlighted circles show areas of high activation in the left and right temporal lobes for novel tasks, but only in the left temporal lobe for practiced tasks.

Similar results were reported from other studies involving a variety of learning tasks, such as recognizing faces and symbols (Henson, Shallice, and Dolan, 2000), learning a complex motor skill (Shadmehr and Holcomb, 1997), and learning and relearning different systems of rules (Berns, Cohen, and Mintun, 1997). The same shifts were detected no matter what type of information was presented to the subjects. In other words, says Goldberg, the association of the right hemisphere with novelty and the left hemisphere with routine appears to be independent of the nature of the information being learned.

Language Functions in the Hemispheres

Although speech seems to be centered in regions of the left hemisphere, studies involving patients with brain lesions indicate that language functions are distributed across the brain. Damage to the rear part of the temporal lobe nearest to the occipital lobe causes the loss of nouns naming objects. On the other hand, damage to the frontal lobe can cause the loss of verbs. These observations suggest that words are closely associated in the brain with the objects or actions they represent, lending further support for the gradiental and not the modular pattern of organization of the cerebral cortex.

The Prefrontal Cortex

Cognitive thought and related activities are located in the foremost part of the frontal lobes, called the *prefrontal cortex*. This area comprises about 29 percent of the total cortex and is interconnected to every distinct functional region (Figure

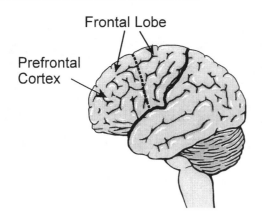

Figure 2.5 The entire area in front of the solid line is the frontal lobe. The area to the left of the dotted line is the general location of the prefrontal cortex.

2.5). Often called the executive control area, the prefrontal cortex is embedded in a rich network of neural pathways so that it can coordinate and integrate the functions of all areas. Like the conductor of an orchestra, the prefrontal cortex blends individual inputs from various regions of the brain into a comprehensive and comprehendible whole. Its interpretations ultimately define personality, and its decision-making abilities determine how successfully an individual copes with each day.

To accomplish this task, the prefrontal cortex must converge the inputs from within an individual with those from the outside world. The brain's organization facilitates this process. Sensory signals from the outside environment pass along the sensory nerves to the thalamus and are routed to other areas toward the back of the brain (reception). These inputs are then directed to specific sites in the parietal and temporal lobes, as well as in the limbic areas, for further analysis (integration). Finally, the frontal lobes combine this input with information from the individual's memory (interpretation) to determine what subsequent action, if any, should be taken (Figure 2.6).

The prefrontal cortex also seems to be strongly interested in task novelty. Several PET studies show that when processing new information, cerebral blood flow levels in the frontal lobes reached their highest levels. But when the subject became familiar with the task, frontal lobe involvement—as measured by blood flow—dropped significantly (Goldberg, 2001). If a somewhat different task was introduced, frontal lobe activation picked up once again. We noted before that the right hemisphere was more associated with novelty than the left. These findings infer that the frontal lobes are more closely aligned with the right hemisphere when dealing with novel learning situations.

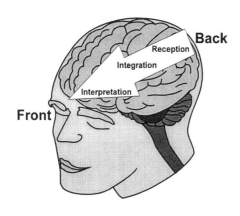

Figure 2.6 Stimuli from the outside world are received toward the rear of the brain, integrated in the center, and interpreted by the frontal lobes.

Decision Making

The prefrontal cortex faces many decisions in the course of a day. Some involve simple concrete problems, such as the following:

"What is my doctor's telephone number?"

"How much money is left in my savings account?"

"When is my nephew's birthday?"

Each question is clear and the situations require searching for a single, indisputable answer. This process is called *veridical decision making*, or finding the single, true answer.

I may be faced with other questions as well:

"Am I sick enough to see the doctor or should I wait a few days?"

"Should I use some of my savings to buy stocks or bonds?"

"What gift should I get for my nephew's birthday?"

These questions are ambiguous and have no intrinsically unique answer. I will choose the answer for a variety of reasons. My decision to see the doctor might depend on whether my body temperature rises or falls. Buying stocks or bonds might depend on where I think the stock market may be headed in the next year. In any event, my

> **Veridical decision making gets us through the day. Adaptive decision making gets us through life.**

brain is engaging in *adaptive decision making,* that is, I adapt the decision on the basis of context and my priorities at the moment. At another time and place, my decision might be different.

No one doubts that finely tuned veridical decision-making skills are valuable in certain technical occupations. But, life in general is fraught with ambiguities, and most critical decisions—personal and occupational—often require choosing from among equally valid options. Deciding among ambiguities is one of the most important functions of the prefrontal cortex. Studies show that individuals with damage to the prefrontal cortex have difficulty dealing with adaptive decision making, while damage to other parts of the brain does not seem to affect this process (Goldberg, 2001).

To be successful, we need to be competent in both types of skills. Veridical decisions help us get through the day: What time do I need to be at work and when is my first appointment? How much gasoline is in the car? Who's picking up the kids after practice? Adaptive decisions, on the other hand, get us through life: Is this the person I should marry? Is this the right job for me? When should we start a family?

Neural Efficiency

As mentioned in Chapter 1, when the frontal lobes gain more experience at making adaptive decisions and solving complex problems, neuronal pathways responsible for these processes should become more efficient and thus require less effort. Indeed, this concept—known as neural efficiency—has long been part of most theoretical models of the gifted brain. The idea is that gifted brains can perform tasks more quickly and accurately because they contain networks comprising neurons working together in vast arrays and with such efficiency that they require less cerebral energy than unorganized networks. One way to measure the level of brain activity is to monitor the pattern of waves produced by the brain's electrical activity. Obtaining experimental evidence to support this idea would require using EEG technology to measure the activity of the brain while it was performing different functions. Even though early attempts were inconclusive, advancements in EEG techniques have spurred new interest in studying this idea experimentally.

EEG Studies

When using the EEG to detect brain functioning, two wave patterns are of particular interest: alpha waves (8-13 cycles per second) and beta waves (14-60 cycles per second). Neurobiologists theorize that alpha activity is the result of neurons firing together (in synchrony) and resting together—an indication of neural pathway efficiency. Thus, alpha activity produces high voltage, rhythmic, and sinusoidal patterns. The higher the amplitude of the alpha wave (called *alpha power*), the more efficiently the neurons are firing, resulting in less mental effort.

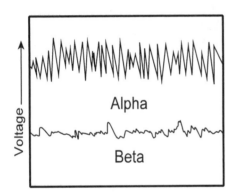

Figure 2.7 The diagram shows typical activity patterns of alpha and beta brain wave activity.

Beta waves, on the other hand, result from the activity of neurons that are doing different things at different times (asynchrony), producing a low voltage, irregular pattern (Figure 2.7). Beatty (2001) offers the analogy of a marching band. When the band members are marching in synchrony, their footsteps are a loud beat with silence between the steps. But as the band members disperse after the march, one hears the constant sound of many steps at random intervals.

Norbert Jausovec (2000) used EEG to study the differences in brain activity during problem solving in about 50 young adults who were separated into four groups based on their intelligence (average or high) and creativity (average or high). On the basis of their scores on various assessment measures, Jausovec placed them into the categories of intelligent, gifted, creative, and average (Figure 2.8). He then measured their alpha wave activity as they were solving closed problems (i.e., requiring convergent and logical thinking) and creative problems (i.e., requiring more adaptive decision making). His findings were threefold:

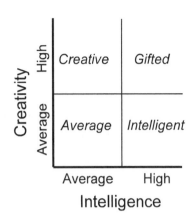

Figure 2.8 Jausovec's system for classifying subjects for the EEG study based on level of creativity and intelligence.

- Alpha wave activity showed that high IQ individuals (gifted and intelligent) used less mental effort than the average IQ individuals (creative and average) when solving closed problems.
- Alpha wave activity showed that high creative individuals (creative and gifted) used less mental effort than average creative individuals (intelligent and average) when engaged in creative problem solving.
- Creative individuals showed more cooperation among brain areas than did gifted ones, who showed greater decoupling of brain areas when solving ill-defined problems.

These results first suggest that when individuals are solving problems in their area of strength, less mental effort is needed so the alpha power is high, an indication of neural efficiency. Second, the results appear to support the concept that creativity and intelligence are different abilities that involve different areas of the cortex while solving closed or creative problems. This finding enhances the position of those who urge that creativity be considered as a separate measure of giftedness.

Creativity and intelligence are different abilities that involve different areas of the cerebral cortex while solving problems.

Implications for Schools

Far too frequently, what is taught in schools emphasizes veridical, rather than adaptive decision making. Most course work—and the resulting tests—ask students to search for the unique answers to concrete and unambiguous questions. Some students adapt to this strategy quickly and excel at veridical decision making. As a result, their test scores are high, and they may even be considered gifted. However, when faced with ambiguous problems, they often vacillate and become indecisive. Seldom do schools offer students consistent opportunities to develop adaptive decision-making skills. Instead, these are acquired individually, through trial and error.

With such emphasis on veridical decision making in schools, one wonders what happens to students who favor adaptive decision making. Do they get bored easily and act out or become withdrawn? Do they get frustrated if teachers insist they find only the unique answer? Are there areas in the curriculum where they can excel with their adaptive skills? Is it possible that those students who prefer adaptive decision making will seem different from the rest of the class? Is it also possible that a high aptitude in adaptive decision making is a characteristic of the gifted brain?

> **Is it possible that a high aptitude in adaptive decision making is a characteristic of the gifted brain?**

Given the appropriate adjustments in curriculum, most students can be taught to improve their adaptive decision-making skills. This process involves helping students to make connections and to discover relationships between the new learning and what they already know. One valuable strategy for accomplishing this is the frequent use of elaborative rehearsal.

The Overlooked Role of Visual-Spatial Abilities

For decades, general intelligence has been measured largely by one's ability to handle verbal skills through language manipulation. Yet, there is mounting evidence that visual-spatial abilities may play just as important a role as language to indicate general intelligence. Recent studies have been able to correlate visual-spatial abilities with the brain's executive functions, which, you will recall, reside in the frontal lobes.

One major study tested 167 participants on a variety of tasks to determine their ability to solve visual-spatial problems, to temporarily store visual-spatial information, and to measure their brain's executive functioning. The study found the following:

- Participants who were good at solving complex visual-spatial problems displayed superior executive functions.
- Executive functioning had the strongest correlation with spatial visualization.
- Executive functioning had the lowest correlation with perceptual speed (the ability to match simple shapes).

In sum, participants who were better visualizers and who solved visual-spatial problems quickly had stronger executive function, even if they had slow perceptual speed. The researchers felt that these findings made sense because spatial visualization is a complex cerebral operation, requiring substantial frontal lobe resources (Miyake, Friedman, Rettinger, Shah, and Hegarty, 2001).

Implications

Because traditional IQ tests are more verbally oriented, it is easy for visual-spatial intelligence to be discounted. Individuals with strong visual-spatial abilities are often not even identified in schools as gifted. But this study highlights the relationships between visual-spatial abilities and executive functions, thereby contributing to our emerging and broader view of intelligence as multifaceted.

EFFECT OF NURTURE ON INTELLIGENCE ■

As mentioned earlier, psychologists long believed that an individual's intelligence was determined primarily by the genetic code. Little credence was given to the notion that the child's environment could have any major or lasting impact on overall intelligence. Today, our view of intelligence is quite different. Few cognitive neuroscientists dispute the substantial impact that environment can have on a child's intellectual development. Intellectual skills once thought to be innate seem instead to be very sensitive to a person's environment.

Thus, IQ can be modified—up or down—by the child's environment. Well-designed day-care programs, for example, can provide the mental stimulation that young brains need during this period of rapid neural growth. Stephen Ceci (2000) has suggested that the following environmental factors can affect IQ:

> **Intelligence can be affected by**
> ★ **Well-designed daycare**
> ★ **School attendance**
> ★ **Breast-feeding**
> ★ **Diet**

- *School Attendance.* Staying in school can elevate IQ above what it would be if the student dropped out. For each year of schooling completed, there is an IQ gain of approximately 3.5 points. This indicates that other factors besides heredity are at work in shaping intelligence.

- *Breast-Feeding.* Despite skepticism over initial reports that breast-fed children grew into adults with higher IQs than siblings who were not breast-fed, more controlled studies, according to Ceci, continue to indicate a three to eight point IQ gain for breast-fed children by age 3. No one knows for sure why, however. It may be that the immune factors in mother's milk boost the infant's immune system, making it less prone to contract diseases that could affect learning. Mother's milk also contains high quantities of omega-3 fatty acids, which are used to build nerve cell membranes as well as the myelin that protects the impulses moving along the neuron.

- *Diet.* Nutritional researchers have long suspected that some of the substances added to today's food can affect brain development. Because controlled studies in this area using human children would be unethical, other types of data analysis are used. Ceci refers to one large-scale study of about 1 million students in the New York City schools, researchers found that IQ scores increased 14 percent after dyes, colorings, preservatives, and artificial flavorings were removed from the lunch food. Further, the weakest students showed the greatest improvement. Researchers also noted that the number of students who were performing two or more grade levels below average had dropped, from 120,000 before the dietary changes to 50,000 afterward.

Scientists are now starting to define the kinds of environmental stimuli that can promote (or delay) intellectual development in children.

Birth Order, Family Size, and Intelligence

The relationship between birth order, family size, and intelligence has been the subject of many research studies. Some articles have suggested that birth order and larger families expose an individual to environmental conditions that influence intellectual abilities. However, the results of a longitudinal study indicate that although low-IQ parents have been making larger families, larger families do not make low-IQ children. Further, the connection between birth order and intelligence seems to be unfounded (Rodgers, Cleveland, van den Oord, and Rowe, 2000).

SOCIAL AND EMOTIONAL CHARACTERISTICS OF GIFTEDNESS ■

Social Characteristics

Despite stories that often circulate in schools about gifted students being loners, surveys indicate that preadolescent and adolescent gifted students were at least as popular as other students their age, and most gifted students felt good about themselves and their relationships with peers. However, highly gifted students had more difficulty with the peer relationships and often developed coping strategies to deal with such circumstances (Mayseless, 1993). Swiatek (1995) found that the three most frequent coping strategies used by highly gifted students were denial of giftedness, popularity/conformity, and peer acceptance. There were no gender differences in the use of the strategies. Students more highly gifted in mathematical talents reported more peer acceptance than students who were gifted predominantly in verbal skills. It may be that verbally gifted students are more obvious to their peers and, therefore, they may feel more different.

> **Highly gifted adolescents**
> - **Often deny their giftedness**
> - **Want to conform**
> - **Seek popularity and peer acceptance**

A more recent study of over 220 gifted and nongifted high school freshmen found that gifted students perceived themselves as being more intimate with friends and assuming fewer family responsibilities. The gifted group also took more sports-related and danger-related risks than nongifted students. Furthermore, gifted students reported feeling that they were the same as or better than their peers in social skills, and, coincidently, their teachers agreed (Field, Harding, Yando, Gonzalez, Lasko, Bendell, and Marks, 1998).

Theory of Mind in Social Situations

Other studies also tend to show that some gifted adolescents and young adults can be very successful in social as well as intellectual situations. Is there some relationship between this capability and the brain functions of gifted individuals? One possible explanation is that a social relationship involves not only understanding how you would react in a given situation, but also forming a judgment about how the other person would think and act. In effect, you form an internal representation of that person's mental processes, what some call a "theory of mind." The more successful you are at predicting the other person's reactions and choices in a given social situation, the more likely you are to select a behavioral response that will make the interaction successful. This insight into other people's mental states is far more complicated than merely solving a puzzle, and the degree of its mastery is a reliable measure of social skills.

Emotional Characteristics

Numerous studies on the emotional, personality, and motivational characteristics of gifted students have yielded similar results. In general, the studies showed that, when compared to average students, gifted students

- Were at least as well or somewhat better adjusted
- Possessed more personality traits considered to be favorable
- Displayed personality traits similar to older students
- Had lower levels of anxiety about school
- Scored higher on measures of self-concept
- Displayed higher levels of intrinsic motivation and autonomy, especially for reading, thinking, and solitude

Some gender and age differences have been noted. For example, gifted high school girls had significantly less self-confidence, more perfectionism, and more discouragement than younger gifted girls. Gifted high school boys, however, felt less discouragement than younger boys, and there were no age differences in self-confidence and perfectionism. High school girls scored higher on discouragement than high school boys (Robinson and Clinkenbeard, 1998).

Although the studies present a useful profile, it is important to remember that some groups of gifted students will look quite different. For example, gifted students who are underachievers, and those whose talents are very far from the norm, are more likely to have difficulty fitting in socially and emotionally with their peers (see Chapter 7).

Frontal Lobe and Emotional Maturity

Why is it that many gifted students seem to be emotionally more mature than other students of the same age? Part of the answer may lie in the difference between the rate of maturation of the frontal lobes and the cerebral areas associated with emotions—the limbic area. You will recall from the previous chapter that the limbic area is located deep within the brain between the two temporal lobes where it generates, interprets, and stores emotional messages. Neurobiologists estimate that the limbic area matures (i.e., is fully functional) by the age of 10 to 12 years.

Maturity of a brain structure can be determined by measuring the amount of myelin covering the axons in the neural pathways. As structures become fully myelinated, nerve impulses can move along the pathways efficiently, making communication between various regions of the brain faster and more reliable.

Complete myelination of the frontal lobes takes a lot longer than for the limbic region, occurring for most individuals around the age of 18 to 20 years. This is because the frontal lobes have to communicate with all areas of the brain, and it takes time for the more distant pathways to be established and fully myelinated. One of the functions of the frontal lobes, you may recall, is to control the excesses of our emotions. We have all experienced situations in

> **For highly intelligent adolescents, it is possible that faster myelination in the frontal lobes may lead to earlier maturation of that area.**

which our impulses could easily have got out of control if the frontal lobes had not reined them in. The approximate 8-year time lag between the full maturity of the limbic region and the frontal lobes is largely responsible for the impulsive, high-risk behavior that is typical of most adolescents. Field and her colleagues (1998) found that gifted high school students do engage in high-risk behavior. However, she suggested that this finding may be because, as gifted children, they may have had earlier psychological separation from their parents and greater intimacy with peers. Thus, as adolescents, their distance from parents, association with peers, and a self-perception of social maturity may increase their desire and need to take more risks.

But neuroscience may provide us with another possible explanation as to why gifted students display more mature behavior and decision-making skills than other students of the same age. It may be that the greater frontal lobe volume found in more intelligent individuals (Thompson, et al., 2001) indicates that faster and more widespread myelination is occurring in those brains, thereby leading to earlier maturation of the frontal lobes. Supporting evidence for this concept may come from an EEG study that measured different alpha wave activity in 30 gifted adolescents, 30 average ability adolescents, and 30 college-age subjects. When given a series of cognitive tasks to complete, the overall alpha wave levels of the 30 gifted adolescents more closely matched that of the college-age subjects than the alpha levels of the average ability adolescents. These findings suggest that the gifted adolescents may have a more enhanced state of brain development than their average ability peers (Alexander, O'Boyle, Benbow, 1996).

■ GENDER DIFFERENCES

One always has to tread lightly when suggesting that males and females are different. No one disputes the obvious biological and anatomical differences that exist between the sexes. However, people often misinterpret discussions of differences in how the genders think or act to mean that one gender is inferior to another. This is not the case here. The intent is to present some valid observations from cognitive neuroscience to support the self-evident notion that males and females, in general, look at life through different lenses and approach decision making with specific gender-related preferences.

Differences in Cognitive Styles

Years of anecdotal studies, learning styles research, and real-life experiences seem to indicate that male and female brains do not think alike. Television programs, best-seller books, and even standup comedians have all tried to demonstrate and explain the different ways males and females deal with solving daily problems and arriving at important decisions. Much of the early research on male-female differences focused on veridical decision making and on the acquisition of specific skills. For instance, studies suggested that males were better at visual-spatial skills and at mathematics and that females were better at learning language. Until recently, little research was done to examine each gender's general approach to adaptive decision making and problem solving, better indicators of cognitive style.

Now, neuroscience is joining the fray by offering new evidence that male and female brains are generally different in structure, in basic biochemistry, and in cognitive style. In studies on cognitive problem solving, males tended to be more *context-dependent*, that is, they changed their choice of answer depending on how the type of question changed. Females, on the other hand, were far more *context-independent*, that is, they made their choices based on a stable set of preferences, regardless of the changes in the question type (Goldberg, 2001).

> **In terms of cognitive style, more males prefer a context-dependent approach and more females prefer a context-independent approach.**

People who are context-dependent tend to size up the problem at hand and then tailor a response that is appropriate to the specific context. In a new situation, a different choice is made, depending again on the new context. In Goldberg's example, a context-dependent person would vary the amount put into a savings account each month, depending on that month's income. By contrast, context-independent people tend to seek solutions that can apply across a number of different situations. When the context changes, little or no change in response is usually required. Here, a context-independent individual is likely to save the same amount each month, regardless of variations in monthly income. Neither strategy works better in all situations, and few people stick entirely to just one strategy. Nonetheless, although most people can move between the two strategies at will, more males prefer context-dependence and more females prefer context-independence.

Other studies have found that, when trying to exit a virtual 3-D maze, women activated the right parietal cortex and right prefrontal cortex, but that men triggered only the left hippocampus. When viewing emotionally disturbing images, women activated the amygdala on the left side, but men activated the right side. All of these findings lead to an obvious question: Can the gender differences in decision-making strategies be explained through gender differences in brain structure and brain biochemistry?

Differences in Brain Structure and Biochemistry

The male brain is about 10 percent larger than the female brain. One major difference in brain structure between the genders relates to the thickness of the cerebral cortex covering the frontal lobes. In males, the right frontal lobe cortex is thicker than the left, and in females, the cortical thickness is about the same for both frontal lobes. The corpus callosum tends to be proportionally thicker and denser in females than in males. Biochemical differences are also found. Estrogen receptors are distributed symmetrically across the frontal lobes in females, but asymmetrically in males. Gender differences also exist in the prevalence of neurotransmitter pathways—especially dopamine and norepinephrine—in the two lobes.

Given these variances, it is highly probable that the frontal lobes of males and females function differently. It is also highly probable that the left frontal lobe is functionally different from the right frontal lobe and that these differences are greater in male brains than in female brains. This may be because the female's proportionally larger corpus callosum allows for greater integration of functions (and less differentiation) between the cortical hemispheres than in males. In other words, most female brains are better at communicating *between* hemispheres, while most male brains are better *within* hemispheres.

Several recent MRI studies found that the volume of the cerebral hemispheres in most females was symmetrical, but the volume was not symmetrical in most males. The parietal lobe was significantly larger in males than in females. On tests of cognitive performance, the females outperformed males on verbal tasks, while males did better than females on visual and spatial tasks (Gur, Turetsky, Matsui, Yan, Bilker, Hughett, and Gur, 1999; Frederikse, Lu, Aylward, Barta, and Pearlson, 1999). Although researchers in learning styles observed similar results long before the advent of MRI, these imaging studies support the idea that differences in cognitive performance are related, at least in part, to differences in brain structure.

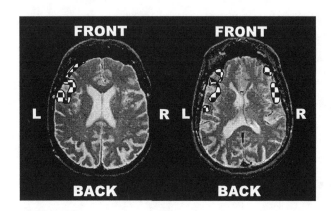

Figure 2.9 While processing phonetic language, fMRI scans show that male brains (left) use left hemisphere regions and that female brains (right) activate regions in both hemispheres (checkered areas).

Another area where gender differences in brain architecture seem to matter is in the processing of language. When doing phonological processing, fMRI scans showed that although both sexes carried out the task with equal speed and accuracy, males activated the left temporal lobe's speech center (Broca's area), which is involved in the processing of speech, while females activated both the left and right temporal regions (see Figure 2.9). This observation helps to explain why a left hemisphere stroke often results in speech problems in men but less so in women (Shaywitz, Shaywitz, and Gore, 1995).

■ IMPACT OF PRAISE ON GIFTED STUDENTS

Gifted children should be commended for their good grades and high test scores. However, recent research seems to indicate that excessively complimenting children for their intelligence and academic performance may lead them to believe that good test scores and high grades are more important than learning and mastering something new (Mueller and Dweck, 1998). Six studies of 412 fifth-graders compared the goals and achievement behaviors of children praised for intelligence with those praised for effort and hard work under conditions of failure as well as success. Through their studies, the psychologists demonstrated that commending children for their intelligence after good performance might backfire by making them highly performance-oriented and thus extremely vulnerable to the effects of subsequent setbacks. In contrast, children who are commended for their effort concentrate on learning goals and strategies for achievement.

The researchers also observed that children who were commended for their ability when they were successful learned to believe that intelligence is a fixed trait that cannot be developed or improved. The children who were explicitly commended after their successes were the ones who blamed poor performances on their own lack of intelligence. However, when children praised for their hard work performed poorly, they blamed their lack of success on poor effort and demonstrated a clear determination to learn strategies that would enhance subsequent performances.

The studies demonstrated that children who are praised for their intelligence learn to value performance, while children praised for their effort and hard work value learning opportunities. Virtually all of the findings were similar not only for boys

> **Studies show that children who are praised for their intelligence learn to value performance, while children praised for their effort and hard work value opportunities to learn.**

and girls but also among children from several different ethnic groups in rural and urban communities.

These findings may also explain why bright young girls who do well in grade school often perform poorly in upper grades. In their desire to bolster young girls' confidence in their abilities, educators have praised them for their intelligence which, these studies have shown, could have an undesired impact on their subsequent motivation and performance.

Labeling children as gifted or talented too soon may also have a negative impact on them. Such labeling may cause the children to become overly concerned with justifying that label and less concerned with meeting challenges that enhance their learning and mastery skills. They may begin to believe that academic setbacks indicate that they do not deserve to be labeled as gifted. The researchers advised that gifted and talented programs should emphasize how to meet challenges, apply effort, and search for new learning strategies. Furthermore, when students succeed, attention and approval should be directed at their effort and hard work rather than for the final product or their ability.

APPLICATIONS

USING ELABORATIVE REHEARSAL

Rehearsal refers to the learner's reprocessing of new information in an attempt to determine sense and meaning. It occurs in two forms. Some information items have value only if they are remembered *exactly* as presented, such as the letters and sequence of the alphabet, spelling, poetry, telephone numbers, notes and lyrics of a song, and the multiplication tables. This is called *rote rehearsal*. Sense and meaning are established quickly, and the likelihood of long-term retention is high. Most of us can recall poems and telephone numbers that we learned years ago.

More complex concepts require the learner to make connections and to form associations and other relationships in order to establish sense and meaning. Thus, the information will need to be reprocessed several times as new links are found. This is called *elaborative rehearsal*. The more senses that are used in this elaborative rehearsal, the more reliable the associations. Thus, when visual, auditory, and kinesthetic activities assist the learner during rehearsal, the probability of long-term storage rises dramatically. That is why it is important for students to talk about what they are learning *while* they are learning it, and to have visual models as well.

Elaborative rehearsal can also develop adaptive decision-making skills because students will have more opportunities to make new connections and to see relationships that would otherwise not be possible through rote rehearsal.

Rehearsal is teacher-initiated and teacher-directed. Much of what students practice in schools is rote rehearsal. Recognizing the value of elaborative rehearsal as a necessary ingredient for retention of learning, teachers should consider the following when designing and presenting their lessons:

Elaborative Rehearsal Strategies

- *Paraphrasing*. Students orally restate ideas in their own words, which then become familiar cues for later storage. Using the auditory modality helps the learner attach sense, making retention more likely.

- *Selecting and Note Taking*. Students review texts, illustrations, and lectures, deciding which portions are critical and important. They

USING ELABORATIVE REHEARSAL— Continued

make these decisions on the basis of criteria from the teacher, authors, or other students. Students then paraphrase the idea and write it into their notes. Adding the kinesthetic exercise of writing furthers retention.

- *Predicting*. After studying a section of content, the students predict the material to follow or what questions the teacher might ask about that content. Prediction keeps students focused on the new content, adds interest, and helps them apply prior learnings to new situations, thus aiding retention.

- *Questioning*. After studying content, students generate questions about the content. To be effective, the questions should range from lower-level thinking of recall, comprehension, and application to higher-level thinking of analysis, synthesis, and evaluation. When designing questions of varying complexity, students engage in deeper cognitive processing, clarify concepts, predict meaning and associations, and examine options—all contributors to retention and to improving adaptive decision-making skills.

- *Summarizing*. Students reflect on and summarize in their heads the important material or skills learned in the lesson. This is often the last and critical stage, in which students can attach sense and meaning to the new learning.

3

Challenging the Gifted Brain

Understanding the nature of the gifted brain is one thing; deciding how to help it learn is quite another. Addressing the needs of gifted students can occur in different classroom settings, using a variety of curriculum resources and teaching strategies and having expectations of specific student products that demonstrate learning. As for classroom settings, elementary and middle school students identified as gifted might participate in a special pull-out class, and high school students can opt for advanced placement courses. But apart from these limited choices, most gifted students—except for those few with extraordinarily abilities—will get their learning opportunities in the normal school setting. Consequently, this chapter examines some considerations for selecting curriculum content, choosing teaching strategies, and deciding on the learning products of gifted students in the regular classroom.

Figure 3.1 illustrates the relationship between the elements of curriculum, process, and product and their setting within the total learning environment. Curriculum identifies *what is being taught* as well as the classroom structures and environment in which the teaching occurs. Process refers to *how the curriculum is taught*, that is, the

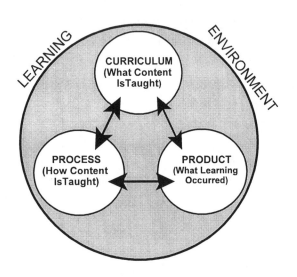

Figure 3.1 The diagram shows the relationship between the elements of curriculum, process, and product and their setting within the learning environment (dark circle).

teaching strategies and resulting learning behaviors that are used in the classroom during the teaching/learning episode. Product describes the various ways students can demonstrate *what they have learned*. Of course, there will be some overlap among the three components, and the learning environments affect all three. But the essential areas focus on what and where material is taught (curriculum), the teacher (process), and the student (product).

DIFFERENTIATED CURRICULUM AND LEARNING ■

Because most gifted students—especially in elementary and middle school—will be taught primarily in the regular classroom, teachers need to find ways to differentiate the learning experiences for these students.

- Differentiating the curriculum means moving students beyond grade-level standards or connecting what is taught to their personal interests.
- Differentiating the processes means using the learning strategies that provide depth and complexity appropriate to the students' abilities.
- The products are differentiated in that they demonstrate student learning at an advanced level, going beyond paper-and-pencil tests and allowing students to develop their talents and curiosities and to present their findings to an appropriate audience.
- Differentiating the learning environment means allowing students to work more independently on their own projects, collaborate with other students, or pursue interests outside the regular classroom (Winebrenner, 2000).

Gifted students are expected to learn the same basic concepts, facts, issues, and skills as all other students. However, they make connections faster, work well with abstractions, and generally have the deep interests found in older individuals. Consequently, they need to work with the curriculum at higher instructional levels, at a faster pace, and using a variety of materials appropriate for their learning style.

Federal regulations and those of most states require that school districts establish curriculum modifications to meet the needs of students identified as gifted. (Federal regulations on educational programs can be found on the Internet at: *http://www.ed.gov/legislation/FedRegister*.) However, the standards movement will be of little value if it does not respond to the needs of all students, including the gifted. The standards need to be flexible so that gifted students can be assured access to a stimulating, rich, and thought-provoking curriculum. Furthermore, standardized tests should not be the primary means for measuring student achievement. A wide range of assessment tools, e.g., journals, learning logs, self-evaluation questionnaires, interviews, and portfolios, are likely to yield more accurate information about how much a student has learned.   To assist districts in deciding what those modifications should be, the National Association for Gifted Children (NAGC) has published standards for pre-K through grade 12 gifted programs. Specifically, the standards suggest (NAGC, 1998) that

- Curriculum for the gifted learner should be differentiated and span grades pre-K through 12.
- Regular classroom curricula must be adapted, modified, or replaced to meet the needs of the gifted.
- The pace of instruction must be flexible to allow for the accelerated learning of the gifted.
- Gifted students must be allowed to skip subjects and grades.
- Gifted learners must have opportunities that provide a variety of curriculum options, instructional approaches, and resources.

Exactly how to best address the different learning styles and needs of the gifted has been a question that schools have pondered for years. Some schools offer pull-out programs at the elementary and middle school levels, where gifted children can interact with their peers for a set time period. But for budgetary and philosophical reasons, schools in recent years have been moving away from pull-out programs and toward providing enrichment services to all students in the regular classroom environment. Some researchers in

> **Teachers need to establish a flexible learning environment and differentiate the curriculum so that gifted students will be challenged rather than bored.**

gifted education are alarmed at this trend, fearing that gifted students will not be appropriately challenged in this format.

The reality is that, as budgetary reductions take their toll on pull-out programs for the gifted, an increasing number of these elementary and middle school students will have to get their needs met in their regular classroom. To accomplish this successfully, teachers need to establish a flexible learning environment and differentiate the curriculum content so that gifted students will be challenged rather than bored.

A SUPPORTIVE LEARNING ENVIRONMENT ■

Teaching gifted students in an inclusive classroom requires a flexible and supportive learning climate that encompasses both the physical setting of the classroom and its climate. The teacher maintains a challenging environment by encouraging responsibility and autonomy, emphasizing student strengths, and addressing individual student needs.

Classroom Organization and Management

To organize the classroom for flexibility and openness, the teacher provides space for students to work independently and in small groups. Students may move around the room freely as long as they remain on task. They may also go to the computer lab, library, or other in-school location, if appropriate. In this setting, the teacher's role changes from presenting the curriculum to selecting and creating learning opportunities, guiding students, and assessing their progress. Students are given choices and allowed to schedule their activities, at least for part of the classroom time. Of course, students are still responsible for completing specific activities or periodically demonstrating what they have learned. However, they can choose how and when they will work.

Social and Emotional Climate

A positive learning environment includes the elements of safety and acceptance. Teachers create this atmosphere by modeling care and respect for all members of the classroom, emphasizing every student's strengths. All students need to recognize and appreciate their own strengths and those of others. Acceptance is a particularly important component of classroom climate because gifted learners are prone to being perfectionists and thus place great emphasis on completing a task quickly and getting the right answer. Their unusual abilities may make them outsiders among their classmates, or they may be accustomed to having a higher status than others in the classroom.

Gifted students sometimes feel insecure when presented with problem-solving activities or open-ended inquiry. They want to know the procedures that will ensure that they do it the right way. Here the teacher needs to remind these students that mistakes are an important part of the learning process and that there may be several "right" ways to solve a problem.

Not all gifted students like to display or explain their work. Some see this as redundant or as slowing them down. Teachers need to assure students that explaining how they got an answer is as important as being correct. Using a scoring guide or rubric may help these students recognize the value of the steps used to work through a problem.

■ CURRICULUM CONTENT INITIATIVES FOR GIFTED LEARNERS

Gifted students need to work at higher instructional levels and at a faster pace than non-gifted students. Several initiatives have emerged to enhance content within the context of the self-contained classroom as well as within the middle and high school curricular formats. Numerous studies in recent years have investigated the impact of these initiatives on student performance, the extent of which is assessed by a statistical measure known as *effect size*.

A Note About Research and Effect Sizes

One way to measure the impact of an educational strategy on student achievement is with a statistical measure known as *effect size* (ES). It is determined by dividing the standard deviation of the control group into the difference between the mean scores of the treatment and control groups.

$$\text{Effect Size} = \frac{(\text{Mean of Treatment Group}) - (\text{Mean of Control Group})}{\text{Standard Deviation of Control Group}}$$

An effect size of 0.25 or greater is considered educationally significant. In classroom terms, an effect size of 1.00 is approximately equal to one school year. Thus, if a study found an effect size of 0.33, it would mean that the treatment group outperformed the control group by 1/3 of a school year, or about 3 grade-equivalent school months of additional achievement.

In the following sections, references are made to effect size results if they are available. (For more information on effect size, see Glass, McGaw, and Smith, 1981.)

Acceleration

Acceleration assumes that different students of the same age are at different levels of learning. This requires a diagnosis of the learning level and the introduction of curriculum at a level slightly above it. Essentially, acceleration recognizes that different students will learn different material at different rates in different subject areas and at different stages of their development. However, schools have found great difficulty in achieving the flexibility required to meet these varying student needs. No one pretends that this is easy, and several components need to be considered.

Early Entrance and Exit

One component should allow for early entrance and early exit of students who complete the curricular requirements and any grade level. Getting into high school early eliminates the slower moving middle school years. Despite the cry over standards, they do provide a clear way to determine mastery of curriculum, thus allowing students to move ahead.

Content-Based Acceleration

Another component involves content-based acceleration in all subject areas while the student remains in grade. Although schools have become more open to acceleration in mathematics, other areas of acceleration languish. Gifted learners with verbal, scientific, and artistic abilities need access to accelerated programs in these subjects as well. Some educators and parents express concern that gifted children should not accelerate more than six months to a year for fear they will get too far out of step with the curriculum or socially with their peers. Yet, there is little reliable research to support either of these fears.

Telescoping

Courses often overlap material and skills from one grade level to the next. Because gifted students learn and remember material faster, telescoping reduces the amount of time a student takes to cover the curriculum. An example is when a student completes grades 7 and 8 mathematics in one year, thus allowing the student to move on to more challenging work.

Grade-Level Advancement

Acceleration can involve advancing students who have learned all areas of a grade's curriculum, to the next grade. This step is particularly warranted for students who demonstrate more than 2 years' advancement in all school subjects. Once again, the concerns raised about the students, potential mismatch of social and emotional growth between these students and their new peers seems unfounded, especially when compared with how grade acceleration can counter the boredom and disenchantment of our most able learners. Given its powerful effect sizes (see box that follows), grade advancement should be far more common than it is.

Yet, many practitioners continue to have concerns about this practice and use it infrequently (Southern, Jones, and Stanley, 1993). However, when it does occur, skipping a grade is not always accompanied by adaptations to the curriculum to meet the needs of the advancing student (Southern, et al., 1993; Shore and Delcourt, 1996). Because grade skipping is applied to an individual student, a curriculum plan needs to be designed to ensure that appropriate curriculum experiences will occur for that student in the new placement.

Problems With Advanced Placement and International Baccalaureate Programs?

Advanced Placement (AP) and International Baccalaureate (IB) programs have recently come under scrutiny. A study in 2002 by the National Research Council criticized AP and IB mathematics and science courses as
- cramming too much material at the expense of depth of understanding
- failing to keep up-to-date with developments in the area
- not providing adequate guidance to teachers on modern methods of instruction
- lacking research on what the examinations actually measure
- lacking systematic and continuing professional development for teachers.

(Gollub, Bertenthal, Labov, and Curtis, 2002)

Advanced Study Programs

In high school, acceleration has traditionally meant enrollment in the College Board's Advanced Placement (AP) Program or the International Baccalaureate (IB) program. Both programs allow students to engage in college-level work and get the reward of college placement or credit for work done during their high school years. However, recent concerns about the integrity of both these programs have led some colleges to give credit only to students who score a five (the highest grade) on the AP exam.

Dual Enrollment

Acceleration can also mean dual enrollment at local community and 4-year colleges, where students can sample the college environment and gain the opportunities needed for early academic and socialization processes to occur.

Acceleration Through Technology

Advances in telecommunications now permit university on-line courses to reach distant rural areas. Some of these distance learning courses (e.g., the

Stanford Education Program for Gifted Youth) are tailored for younger students, and others offer the equivalent of freshman-level college courses. On-line communications also offer independent study with university faculty and opportunities to work on research projects.

Acceleration and Effect Sizes

After conducting an exhaustive search of research literature on gifted education through 1998, Rogers (1998) performed an analysis of acceleration formats and found the following effect sizes (ES):

- ◆ Early Entrance and Exit: ES = 0.49
- ◆ Content-Based Acceleration: ES = 0.57
- ◆ Telescoping: ES = 0.40
- ◆ Grade-Level Advancement: ES = 0.49 (Academic effect); 0.31 (Socialization effect)
- ◆ Advanced Study Courses: ES = 0.27
- ◆ Dual Enrollment: ES = 0.22

Curriculum Compacting

Compacting is one of the most common curriculum modifications for academically gifted students. This strategy reduces the amount of time the student spends on the regular curriculum. It allows students to demonstrate what they know, to do assignments in those areas where work is needed, and then to move on to other curricular areas. The strategy makes appropriate adjustments for students in any curriculum area and at any grade level. Essentially, the process involves defining key concepts and skills of a specific curriculum unit, determining and documenting which students have already mastered most or all of the learning objectives, and providing replacement strategies for material already mastered that result in a more challenging and productive use of the student's time (Reis, Burns, and Renzulli, 1992).

Occasionally, there will be specific areas in which the student is still developing competence. In this instance, the teacher can ask the student to rejoin the class at strategic points during the unit. The student may also need to join the class for discussions and inquiry or for problem-solving activities.

Teachers can compact basic skills as well as course content. Compacting basic skills involves determining which ones the students have mastered and eliminating the repetition or practice of those skills. For example, beginning algebra students who demonstrate mastery of some algebraic functions have little need for drill and practice in those areas and should move on to more complex course content.

Compacting is also useful for those gifted students who have not mastered the course material at the regular classroom pace but can do so at an accelerated pace. They usually have some understanding of the content but may require only minimal instructional time to reach mastery.

> **A teacher's fear that curriculum compacting will cause decreases in students' achievement scores is not supported by research studies.**

Some elementary teachers are reluctant to use curriculum compacting for fear that doing so could cause declines in students' scores on achievement tests. However, a recent study looked at the achievement scores of a national sample of 336 high-ability students from second- through sixth-grade heterogeneous classrooms in urban, suburban, and rural settings. The teachers selected one to two students who demonstrated superior knowledge of the material prior to instruction and eliminated 40 to 50 percent of the curriculum across content areas for those students. The results of the Iowa Test of Basic Skills indicated that the achievement scores of the students whose curriculum was compacted did not differ significantly from the scores of similar students whose curriculum was not compacted (Reis, Westberg, Kulikowich, and Purcell, 1998).

In a study of language arts curriculum for advanced learners in grades 4 through 6, teachers replaced the regular readings with selections that were advanced for the grade levels in which they were introduced. The readings emphasized abstract concepts in literary analysis, such as mood, tone, theme, and

---

Curriculum Compacting and Effect Sizes

♦ Compacting: ES = 0.83, 0.26;
         11, 0.99, 1.57

Different effect sizes were found in the research literature on curriculum compacting, depending on the type of replacement activity provided. The 0.83 represents the replacement of math and science curriculum with advanced math and science at the student's true learning level and at an accelerated pace. The 0.26 represents the replacement of social studies and reading curriculum with enrichment activities in those areas (Rogers, 1998).

When regular readings in grades 4 through 6 were replaced with advanced-level readings for gifted students, the effect size of 11 represents literary analysis, the 0.99 represents writing, and the 1.57 is grammatical understanding (VanTassel-Baska, et al., 1996).

motivation. Outcome measures showed that the learners who received the advanced material outperformed students in the comparison groups in three areas: on a reading assignment that focused on literary analysis, on a persuasive writing assignment, and on an objective measure of grammatical understanding (VanTassel-Baska, Johnson, Hughes, and Boyce, 1996).

Grouping

Grouping can be an effective component in educating all students. But this technique is particularly effective with gifted students because it is an ideal medium for differentiation. Furthermore, several studies have found that gifted students benefit most from like-ability grouping because they are able to access more advanced knowledge and skills and to pursue their learning tasks in greater depth (Pallas, Entwisle, Alexander, and Stluka, 1994; Gamoran, Nystrand, Berends, and LePore, 1995). Grouping formats run the gamut from within-class ability groupings to independent grouping options, such as internships and mentor programs.

Within-Class Ability Grouping

This format can occur at all grade levels. In elementary schools, many classes are now heterogeneous and inclusive—settings where little challenge or differentiation is provided for the gifted learner. In secondary schools,

> **Gifted students benefit most from like-ability grouping because they can get more deeply involved in the learning task.**

instruction in even the honors, Advanced Placement, or International Baccalaureate programs are set for the norm. Thus, high ability students may find the instructional pace too slow and miss out on opportunities for more in-depth and challenging work. Within-class groups can be formed around term papers, for example, allowing advanced students more latitude for their work. Groups for differentiated reading assignments can have the same effect.

Pull-Out Grouping

This program is particularly popular at the elementary level and is one of the primary ways to deliver differentiated curriculum. Students identified as gifted from different classes meet as one group on a regular basis. In this setting, effective acceleration practices can be used for individual students because the content level of the class, by its very nature, needs to be more advanced.

Full-Time Ability Grouping

Also known as tracking, this format usually starts in upper elementary grades. Students are in the same group for most of the day and tend to remain in the same track throughout their school year. Tracking allows students to pursue a more advanced series of courses through middle and high school. The recent trend toward heterogenous classes has diminished tracking, especially in middle school where it all started. Where it still occurs, tracking usually provides for special grouping in mathematics and language arts, but not in science and social studies. To be truly successful, full-time grouping should apply across all subject areas, where the school size allows.

A Word About Cooperative Learning

Cooperative learning is an effective instructional strategy, especially in heterogeneous classes. However, when the range of abilities gets very wide, gifted students may not benefit from the heterogenous cooperative group. One study found that gifted students participated in higher-level discussions when grouped with other gifted students (Lando and Schneider, 1997), and that their absence from the heterogeneous group did not adversely affect the learning of other students in the group (Kenney, Archambault, and Hallmark, 1994). These findings suggest that teachers may want to use caution when using this practice with gifted students.

Cluster Grouping

Cluster grouping is different from tracking in that the group is composed of only three to six students, usually the top 5 percent of ability in the class. This format allows the gifted children to learn together while avoiding permanent grouping arrangements with students of other ability levels. If the cluster group is kept to a manageable size, teachers report a general improvement in achievement for the whole class. This is probably because teachers who learn how to provide opportunities for gifted students also modify those opportunities for the rest of the class, raising achievement for all. Cluster groups can also be formed in secondary schools in any heterogeneous classroom, especially in smaller schools, where there may not be enough students to form an advanced section in a particular subject (Winebrenner and Devlin, 2001).

Independent Work Grouping

This format offers students options for more personalized opportunities for intellectual growth. It can occur by one or two students working on a well-designed independent project, interning in a professional setting (e.g., a hospice or senior care center), or associating with an adult mentor who has expertise in an area of the student's interest. Such options require close collaboration between school and community leaders.

Grouping Formats and Effect Sizes

- ◆ Within-Class Ability Grouping: ES = 0.34
- ◆ Pull-Out Grouping: ES = 0.65, 0.44, 0.32
- ◆ Full-Time Ability Grouping: ES = 0.49, 0.33
- ◆ Cluster Grouping of Gifted Students: ES = 0.62
- ◆ Independent Work With Mentors: ES = 0.47, 0.42, 0.57

There are only a few reliable studies on pull-out groups, so the effect size numbers may be inflated. The 0.65 refers to pull-outs that are a direct extension of the regular school curriculum; the 0.44, to pull-outs that focus on thinking skills; the 0.32, to pull-outs that focus on creative skills.

For full-time ability grouping, the 0.49 represents the yearly effect for all academic areas for elementary gifted students (grades K-6); the 0.33, for secondary students (grades 7-12).

Mentor programs can advance gifted students in many ways. The 0.47 represents the socialization effect; the 0.42 is the self-esteem effect; and 0.57 is the academic effect (Rogers, 1998).

INSTRUCTIONAL PROCESSES FOR GIFTED LEARNERS ■

Processes refers to the instructional strategies that engage students during the learning episode that will help them find sense and meaning. This is more likely to happen if the instructional techniques help students see purpose to the new learning and have opportunities to probe for understanding and relevancy. Such process skills might involve higher-level thinking, creative thinking, problem solving, and independent or group research.

Higher-Level Thinking

Trying to classify levels of human thought is no easy feat. But that has not kept psychologists from trying. One model, published nearly 50 years ago by Benjamin Bloom (1956), still passes the test of time and remains useful as a starting point for understanding the complexity of human thought. I have discussed the value of Bloom's Taxonomy at great length in a previous publication (Sousa, 2001a) so my purpose here is just to present a short version to set the stage for discussing thought processes further.

Bloom's model is a hierarchy of six levels describing human thought, from the least to the most complex: knowledge, comprehension (understanding), application, analysis, synthesis, and evaluation. Although there are six levels, the hierarchy is not rigid, and an individual may move easily among the levels during extended processing. Here are brief definitions of each level:

- **Knowledge:** The mere recall of rote learning, from specific facts, to a memorized definition or complete theory. This is semantic memory and there is no presumption that the learner *understands* what has been recalled.

- **Comprehension:** This level describes the ability to make sense out of the material, goes beyond recall, and represents the lowest level of understanding. Here the material becomes available for future use to solve problems and to make decisions.

- **Application:** Application refers to the ability to use learned material in new situations with a minimum of direction. It includes the application of such things as rules, concepts, methods, and theories to solve problems. The learner activates procedural memory and uses convergent thinking to select, transfer, and apply data to complete a new task. Practice is essential at this level.

- **Analysis:** Analysis is the ability to break material into its component parts so that its structure may be understood. It includes identifying parts, examining the relationships of the parts to each other and to the whole, and recognizing the organizational principles involved. The learner must be able to organize and reorganize information into categories. The brain's frontal lobes are working hard at this level. This stage is more complex because the learner is aware of the thought process in use (metacognition) and understands both the content and structure of the material.

- **Synthesis:** Synthesis refers to the ability to put parts together to form a plan that is new to the learner. It may involve the production of a unique communication (essay or speech), a plan of operations (research proposal), or a scheme for classifying information (a taxonomy). This level stresses creativity, with major emphasis on forming *new* patterns or structures. This is the level where learners use divergent thinking to get an *Aha!* experience. Although most often associated with the arts, synthesis can occur in all areas of the curriculum.

- **Evaluation:** Evaluation describes the ability to judge the value of material on the basis of specific criteria. The learner examines criteria from several categories and selects those that are the most relevant to the situation. Activities at this level almost always have multiple and equally acceptable solutions. This is the highest level of cognitive thought in this model because it contains elements of all the other levels, plus conscious judgments based on definite criteria. At this level, learners tend to consolidate their thinking and become more receptive to other points of view. (Note: The name of this level often creates confusion because one immediately thinks of testing. Bloom intended for *evaluation* to mean a judgment or assessment of different individual options within a group and the selection of one option supported by a defensible rationale.)

Convergent/Critical and Divergent/Creative Thinking

The first three levels of Bloom's taxonomy describe what can be called *convergent* or *critical* thinking whereby the learner recalls and focuses what is known and comprehended to solve a problem through application. While using the upper three levels, the learner often gains new insights and makes discoveries that were not part of the original information. This describes a *divergent* or *creative* thinking process.

The Important Difference Between Complexity and Difficulty

Complexity and difficulty describe completely different mental operations, but are often used synonymously (Figure 3.2). This error, resulting in the two factors being treated as one, limits the use of the taxonomy to enhance the thinking of all students. By recognizing how these concepts are different, the teacher can gain valuable insight into the connection between the taxonomy and student ability. *Complexity* describes the *thought process* that the brain uses to deal with information. In Bloom's Taxonomy, it can be described by any of the six words representing the six levels. The question, "What is the capital of Florida?" is at the knowledge level, but the question, "Can you tell me in your own words what is meant by a state

Levels of Bloom's Taxonomy

Difficulty and Complexity

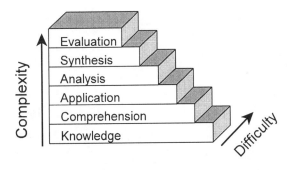

Figure 3.2 Complexity and difficulty are different. Complexity establishes the level of thought; difficulty determines the amount of effort within each level.

capital?" is at the comprehension level. The second question is more *complex* than the first because it is at a higher level in Bloom's Taxonomy.

Difficulty, on the other hand, refers to the *amount of effort* that the learner must expend *within* a level of complexity to accomplish a learning objective. It is possible for a learning activity to become increasingly difficult without becoming more complex. For example, the question, "Can you name the states of the Union?" is at the knowledge level of complexity because it involves simple recall (semantic memory) for most students. The question, "Can you name the states of the Union and their capitals?" is also at the knowledge level but is more difficult than the prior question because it involves more effort to recall more information. Similarly, the question, "Can you name the states and their capitals in order of their admission to the Union?" is still at the knowledge level, but it is considerably more *difficult* than the first two. It requires gathering more information and then sequencing it by chronological order.

Bloom's Taxonomy and Gifted Students

These are examples of how a student can exert great effort to achieve a learning task while processing at the lowest level of thinking. When seeking to challenge students, classroom teachers are more likely (perhaps unwittingly) to increase difficulty rather than complexity as the challenge mode. This may be because they do not recognize the difference between these concepts or that they believe that difficulty is the method for achieving higher-order thinking. Moreover, for all sorts of reasons including the overcrowded curriculum and the continued educational emphasis on fact acquisition, more class time is spent with instruction at the lower levels of the taxonomy. Obviously, all students benefit when teachers include activities that engage students at the upper levels of analysis, synthesis, and evaluation. Gifted students, particularly, can pass through the first three levels quickly and schools do these students a great disservice if they fail to provide opportunities for higher-level thinking.

Creative Thinking

Is creativity the result of innate abilities or of a learned set of behaviors? Psychologists and others have debated this question for decades, more often siding with the view that creativity is a gift from nature or the result of genetic heritage. Now studies in cognitive neuroscience seem to be indicating that creativity is more likely the result of a series of cognitive processes that can be developed in most individuals. Surely, genetic heritage still has some influence. But the notion that some degree of creativity can be *taught* is exciting, and strategies to accomplish this will make valuable additions to a teacher's repertoire.

In Bloom's model, synthesis is the level most closely associated with creativity, but there certainly are other ways to define creative thinking, usually in terms of the learning behaviors creativity evokes. Four behaviors often associated with creativity are

> **Fluency:** This describes the ability to generate new ideas. This skill is required for students to explain what they know, to think of ways to solve a problem, to develop ideas for writing or speaking, and to draw diagrams or models. A question like, "In what ways can we do this?" evokes fluency.
>
> **Flexibility:** This behavior requires generating a broad range of ideas, such as "How many different ways can we do this?"
>
> **Originality:** This behavior refers to unusual or unique responses to a situation. Original responses usually occur at the end of an idea-seeking activity and after the more obvious ideas have been rendered. A question stem might be, "What is the most unusual way to accomplish this?"
>
> **Elaboration:** Here, other ideas and details are added to the reasoning. "What else can we do here?" and "Can you tell me more?" are questions that elicit elaboration.

Mental Imagery and Creativity

At least three of these creativity behaviors—fluency, originality, and elaboration—seem to be closely associated with mental imagery. One large study of 560 high school students compared scores on tests of imaging ability with those on tests of creative thinking. The results indicated a significant correlation between imaging ability and creativity in general and that imaging ability had strong effects on fluency, originality, and elaboration (González, Campos, and Pérez, 1997). The researchers did not offer an explanation for the correlation. However, it seems reasonable to speculate that because other scanning studies have shown separately that imagery and creative activities engage the right frontal and temporal

> **Creativity appears to be closely associated with the ability to do mental imagery.**

lobes of the brain, individuals having high imaging capabilities would also have high capabilities in creativity as well.

Creativity as Decision Making

If being creative is more a learned pattern of behavior than genetic heritage, the question arises as to what behaviors or skills are likely to develop creativity. Sternberg (2000) suggests that students can develop their creativity by learning the attitudes they will need to be successful in their work. Thus, they develop what Sternberg calls "creative giftedness" as a decision-making skill. He describes ten decisions that students can make to be more creative:

> **Creativity is a decision-making skill that can be developed.**

1. **Redefine Problems.** Creative people take a problem and force themselves to see it differently from the way most other people see it. For example, Manet and Monet challenged artistic representations, Beethoven redefined classical music, and Einstein totally altered our views of the universe.

2. **Analyze One's Ideas.** Creative people analyze the value of their ideas, recognizing that not all of them are worthy of pursuit and that they will make mistakes. This self-skepticism prevents them from believing that they have all the answers and encourages them to admit when they are wrong.

3. **Sell One's Ideas.** Because creative ideas usually challenge existing methods, they will not be easily accepted and thus need to be sold to the public.

4. **Knowledge Is a Double-Edged Sword.** Knowledge can help people decide what new areas need to be explored, or it can entrench people so that they lose sight of other perspectives.

5. **Surmount Obstacles.** Creative people inevitably confront obstacles and must have the determination to surmount them.

6. **Take Sensible Risks.** Creative people must be willing to take reasonable risks, recognizing that they will sometimes fail and sometimes succeed.

7. **Willingness to Grow.** Creative people avoid getting stuck with one idea forever. Rather, they look for new ways to expand the idea or add new ones.

8. **Believe in Yourself.** Creative people maintain their belief in themselves even when their ideas are poorly received and when other sources of intellectual and emotional support are gone.

9. **Tolerance of Ambiguity.** Creative people often face ambiguity when trying creative things. A high tolerance for ambiguity is important if the creative venture is to succeed.

10. **Find What You Love to Do and Do It.** Creative people are at their best when they are doing what they love to do.

Sternberg proposes that anyone can make the decision to be creative. Because the ten decisions are not fixed abilities, teachers can encourage students to decide in favor of creativity and to reward those students who do.

Problem-Based Learning

Problem-based learning places students in the position of trying to solve a multifaceted problem of significant complexity. The problem resembles a real-life situation in that the students lack some of the information they need to solve the problem or are not clear on the steps they will need to take. The students critically analyze the problem from different points of view, look for alternative solutions, select a solution, and develop a plan of action for its implementation.

Students usually work in groups and are responsible for retrieving the additional information and resources they will need. In addition, students decide which group members will focus on the various parts of the problem and on how to present their findings to demonstrate what they have learned. Their presentations can be in the form of portfolios, videotapes, exhibits, or written reports (Burruss, 1999).

The teacher's role in problem-based learning is to act as a metacognitive coach by asking questions, helping students plan their work, guiding them toward the questions they need to pursue, and assessing their progress. In this format, the teacher is more of a guide than a provider of information.

The open-ended nature of problem-based learning allows for considerable differentiation of curriculum and instruction. The process calls upon the varied strengths of the learners, involves a multitude of in-school and out-of-school resources, and provides opportunities for students to pursue their interests. Sources of real problems to study may be

- Environmental: Why is the amount of mercury increasing in our drinking water?
- School: What are the implications of starting high school an hour later?
- Community: Should we adopt an evening curfew for teenagers?

- Political: Should city councilors be subject to term limits?
- Global: What can be done to stem the rise of AIDS in Africa?

The Triarachic Approach

The text in Chapter 2 explains the Triarchic Theory of Intelligence (Sternberg, 1985). To apply the theory in the classroom, teachers need to present instruction so that at different times it engages the students in analytical, creative, and practical thinking while solving problems. The problem-solving cycle involves five steps: identifying the problem, acquiring the resources for solving the problem, devising a strategy for solving the problem, and monitoring and evaluating the problem solving (see Figure 3.3). Properly implemented, the cycle promotes the three different types of thinking. For example, evaluating the problem-solving approach might involve analytical thinking. Creative thinking would help to formulate the strategy, and practical thinking would be helpful in determining and acquiring the resources for solving the problem at hand.

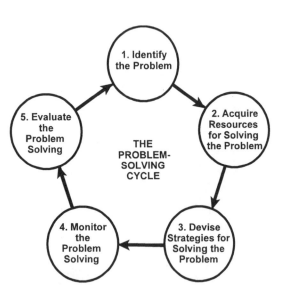

Figure 3.3 The five steps in the problem-solving cycle.

In the triarchic approach, teachers plan their lessons not only for memory but also for analytical, creative, and practical processing. Analytical thinking occurs then teachers ask students to judge, compare and contrast, evaluate, and critique. Creative thinking activities would have students suppose, invent, imagine, explore, and discover. Practical thinking is involved when students implement, use, apply, and contextualize. Classroom applications of the theory have shown positive results in terms of student achievement (Sternberg, et al., 1996; Sternberg, et al., 2000).

Independent Study

Independent study can be a useful strategy for differentiating curriculum. However, students generally need help in learning how to become independent workers. But with proper teachers' guidance, students can learn to pursue interests on their own by setting learning goals, establishing criteria for judging their work, assessing their progress, and presenting their work products to an audience. The goal of this program is to help the student move from being teacher-directed to being self-directed.

These ventures are more likely to be successful if the student has a clear focus on what material and skills are to be learned. The selected independent learning activities should help develop creative and critical thinking skills as well as time management strategies and research skills. Maintaining a learning log and a portfolio of results also is an important component of a successful independent study program. It should be noted that assessment results of the effect size of independent study are inconclusive.

Tiered Assignments

Tiered assignments provide for differentiation by allowing students at different ability levels to work on the same content. However, students seek out the answers to different questions and are assigned different activities based on their ability. One approach is to teach Bloom's Taxonomy and to ask them to design questions and activities at the different levels of complexity. The teacher then works with the students to decide which questions they will pursue and to set the criteria for evaluating their results.

Before starting on tiering, the teacher needs to identify the core elements—those components that *all* students should master. The teacher then devises separate versions of the activities so that the low-, middle-, and high-ability students are adequately challenged. The advantage of this approach is that, with a little advance planning, the teacher can keep students of differing ability levels engaged and working toward the same learning objective through differentiated tasks.

THE PRODUCTS OF GIFTED LEARNERS ■

Products are the vehicles through which students demonstrate what they have learned as a result of their engagement with a particular body of knowledge and skills. The products referred to in this context are culminating activities that result from a considerable amount of student time and involvement with the learning unit; they are not the worksheets or quizzes that are part of daily routine.

To be effective, the culminating products need to be able to do the following (Tomlinson, 1995):

- Offer students opportunities to extend their knowledge, stretch their abilities, and pursue authentic and challenging learning experiences.
- Evolve from advanced materials, original research, or primary documents.
- Transform information so that students are not merely repeating information but creating a new idea or product.
- Be similar to those created by professionals in that the products address real-world problems and are intended for real audiences, for example, are published in student literary magazines, displayed in public places (banks, malls, and shop windows), or prepared as oral history tapes for a library.
- Be assessed by experts associated with the field of endeavor, such as researchers, college professors, or other professionals.

Student products can be centered around tiered assignments, independent studies, the Triarchic and Multiple Intelligences models, and any complex investigations that result in the learning of a body of knowledge and skills. They can include the following:

☞ Written reports	☞ 3-D sculptures
☞ Oral reports	☞ Storyboard displays
☞ Plays, skits, or pantomimes	☞ Audiotapes
☞ Songs	☞ Poems
☞ Charts and graphs	☞ Oral history tapes
☞ Photo essays	☞ Charcoal sketches
☞ Demonstrations	☞ Watercolors
☞ Videotapes	☞ Puppet shows

■ GIFTED VISUAL-SPATIAL LEARNERS

The information in human brains can be organized in specialized patterns that result in different views of the world, as discussed in Chapter 2. Left-hemisphere-preferred individuals develop a highly-organized sequential system that is strong on analysis, progression from simple to complex, and specializing in linear deductive reasoning. This system seems to be greatly influenced by auditory input and language. By contrast, right-hemisphere-preferred individuals develop thinking patterns that use synthesis, have an intuitive grasp of complex systems, process concepts simultaneously, and specialize in inductive reasoning.

Visualization and spatial abilities are thought to be strongly associated with this preference. Although more males are right-hemisphere preferred and more females are left-hemisphere preferred (Sousa, 2001a, Ch. 5), it is important to remember that integration of both hemispheres is necessary for higher-level thought. All learners use both hemispheres, but not with equal fluency.

Linda Silverman (1989) was among the first researchers to identify visual-spatial learners as a result of working with children with many types of giftedness. She identified two groups of gifted visual-spatial learners. The first group scores extremely high on IQ tests because they have high ability in tasks requiring visual-spatial processing as well as those tasks requiring sequential thinking processes. The second group consists of students who are brighter than their IQ scores would indicate but do not score well because they have weaknesses in sequential processing skills. Although these students may have difficulty achieving their potential in school, they may not have a learning disability, but perhaps a teaching-style disability. That is, traditional teaching methods tend to favor strong sequential learners. Concepts are usually presented step-by-step, practiced with drill and repetition, reviewed, and then tested under timed conditions. Consequently, gifted visual-spatial learners may have greater difficulty in traditional classrooms and their talents may not be fully recognized.

Characteristics of Visual-Spatial Learners

There is no single test to determine visual-spatial giftedness. Identification is best accomplished by looking for a collection of behaviors that often indicate visual-spatial preference. For example, IQ tests generally show higher scores on nonverbal tasks compared with verbal tasks. Essentially, this type of learner enjoys constructing toys and rarely follows directions. These students are reflective and need time to think. Consequently, they may appear off task when they are really probing some inner meaning or mentally creating a new conceptual scheme. As children, they often pull toys apart, trying to determine how they work. Organizational skills are not their strong point and they have difficulty keeping to schedules and being on time. Table 3.1 lists some of the

Table 3.1 Characteristics of Visual-Spatial Learners
■ Rely on vision and visualization ■ Preoccupied with space at the expense of time ■ Intuitive grasp of complex systems ■ Prefer synthesis approach ■ Simultaneous processing of concepts ■ Active use of imagery ■ Prefer visual directions ■ Poorly organized ■ Prefer puzzles, jigsaws, computer games ■ Get difficult concepts, struggle with easy ones

characteristics of visual-spatial learners (Silverman, 1989b), who thrive on complex ideas, abstract concepts, holistic methods, multidisciplinary studies, inductive learning strategies, and any other activities requiring synthesis of thought.

Once visual-spatial learners create a mental image of a concept, it creates a permanent change in the students' understanding and awareness. Repetition is unnecessary and may cause difficulty because it emphasizes their weaknesses instead of their strengths.

These students are ideally suited for the kinds of activities and learning experiences associated with programs for the gifted. However, to reach their full potential, visual-spatial learners must be placed in a learning environment that is a good match between their learning style and the way they are taught.

■ AVOIDING THE PITFALL OF ACADEMICS VERSUS THE ARTS

Much of the research in areas related to programs for the gifted and talented focuses on the education of students with high ability in academic areas. Little research exists that suggests how to develop curriculum, teach, or assess students who are artistically gifted, probably because educators—and the communities they serve—generally place much greater emphasis on the academic areas than the arts. Furthermore, researchers and educators traditionally have used the terms *gifted* and *talented* to describe different things. *Gifted* often referred to high ability in one or more academic areas; *talented* usually meant superior abilities in the visual or performing arts. Researchers in the past often claimed that there was little direct evidence that students who were talented in the arts also exhibited high abilities in academic areas. To this day, it is not unusual to find school districts that have separate programs for the academically and artistically gifted.

Researchers today, who have worked with both types of high-ability students, argue that academically gifted students are often equally gifted in the arts, and vice versa. In a study of teenage students at a summer institute for the arts, all the participants were superior students in academic areas as well (Clark and Zimmerman, 1998). Perhaps we need to adopt a broader view of giftedness that includes all areas of both academic and artistic talents for all students who participate in gifted education programs. The theories of Renzulli, Sternberg, and Gardner discussed in Chapter 2 define a wide range of abilities that can contribute to a more inclusive description of what constitutes programs for gifted students. This multidimensional approach allows for the inclusion of students with abilities in a wide range of school subjects and from all racial, ethnic, and socioeconomic groups.

Fortunately, the growing recognition that students may have multiple abilities, such as mathematics and music, has prompted some school districts to use multiple criteria to identify students for special programs. Regrettably, this process is moving much too slowly. Given the enormous economic and technological threats facing our society, we need to accelerate and expand our efforts to identify and support all the gifts of our children, for it is their knowledge and skills that will ultimately determine the nature and quality of our lives in the future.

APPLICATIONS

ASSESSING THE LEARNING ENVIRONMENT

The following list of questions is designed to help teachers assess the effectiveness of the learning environment for gifted students in their classroom:

- Have you helped students become more aware of their learning styles?

- Have you asked students what helps them learn effectively?

- Do you model the process of talking about *how* we learn, rather than just *what* is learned?

- Have you established an environment in which wrong answers are a productive opportunity for learning?

- Do you actively encourage creative thinking by asking open-ended questions to which there are no single right answers?

- Do you encourage students to question themselves, each other, and other adults in the classroom?

- Are students involved in self-assessment?

- Do you encourage students through challenging and interactive displays?

- Have you developed a resource collection including websites and in-school and out-of-school resource centers, and how do you know if the resources are being well used?

APPLICATIONS

PROCEDURES FOR COMPACTING CURRICULUM

Compacting curriculum simply means determining what students already know about a particular unit of instruction, deciding what they still need to learn, and replacing it with more interesting and challenging material that they would like to learn. There are eight basic steps to the process (Reis, Burns, and Renzulli, 1992a):

Define and Assess Key Concepts and Skills	1. The first step is to identify and define the key concepts and skills for the unit to be taught. Teachers' manuals, district curriculum guides, scope-and-sequence charts, and even some textbooks list the goals and key learning objectives for each curriculum unit. 2. Examine these key objectives to decide which represent the acquisition of new learning and which review and practice material is already presented in earlier grades or courses. Comparing the scope-and-sequence charts or tables of contents of basic textbooks will often reveal new versus repeated material.
Identify and Assess Student Candidates for Compacting	3. Identify the students who have the potential for mastering the new material at a faster than normal pace. Use completed assignments, scores on previous tests, classroom participation, and standardized achievement tests as some of the measures for identifying potential candidates for compacting. 4. Develop appropriate techniques for assessing specific learning objectives. Any unit pretests can be helpful here. The analysis of the pretest results will help determine proficiency and identify instructional areas that may need additional practice.

PROCEDURES FOR COMPACTING CURRICULUM—Continued

5. Streamline the instruction and practice activities for students who demonstrate mastery of the learning objectives.

6. Provide individualized or small group instruction for students who have not yet mastered all the objectives, but who are able to do so more quickly than their classmates.

Provide Acceleration and Enrichment Options and Keep Records	7. Offer more challenging learning alternatives based on student interests and strengths. Deciding which replacement activities to use is guided by space, time, and the availability of resource persons and materials. Resource persons can be other classroom teachers, media specialists, content area or gifted education specialists, and outside mentors. The materials can include self-directed learning activities, instructional materials that focus on developing particular thinking skills, and a variety of experiences designed to promote research and investigative skills. 8. Use a simple three-column form for maintaining a record of the compacting process and of the instructional alternatives provided. In the first column, list the objectives of a particular unit of study and data on the students' proficiency in those objectives. Use the second column specifically to detail the pretest measures and their results. In column three, record information about the acceleration and enrichment options that were used.

PROCEDURES FOR COMPACTING CURRICULUM—Continued

Guidelines. Curriculum compacting takes time and energy at first, but usually saves time once teachers and students are familiar with the process. For educators who are hesitant to try curriculum compacting, here are a few guidelines that are likely to increase your chances of success (Reis, Burns, and Renzulli, 1992b):

■   Start with one or two responsible students who have a positive attitude and who are more likely to welcome the change and be successful with the replacement activities.

■   Talk with these students and discuss the content with which they feel comfortable. Select the appropriate activities, but be sure to give them some options.

■   Try a variety of methods to determine how much they already know about the material. Sometimes a brief conversation with the students is just as reliable as a formal pretest.

■   Compact the topic rather than the time. Because the alternative activities are usually more interesting, students may take more time to complete them than you estimated.

■   Define proficiency in learning the material or skills based on conversations with school staff, administrators, and parents.

■   Do not hesitate to request help from other school personnel or from community volunteers to accomplish the replacement activities.

Teachers who use curriculum compacting on a regular basis report increased interest and enthusiasm among their students and thus often expand the compacting program from just one or two students to a broader segment of the class. The process can be used at any grade level and in any subject area and is not aligned with any specific curricular reform. It is adaptable and flexible to meet the needs of almost any classroom. More information on this strategy is available from the National Research Center on the Gifted and Talented (see **Resources**).

APPLICATIONS

STRATEGIES FOR FLEXIBLE GROUPING

Grouping is common in the elementary school classroom. Creating small groups of gifted students to work together provides a productive learning situation. Here are some guidelines to consider when organizing these groups (Smutny, 2000).

CREATE GROUND RULES

Certain ground rules need to be established to ensure that all participants have an opportunity to participate and share ideas. Discuss these ground rules with the class. The rules should be grade- and age-appropriate, but most need to include the following:

- If you cannot agree on what to do, move on to another idea
- Listen to others in your group and respond to their comments
- Take turns sharing ideas
- Help each other
- Make your best effort
- If you don't understand something, talk it out with your group
- Seek the teacher's help when needed

PROVIDE VARIETY

Organize a variety of groups based on the learning objective. Groups can be formed around student interests, motivation, and the complexity level of the assignment.

OFFER CHOICES

When appropriate, allow students to choose their group members as well as their topic. Of course, teacher discretion may be necessary to allow for variety of groupings over time or to ensure that certain students do not always dominate a group.

STRATEGIES FOR FLEXIBLE GROUPING—Continued

ASSESS STUDENTS INDIVIDUALLY

Although some reward can be given to the group upon completion of their work, it is important to assess each student individually. Assessment measures can include checklists, portfolios, mastery tests, drawings, written compositions, and oral responses.

COMPACT THE CURRICULUM

Compress the essentials so that students can move beyond what they have already mastered. Assess their level of mastery and then allow students to choose activities of particular interest to them. Another option is to design an activity related to the current lesson that challenges their abilities. Some teachers find that signing a learning contract with a student can be effective. The contract stipulates the chosen activities or projects, the conditions for their completion, and the expected outcomes.

INCORPORATE CREATIVE THINKING

Using creative thinking activities benefits all students. The "what if" questions are always interesting to pursue and they challenge students to come up with alternative explanations. Teachers can then suggest other resources to help students with their new explorations. Brainstorming and other metacognitive strategies can stimulate discussions and add to the depth of understanding that students have about a particular subject or theme.

APPLICATIONS

DIFFERENTIATING CONTENT

Content refers to what the student needs to know, understand, and be able to do as a result of a particular unit of study. It should be highly relevant to students, coherent, transferable through instructional techniques, and authentic. Content includes any means by which students acquire information and skills. The teacher promotes differentiation through (Tomlinson, 1999) the use of the following:

✓ Multiple textbooks	✓ Learning contracts
✓ Field trips	✓ Mentors
✓ Supplementary readings	✓ Media centers
✓ Videos	✓ Experiments
✓ Guest speakers	✓ Interest centers
✓ Demonstrations	✓ Audio tapes
✓ Lectures	✓ Internships
✓ Computer programs	✓ Group investigations
✓ Internet	

APPLICATIONS

TEACHING FOR CREATIVITY

Sternberg (2000) proposes that creativity results from a set of 10 decision-making skills that can be learned. He further suggests that teachers can encourage students to be creatively gifted by doing the following:

Decision	Teacher Activity
1. Redefine Problem	• Goal: To help students see an aspect of the world in a different way from which it is usually seen. • Example: Select or have students provide a well-known phenomenon, such as seasonal differences in the northern and souther hemispheres. "Summer vacation" in the USA has to be redefined for students living in Australia.
2. Analyze One's Ideas	• Goal: To help students critique strengths and weaknesses of their ideas. • Example: Have students analyze the phenomenon they presented above. What were its strengths and weaknesses? How can they improve the idea?
3. Sell One's Ideas	• Goal: To teach students the importance of selling their ideas to others. • Example: Have students present an oral or written report in which they explain, defend, and promote an idea in which they truly believe. Remind them to defend their idea against possible criticism.
4. Knowledge Is a Double-Edged Sword	• Goal: To help students realize that theories apply only to a limited range of behavior. • Example: Lead students to study a major idea (e.g., any person born in the United States can become president). What kind of information would we need to determine if this really applies to all children? What other factors could limit this statement's validity?

TEACHING FOR CREATIVITY—Continued

Decision	Teacher Activity
5. Surmount Obstacles	• Goal: To help students realize that new ideas are not immediately accepted. • Example: Ask students to reflect on ideas they may have encountered (e.g., Darwin's Theory of Evolution, the Wright brothers' concept of flight, or the "big bang" theory of the formation of the universe) or on one of their own ideas that others had difficulty accepting. What strategies would help these ideas gain acceptance? Can we relate them to ideas people already accept?
6. Take Sensible Risks	• Goal: To help students realize that creativity involves some degree of risk. • Example: Have students write a brief essay critiquing an interpretation you (the teacher) gave in class. They must support their belief and their criticism must be constructive. Assure the students that you welcome alternative interpretations. Evaluate their essay and offer ways for them to improve their critique. Here they realize they can take a sensible risk and be rewarded.
7. Willingness to Grow	• Goal: To encourage students to grow by challenging their own beliefs. • Example: Ask students to select a belief they have about human behavior, such as why people fall in love, why they get angry, how they chose their friends, or whether capital punishment is effective (or ineffective). Have them commit to this belief in writing and then compose an essay that persuasively supports an opposite point of view. Afterwards, ask if writing this essay helped them to better understand people who disagree with them.
8. Believe in Yourself	• Goal: To show students that if they believe they can do something, they often can. • Example: Ask students to select a task they think would be very difficult to do (e.g., learning to play an instrument, losing weight, or achieving an athletic goal), and then ask them to develop a plan for accomplishing that task. In some cases, students may be encouraged to follow through on their plan and report on their progress periodically.

TEACHING FOR CREATIVITY—Continued

Decision	Teacher Activity
9. Tolerance of Ambiguity	• Goal: To help students recognize and appreciate that ambiguity is inherent in much thinking in the academic disciplines. • Example: Ask students to read a piece that seems to present a theory, analysis, or explanation persuasively. The ask them to read a critique of what they have read and to let you know if the original analysis is still convincing. Why or why not? The reading and critique can be on any set of opposing ideas, such as communism versus capitalism, the North's and South's views of the Civil War, or capital punishment versus life without parole. Students should realize that attaining understanding can be a slow process and that one must tolerate ambiguity for a long time in order to better understand the world.
10. Find What You Love to Do and Do It	• Goal: To show students how any field of endeavor can accommodate a wide variety of outside interests. • Example: Ask students to reflect on an interest they have that is outside a field of study and to relate orally or in writing this interest to the field being studied. These investigations might relate music or art to a scientific field, or compare science fiction to real science, or delve into the psychological makeup of a literary character. The point is to show that they can pursue a diversity of interests while still following a specific area of study.

APPLICATIONS

CREATIVE THINKING THROUGH QUESTIONING

Open-ended questions are effective for encouraging creative thinking because they rarely have one answer and they stimulate further inquiry. They ask for clarification, probe for assumptions, search for reasons and evidence, and look for implications and consequences. Here are a few examples of these types of questions:

What would you have done? Why do think this is the best choice?

Could this ever really happen? What might happen next?

What do you think might happen if … ? What do you think caused this?

Is what you are saying now consistent with what you said before?

How is it different from …? Can you give an example?

Where do we go next? Where could we go for help on this?

What do you mean by that expression?

Can we trust the source of this material?

In what other ways could this be done? How can you test this theory?

What might be the consequences of behaving like that?

Do you agree with this author/speaker? Why or why not?

How could you modify this? How would changing the sequence affect the outcome?

CREATIVE THINKING THROUGH QUESTIONING—Continued

The Question Spinner. Here is a tool to promote creative questioning. Make a copy of this page. Cut out the arrow. Insert a paper fastener through the white dot on the arrow and through the center of the inner circle. A student spins the arrow and answers the indicated question.

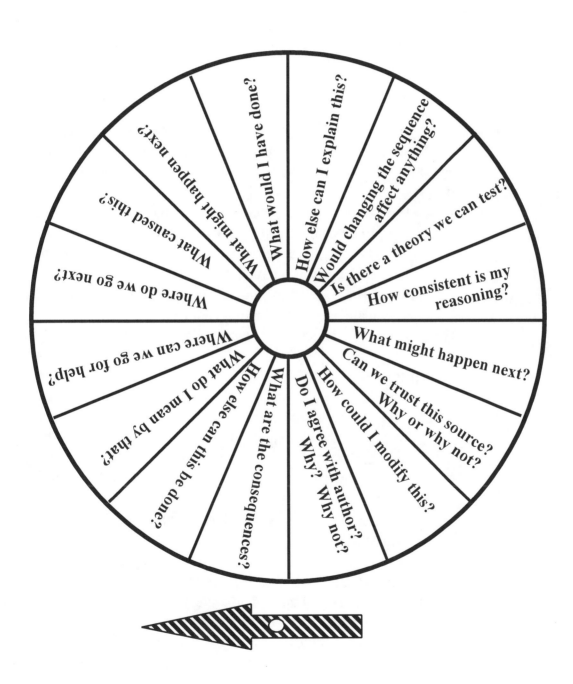

APPLICATIONS

GUIDELINES FOR PROBLEM-BASED LEARNING ACTIVITIES

Problem-based learning activities are usually labor-intensive and time consuming. Before embarking on these activities, the teacher should consider working with other teachers to plan the problem that the students will undertake. Here are some guidelines to consider (Burruss, 1999):

- Identify some complex issues or problem situations. Selecting a local issue, such as environmental preservation or city planning, adds relevancy to the process. The following are examples of local issues:

  ➡ Should a city park be sold for commercial development to increase dwindling property tax revenues?

  ➡ What can be done to prevent or lessen the runoff of fertilizers into the community's water table?

  ➡ What are the advantages and disadvantages of building a strip mall next to the middle school?

  ➡ Should all smoking be banned from local restaurants?

- Examples of regional and national issues can be found in books, newspapers, magazines, and television news and documentary programs. Here are a few examples:

  ➡ Should the elected county commissioners be subject to term limits?

  ➡ What are the pros and cons of electing the US president by popular vote?

  ➡ Should Americans give up some liberties in the fight against terrorism?

- State the problem in a way that is interesting for students and that puts the situation in an intriguing context. The statement should suggest avenues they can pursue but should not provide all the information and resources they need.

PROBLEM-BASED LEARNING ACTIVITIES—Continued

- Because your program may have time restrictions, be sure to align the problems with the curriculum and standards. Think about the curriculum areas involved and the skills the students will use as they pursue the problem and generate solutions.

- Carefully select the best time to discuss and present the problem in class, and make sure to allow sufficient time for students to complete their work.

- To ensure a productive start, give the students a partial list of materials and resources they may need at the onset of their work.

- If the project falters, revise the problems as needed to resume progress.

APPLICATIONS

USING THE TRIARCHIC MODEL IN THE CLASSROOM

Practical applications of Sternberg's Triarchic model in the classroom require that the teacher incorporate activities that provoke analytical, creative, and practical thinking whenever students are involved in complex problem solving (Sternberg, 1985; Sternberg, et al., 2000). This approach to differentiated instruction helps all students, but is particularly beneficial for gifted students who can use their strengths for in-depth study.

General Guidelines

- Use *analytical activities* at times that encourage students to compare and contrast, analyze, evaluate, judge, and critique.

- Use *creative activities* at times that encourage students to discover, imagine, explore, invent, and create.

- Use *practical activities* at times that encourage students to use, contextualize, apply, and put into practice.

- Allow all students occasionally to capitalize on their strengths.

- More often, enable students to correct or compensate for their weaknesses.

- Use assessments that match the analytical, creative, and practical activities you are using, as well as testing for memory skills.

- Value the diversity of learning styles in all students.

USING THE TRIARCHIC MODEL IN THE CLASSROOM—Continued

Examples

Activity	Science	Language Arts	Social Studies
Analytical	• Draw the major parts of an animal cell, and explain what the parts do.	• Identify simile, analogy, and metaphor, and explain their function.	• Describe the steps necessary for a bill to become law in the state legislature.
Creative	• Write a story (or play) using characters representing the parts of an animal cell, and describe a potential conflict.	• Using unusual materials, act out simile, analogy, and metaphor in mime, and see if other students can guess them.	• Become a state senator, and use your position to help us think about the merits and problems of laws to restrict campaign financing.
Practical	• Find a system in the world around you that mimics the activities and relationships in an animal cell, and explain it.	• Demonstrate how someone would use similes, analogies, or metaphors in their work or life.	• Underage drinking is a problem here at school. Devise legislation that would address this problem.

APPLICATIONS

GUIDING STUDENTS FOR INDEPENDENT STUDY

Independent study is another useful strategy for differentiating curriculum and instruction, especially in the self-contained classroom. However, even gifted students often need guidance in pursuing learning objectives independently. Here are some considerations.

- Prepare options in advance for the students to select as part of the curriculum unit's work. These options should include a variety of ability levels, involve different skills, and address different learning styles.

- Encourage students to select the option they feel is most relevant to their topic. The teacher may need to help with this decision by discussing with the students how the options match their needs, strengths, and desires.

- Guide students toward appropriate resources that they can seek out independently.

- Ensure students that they can also develop other options for the curriculum unit, but that they should discuss them with the teacher before embarking on any work with the options.

- Suggest to students that they can occasionally work in small groups if necessary to accomplish their learning objectives.

- Encourage students to seek out other environments (e.g., another classroom, the media center, or computer lab) that will help them with their task.

APPLICATIONS

STEPS FOR DEVELOPING TIERED ACTIVITIES

In a classroom with students of mixed abilities, tiered activities offer choices for accomplishing a learning objective at different levels of complexity. The following guidelines are useful for planning tiered activities (Tomlinson, 1999).

- Decide which concepts, themes, and skills all students will be expected to learn in the instructional unit. These selections are the core fundamentals for developing an understanding of the curricular material.

- Use simple assessments to determine the range of readiness of the students who will be studying this unit. Other measures and previous experience will also allow you to determine the students' interests, talents, and learning styles as they pertain to the learning objectives.

- Select a past activity, or create a new one, that focuses students to use an important skill to understand an important idea. This activity should be interesting, relevant, and able to engage students in higher-level thought (e.g., Bloom's analysis or synthesis levels).

- Next, chart the complexity of the activity along some linear scale (Tomlinson suggests a ladder) that runs from low to high complexity. Think about the students who will be using the activity you developed in the previous step and place it on that scale. Its placement will help you determine what other versions of the activity need to be developed. For example, will the lesson challenge only the average ability students? If so, you need to develop versions for the low- and high-ability learners.

STEPS FOR DEVELOPING TIERED ACTIVITIES—Continued

- Devise the versions of the activity needed along the scale at the different degrees of complexity. These versions can be created by varying the material the students will use (from basic to very challenging), by developing a range of applications of the learning (from those that are close to the student to those that are very remote), and by allowing different products that students can use to demonstrate achievement.

- Finally, match each version of the activity to the appropriate students based on their learning profile and the requirements of the learning task. The goal is to closely match the degree of complexity to the students' readiness, but to add a measure of challenge.

APPLICATIONS

COMPONENTS OF EFFECTIVE CULMINATING PRODUCTS

A culminating product created by students at the end of a major unit of inquiry is an excellent opportunity to assess how much the students have learned. Teachers can use differentiation in their classes when they allow students to select from a broad variety of possible culminating projects. This venture is more apt to be successful if the teacher (Tomlinson, 1999)

- Makes clear to students what they should transfer, demonstrate, explain, or apply to show what they have learned and what they can do as a result of their inquiry.

- Allows students to choose from among a variety of product possibilities, such as videos, photo essays, charts and graphs, and written reports.

- Presents specific expectations about what (1) type of information, concepts, and resources constitute high-quality content; (2) steps should be used in developing the product, such as planning, editing, effective use of time, and originality; and (3) details describe the nature of the product itself, such as size, durability, format, construction, accuracy, and the anticipated audience.

- Supports student efforts by providing in-class workshops on how to use research materials, for brainstorming ideas, for discussing timelines, and for peer reviewing, critiquing, and editing.

- Provides for variations in student learning styles, interests, and learning readiness.

APPLICATIONS

STRATEGIES FOR WORKING WITH GIFTED VISUAL-SPATIAL LEARNERS

Gifted visual-spatial learners do best with a holistic approach to learning. They prefer complex systems, abstract concepts, and inductive reasoning and problem solving. Recognizing the strengths and weaknesses of these learners, and making a few simple academic modifications, can help these students become successful and innovative leaders. Here are some strategies that have been found to be effective with visual-spatial learners (Silverman, 1989b).

- Use visual aids, such as overhead projectors, computers, diagrams, graphic organizers, and other visual imagery.

- Give them the larger scheme at the beginning of each unit and explain the major objectives so that the students understand the instructional goal.

- In spelling, use a visualization approach: Show the word, have students close their eyes and visualize it, have them spell it backward (this is visualization), then spell it forward, and then write it once.

- Find out what they have already mastered about the unit's topics before teaching them.

- Use manipulative materials for hands-on experiences.

- Avoid rote memorization. Use more conceptual and inductive approaches.

- Help students discover their own methods of problem solving. When they succeed, give them a harder problem to see if their system works.

WORKING WITH GIFTED VISUAL-SPATIAL LEARNERS—Continued

- Emphasize concepts over details. Encourage new insights, creativity, and imagination.

- Avoid drill and repetition. Instead, have them try the hardest tasks in the unit with at least 80 percent accuracy. If they accomplish this, then the students may not have to complete the rest of the assignment.

- Group gifted visual-spatial learners together for instruction. Give the group handouts if they have difficulty with dictation.

- Allow them to accelerate in school.

- Give them abstract, complex material at a faster pace.

- Use real-life scenarios and service-oriented projects whenever possible.

- Allow students to construct, draw, or create other visual representations of concepts.

- Have students discuss the moral, ethical, and global implications of their learning.

- For foreign language learning, total immersion is much more effective than being in the typical classroom setting for these students.

- At the end of each class or school day, ask the students to take a few deep breaths, close their eyes, and visualize what happened during the class (or day) and what they will need to do for homework.

APPLICATIONS

INTEGRATING ACADEMIC AND ARTS-RELATED ACTIVITIES FOR ALL GIFTED STUDENTS

Many academically talented students are also capable of being high performers in artistic endeavors. Because the artistic areas are often ignored in gifted programs, educators should incorporate the visual and performing arts into comprehensive gifted and talented programs. Here are some recommendations for accomplishing this task (Clark and Zimmerman, 1998).

- The arts should be included as an integral part of all comprehensive gifted and talented programs. This type of program will more likely accommodate the varying needs of the wide variety of abilities represented in a comprehensive program that includes academically and artistically gifted students.

- Just as scientifically talented students need access to modern, well-equipped laboratories, artistically gifted students should have access to facilities that resemble the studios, stages, and other workplaces of artists who are trying to solve problems in the arts. The goals of programs designed to educate artistically gifted students should be carefully integrated with those for students who are academically gifted so that all students benefit from comprehensive and enriching experiences.

- Traditionally, schools often encourage academically gifted students to take advanced classes in academic subjects within the school but suggest that they pursue artistic endeavors outside the school. Teachers, administrators, and parents need to be educated about the importance of including the arts as an integral part of the gifted education program, and to encourage all students to pursue the arts within the school setting.

ACADEMIC AND ARTS-RELATED ACTIVITIES—Continued

- Educators who teach academically and artistically talented students should collaborate in planning programs that provide equity and excellence, that reinforce shared goals, and that emphasize common strengths for the benefit of their students and the entire school community. Such collaboration would inevitably benefit all students who participate in programs that develop talent.

- More work needs to be done on developing resources and teaching strategies that incorporate the arts into the comprehensive programs for gifted students. If these resources are available, teachers are more likely to include them as a regular part of their repertoire. Furthermore, these strategies need to be appropriate to the learning styles and cultural backgrounds of individual students.

Developing integrated programs should not be solely the responsibility of teachers. Local, community, and state resources should be gathered to support these efforts and to establish liaisons with out-of-school entities (e.g., organizations, government agencies, and businesses) that can contribute to the success of the comprehensive program.

4

Language Talent

One of the most extraordinary features of the human brain is its ability to acquire spoken language quickly and accurately. We are born with an innate capacity to distinguish the distinct sounds (phonemes) of all the languages on this planet. Eventually, we are able to associate those sounds with arbitrary symbols to express our thoughts and emotions to others. Ever since Paul Broca discovered evidence in 1861 that the left hemisphere of the brain was specialized for language, researchers have attempted to understand the way in which normal human beings acquire and process their native language.

■ SOURCES OF LANGUAGE ABILITY

In most people, the left hemisphere is home to the major components of the language processing system (Figure 4.1). Broca's area is a region of the left frontal lobe that is believed to be responsible for processing vocabulary, syntax, and rules of grammar. Wernicke's area is part of the left temporal lobe and is thought to process the sense and meaning of language. However, the emotional content of language is governed by areas in the right hemisphere.

Brain imaging studies of infants as young as 4 months of age confirm that the brain possesses neural networks that specialize in responding to the auditory components of language. Dehaene-Lambertz (2000) used EEG recordings to measure the brain activity of sixteen 4-month-old infants as they listened to language

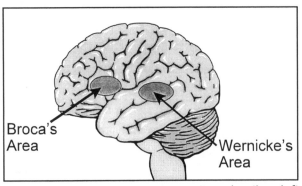

Figure 4.1 The language system in the left hemisphere is comprised mainly of Broca's area and Wernicke's area.

Broca's Area

Wernicke's Area

syllables and acoustic tones. After numerous trials, the data showed that syllables and tones were processed primarily in different areas of the left hemisphere, although there was also some right hemisphere activity. For language input, various features, such as the voice and the phonetic category of a syllable, were encoded by separate neural networks into sensory memory. These remarkable findings suggest that, even at this early age, the brain is already organized into functional networks that can distinguish between language fragments and other acoustical input.

The apparent predisposition of the brain to the sounds of language explains why normal young children respond to and acquire spoken language quickly. How long the brain retains this responsiveness to the sounds of language is still open to question. However, there does seem to be general agreement among researchers that the window of opportunity for acquiring language within the language-specific areas of the brain tapers off for most people around 10 to 12 years of age. Obviously, one can still acquire a new language after that age, but it takes more effort because the new language will be spatially separated in the brain from the native language areas (Sousa, 2001a).

Structure of Language

Languages consist of distinct units of sound called *phonemes*. Although each language has its own unique set of phonemes, only about 150 phonemes comprise all the world's languages. These phonemes consist of all the speech sounds that can be made by the human voice apparatus. Around the age of 6 months or so, infants start babbling, an early sign of language acquisition. Their babbling consists of all those phonemes, even ones they have never heard. Within a few months, however, pruning of the phonemes begins, and by about one year of age, the neural networks focus on the sounds of the language being spoken in the infant's environment (Beatty, 2001).

Syntax and Semantics

With more exposure, the brain begins to recognize the hierarchy of language (Figure 4.2). Phonemes, the basic sounds, can be combined into morphemes, which are the smallest units of language that have meaning. Morphemes can then be combined into words, and words can be put together according to the rules of syntax to form phrases and sentences. Toddlers show evidence of their progression through these levels when simple statements, such as

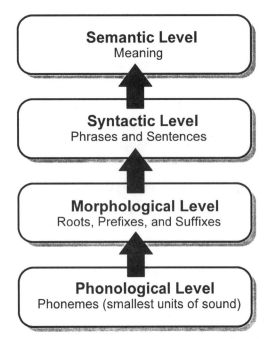

Figure 4.2 These four levels represent the hierarchical structure of language and language acquisition.

"Candy," evolve to more complex ones, "Give me candy." They also begin to recognize that shifting the words in sentences can change their meaning.

The brain's ability to recognize different meanings in sentence structure is possible because Broca's and Wernicke's areas establish linked networks that can understand the difference between "The dog chased the cat" and "The cat chased the dog." In an fMRI study, Dapretto and Bookheimer (1999) found that Broca's and Wernicke's areas work together to determine whether changes in syntax or semantics result in changes in meaning. For example, "The policeman arrested the thief" and "The thief was arrested by the policeman" have different syntax but the same meaning. The fMRI showed that Broca's area was highly activated when subjects were processing these two sentences. Wernicke's area, on the other hand, was more activated when processing sentences that were semantically—but not syntactically—different, such as "The car is in the garage" and "The automobile is in the garage."

How is it that Wernicke's area can so quickly and accurately decide that two semantically different sentences have the same meaning? The answer may lie in two other recently discovered characteristics of Wernicke's area. One is that the neurons in Wernicke's area are spaced about 20 percent further apart and are cabled together with longer interconnecting axons than the corresponding area in the right hemisphere of the brain (Galuske, Schlote, Bratzke, and Singer, 2000). The implication is that the practice of language during early human development results in longer and more intricately connected neurons in the Wernicke region.

> The ability to understand language may be rooted in the brain's ability to recognize predictability.

The second recent discovery regarding Wernicke's area is its ability to recognize predictable events. An MRI study found that Wernicke's area was activated when subjects were shown differently colored symbols in various patterns, whether the individuals were aware of the pattern sequence or not (Bischoff-Grethe, Proper, Mao, Daniels, and Berns, 2000). This predictability-determining role for Wernicke's area suggests that our ability to make sense of language is rooted in our ability to recognize syntax. The researchers noted that language itself is very predicable because it is constrained by the rules of grammar and syntax.

Genes, Language, and the Environment

The production of phonemes by infants is the result of genetically determined neural programs; however, language exposure is environmental. These two components interact to produce an individual's language system and, assuming no pathologies, sufficient competence to communicate clearly with others. Scientists, of course, are interested in the exact nature of that interaction in an effort to determine how genes can be modified by the environment, and vice versa. These gene-environment relationships are called *genotype-environment correlations* (GECs). Research on GECs helps to explain the degree to which a child's genetic destiny can be modified by environmental experiences. Three types of GECs have been described: evocative, active, and passive (Scarr and McCartney, 1983).

Evocative GEC occurs when young students who are talented in language are identified by their teachers and provided with special opportunities to enhance their gifts. In other words, they evoke reactions from other individuals on the basis of their genetic predispositions. Consequently, these students will receive more verbal input and be better stimulated than students without such talents. Over time, the talented group's environment and genetics mutually influence each other, favoring the development of greater language ability.

Active GEC occurs when students talented in language arts seek out environments that are rich in language experiences. For example, they may want to associate with like-talented peers or take part in poetry or

> **Environmental variables in the home may not be reliable predictors of a child's language ability.**

essay contests. Once again, this type of GEC can enhance language skills due to the different groups that the students place themselves into over time.

Passive GEC occurs when students talented in language arts inherit both the genes from their similarly talented parents *and* the environment that promotes the development of language ability. Hence, the children passively receive a family environment that is closely correlated to their genetic predispositions.

Evocative and active GECs can occur inside or outside the family and become increasingly important as the child moves outside the family and becomes involved in other environments. Passive GEC, on the other hand, occurs only within the biological family and tends to decrease in importance as the child matures. Consequently, children who are passive GEC candidates are the most appropriate group to study when trying to determine how much various environmental factors moderate genetic traits.

To that end, a major longitudinal study of passive GEC, by Jeffrey Gilger and his colleagues, looked at language development in children from about 400 families over a 12-year period (Gilger, Ho, Whipple, and Spitz, 2001). In order to isolate the genetic propensities from the environmental influences on linguistic development, the children were selected from an almost even split of adoptive and nonadoptive families. Language-related assessment measures were administered to the subjects during the second, fourth, seventh, tenth, and twelfth years.

Evidence emerged from this study that genetic predispositions *can* dampen the influence of four environmental variables: the provision of toys and games in the home, the degree of maternal involvement in the child's language development, the number of people living in the home, and the degree of intellectual/cultural orientation in the home. Using statistical analysis, the researchers estimated the genetic contribution to these variables to range from 11 to 100 percent.

Keep in mind that passive GECs decrease in importance as the child ages because the family becomes less significant than peers and other adults in the child's environment. Two major implications arise from this study: (1) It is important to avoid drawing conclusions from family data about the impact of the environment on language-based skills, and (2) children possessed of genetic predisposition for high language ability, but raised in family environments that do not evoke the ability, can still realize their potential when they encounter teachers who recognize and nurture these talents.

Learning to Read

Speech will develop in the human brain without any specific instruction. Reading, on the other hand, is an acquired skill. To read correctly, the brain must learn to connect abstract symbols (the alphabet) to those sound bits (phonemes) it already knows. In English, the brain must first learn and remember the alphabet, and then connect those 26 letters to the 44 sounds of spoken English that the child has been using successfully for years. Thus, reading involves a recognition that speech can be broken into small sounds and that these segmented sounds can be represented by symbols in print called *graphemes*. The brain's ability to recognize that written symbols can represent sounds is known as the alphabetic principle. Unfortunately, the human brain is not born with the insight to make these sound-to-symbol connections, nor does it develop naturally without instruction. Children of literate homes may encounter this instruction before coming to school. If these children possess any type of genetic predispositions for high language ability, they are likely to learn quickly the complex process of reading earlier than other children of the same age.

Successful reading involves the coordination of three neural networks: visual processing (orthography), sound recognition (phonology), and word interpretation (semantics). In reading the word *dog*, for example, the visual processing system puts the symbols together.

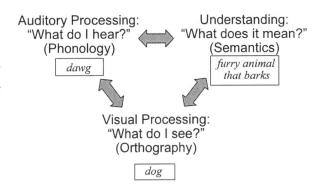

Figure 4.3 Successful reading requires the coordination of three systems: visual processing to see the word, auditory processing to hear it, and semantic processing to understand it.

The decoding process alerts the auditory processing system that recognizes the alphabetic symbols to represent the sound "dawg." Other brain regions, including the frontal lobe, search long-term memory sites for meaning. If all systems work correctly, a mental image emerges of a furry animal that barks (Figure 4.3).

Learning to read also requires good memory systems. Working memory has to keep words available so that letter sounds found at the beginning of the word can be connected to those found at the end of the word. Eventually, the learner has to be able to remember the meaning of the word if future reading is to be successful. Because so many words in English have different meanings in different contexts, the learner must also remember every word in the sentence in order for the brain to select the correct meaning and put everything together.

Some brains acquire the skills associated with reading, such as phonemic awareness and the alphabetic principle, very quickly, and reading becomes an easy task. Most neuroscientists who study how the brain reads agree that genetic predispositions likely enhance processing within various neural networks that contribute to reading. In rare cases, the predisposition is so strong that it produces a condition known as *hyperlexia*, where the child becomes a voracious reader at the expense of developing spoken language and communication skills. See Chapter 8 for more about hyperlexia.

IDENTIFYING STUDENTS GIFTED IN LANGUAGE ARTS ■

Students who are gifted in the language arts of reading, writing, and communication skills will demonstrate competencies in some or all of the following areas:

Awareness of language. These students understand the nature of language and show special interest in language features, such as rhyme, accent, and intonation in spoken language, and the use of grammar in written texts. They often have an interest in other languages and demonstrate an awareness of the relationship between the sounds and words of other languages.

Communication skills. These students can easily gain the attention of an audience by exploiting the humorous or dramatic components of a situation in imaginative ways. They tend to write and talk with a creative flair that is exceptional for their age, often using metaphors and poetry. They can also express ideas elegantly and succinctly, in ways that reflect the knowledge and interests of specific audiences. They will guide a group to achieve its shared goals, while being sensitive to the participation of others.

Reasoning and arguing. These students can use reasoned arguments at an abstract and hypothetical level in both spoken and written language. They can justify their opinions convincingly, and they know how to use questioning strategies to challenge the points of view of others.

■ DEVELOPING LANGUAGE ABILITY

Students talented in language arts will develop their abilities when they are challenged by experiences involving sophisticated language. Too often in the regular classroom, the reading materials and language activities are not sufficiently challenging for gifted students, who then become bored when their learning needs are not being adequately met. For these students to grow, they should be given language problems that are not easily solved, that are open-ended, and that force them to think, study, reread, and reformulate. Thus, a curriculum designed for these students should build upon the characteristics of the intellectually gifted. It should carefully identify which components and strategies will be used at each grade level in order to eliminate the content redundancy that plagues too many curriculum guides.

As explained earlier, teachers can have a great impact on evoking language-related talents in students. The teachers in this program should be highly intelligent, emotionally secure, comfortable interacting with gifted students, and able to demonstrate advanced knowledge of the subject matter. Evaluate the success of the program through the students' work product and not by tests of mastery of lower-level skills. This may require developing new assessment instruments because most current tests evaluate acquisition of knowledge rather than the application of knowledge in creative ways.

Some Instructional Approaches and Strategies

In an effort to address the needs of students who are gifted in language arts, teachers have devised various instructional approaches and strategies to generate exciting experiences in all aspects of language including vocabulary development, grammar, reading, and writing. Here is just a sampling of those ideas, which, of course, could be appropriate for all students. The activities are explained in greater detail in **Applications** at the end of this chapter.

Focus on the Classics (Grades 5 and Higher)

Thompson (1999) suggests that to develop verbal talent, students need go beyond the regular basal texts and be exposed to classical literature. Great books are called great because they can have different meaning for different readers. The classics stretch imaginations, challenge ideas, and open a new world of possibilities for expressing the human condition in language. Gifted students often see themselves in classic stories, whose characters can become their virtual mentors.

The classics also provide an exposure to rich vocabulary somewhat lacking, according to Thompson, from the literature anthologies used in today's classrooms. In addition to their value as sources of mentors and vocabulary, the classics expose students to a wealth of divergent and often conflicting ideas. They shock students into thought, forcing them to confront new concepts.

Author's Chair (Grades 3 and Higher)

This is an opportunity for writers to share their final compositions with an audience in order to receive positive feedback that will assist them in future writing efforts. A particular chair in the classroom is designated for this activity. In addition to the value of the feedback, this strategy also develops listening skills for students in the audience.

Student Journal Writing (Grades 3 and Higher)

Journal writing provides a natural way to integrate language through reading, writing, and discussion. Gifted students generally enjoy expressing their ideas verbally, but keeping a continuous written journal requires them to write, rephrase, and reflect on their thoughts. Different types of journals can be used for different purposes. *Dialogue journals* are conversations in print, designed to promote fluent oral and written communication. In *literary journals*, students enter their responses to works of literature that they have read. A third type is the *subject journal*, in which students record information related to specific topics (e.g., ecology, dinosaurs, and minerals).

Literature Circles (Grades 3 and Higher)

In literature circles, small groups of students discuss a literary work in depth, guided by their responses to what they have read. The circles help students engage in reflection and critical thinking, building on their understanding and ability to construct meaning with other readers.

Writer's Workshop (Grades 7 and Higher)

Writer's workshops were first used to develop the work of adult writers who were pursuing writing as a profession. However, the format can be adapted to younger individuals. Essentially, writer's workshop is a thoughtful and more sophisticated form of Author's Chair that is best suited for older middle and high school students who are gifted in language arts. As in Author's Chair, students who have read a writer's paper give feedback that identifies positive features, such as the literary forms and patterns that the author used, and offer constructive criticism as well. The comments are intended to help the author improve the paper, but the author is not obligated to follow all the suggestions. Because it is time consuming, this strategy should be used sparingly and only with students who are comfortable with feedback that includes constructive criticism.

Out-of-School Activities (High School)

Opportunities often exist in the local community and region for these students to extend and enrich their experiences with language arts.

APPLICATIONS

IDENTIFYING STUDENTS WITH LANGUAGE TALENT

Students with high ability in language do tend to display common characteristics, especially by the time they reach middle school where language fluency rapidly develops. Use the scale below to help decide if a particular student is gifted in language arts. If you rate the student with scores of 4 or 5 on more than half of the characteristics, then further assessment is warranted.

The student...	A little Some A lot
1. Writes or talks in imaginative and coherent ways.	1 — 2 — 3 — 4 — 5
2. Organizes text in a manner that is exceptional for the student's age.	1 — 2 — 3 — 4 — 5
3. Expresses ideas succinctly and elegantly.	1 — 2 — 3 — 4 — 5
4. Writes with a flair for metaphorical and poetic expression.	1 — 2 — 3 — 4 — 5
5. Takes the lead in helping a group reach its writing goal.	1 — 2 — 3 — 4 — 5
6. Easily grasps the essence of a writing style and adapts it for personal use.	1 — 2 — 3 — 4 — 5
7. Can capture and maintain the attention of an audience by using drama and humor in imaginative ways.	1 — 2 — 3 — 4 — 5
8. Engages creatively and seriously with social and moral issues expressed in literature.	1 — 2 — 3 — 4 — 5
9. Justifies opinions convincingly.	1 — 2 — 3 — 4 — 5
10. Shows special awareness of language features, such as intonation, rhyme, accents in spoken language, and grammatical organization in written texts.	1 — 2 — 3 — 4 — 5
11. Presents reason arguments at the hypothetical or abstract level in both spoken and written language.	1 — 2 — 3 — 4 — 5

APPLICATIONS

WORKING WITH GIFTED READERS

Young gifted readers are those who start to read early, read better with less drill, read longer, and read a variety of literature. Teachers promote the intellectual development of gifted readers by selecting books and materials that allow the students to (Halsted, 1990)

- Work with intellectual peers
- Build skills in productive thinking
- Have more time for processing ideas and concepts
- Share ideas in depth verbally
- Pursue ideas as far as their interests take them
- Encounter and use increasingly difficult vocabulary and concepts
- Draw generalizations and test them

Promoting Intellectual Development

Teachers can use books to promote intellectual development by requiring students to read whole books in addition to their reading in the basal series. This approach is positive for gifted students because it rewards them for something they already enjoy. To ensure quality control and choice, the teacher should prepare the reading list from which students can choose their required books. Teachers may also suggest that students keep notebooks for recording the title, author, short comments about the book, and the dates the book was read.

Librarians, teachers, and volunteers can lead discussion of the books that students have read. These group discussions should focus on main themes and ideas, encouraging students to pursue higher-level thinking, such as analysis and syntheses, rather than to give just plot summaries and statements of fact.

Books can also be a part of the educational program for individual students, provided that an adult (teacher, parent, librarian, or other mentor) offers guidance appropriate to the student's interests, reading ability, and reading background.

WORKING WITH GIFTED READERS—Continued

Nurturing Emotional Development

Gifted children may experience feelings of difference and even inferiority, isolation, and a sense of being misunderstood by others. They must constantly choose between the alternatives of using their abilities and the need to fit into their group. Choices like this make growing up more difficult for them. Consequently, teachers need to nurture the social and emotional development of gifted children, in addition to meeting their intellectual needs. Many novels written for children address these affective concerns. The adults who discuss these books with gifted young students can help them cope with the additional considerations that being gifted add to the process of maturing.

Promoting Emotional Development

Books can be used to help individuals who are facing a particular situation, such as giftedness, become better prepared through reading and discussion. This process, known as developmental bibliotherapy, includes three components: a book, a reader, and a leader who reads the same book and prepares a productive discussion on the issues raised in the book. The goal is to help the reader identify with a character in the book, experience that character's emotions, and apply the experience to the reader's own life. The leader's role is to guide this process and to develop questions that will confirm and expand on these elements. Used appropriately, developmental bibliotherapy can be an effective tool for helping young students cope successfully with their giftedness.

APPLICATIONS

LANGUAGE ARTS STRATEGIES FOR GIFTED ELEMENTARY STUDENTS

Gifted students who have already mastered much of the required oral and written language skills for their grade level need strategies to stimulate imaginative and higher-order thinking. Although the following strategies, suggested by Smutny (2001), are appropriate for all students, they encourage gifted students to work at their own pace and level of complexity.

Exploring Poetic Language: Free Verse

Teachers can use poetry to help gifted students explore the quality of words, the power of metaphoric language, and the subtly and complexity of meaning. Without the constrictions of a rhyming scheme, free verse allows students to focus on imagery and to experiment with various writing styles.

Creating a group poem. One method for demonstrating the different ways to write free verse is to have the students work as a group to create a free verse poem together. Using a picture or poster as the theme, ask the students to think about the picture's color, any feelings they get, and what the picture's components mean to them. Ask questions that will provoke their imagination: "If you were to think of the animals in this picture as colors, what colors would they be? If they were music, what sounds would you hear?" Write on the chalkboard the words and phrases that the students contribute. Read the words as a poem and talk about the images that are generated.

Creating individual poems. All kinds of media, such as music recordings, games, pictures, posters, puzzles, films, and paintings, can be used as the basis for creating poetry. Help the students select the medium and stimulate original thinking by asking focused questions: "What is the main character in this painting staring at? What mood is he in? What else could be happening around him? What could have happened minutes later?"

LANGUAGE ARTS STRATEGIES—Continued

Exploring the Elements of Fiction

Divergent thinking. Exploring fiction becomes much more exciting if students think divergently about their stories. Divergent thinking involves pursuing the answers to open-ended questions, such as "How would you change this story, and why? Given all that has happened so far, what are some possible endings to this story? What would you have done in these circumstances, and why?"

Exploring fiction with fractured fairy tales. Altering the plot, setting, or character of a fairy tale in an unexpected way can produce a humorous twist of fiction and stimulate the imagination. For example: What if the big, bad wolf fails to blow down any of the pigs' homes, or the pigs come out and confront the wolf? What if the three bears return home while Goldilocks is still snooping around the place? After presenting a fractured fairy tale, asking some questions can help the students think through what changes have been made and what they mean: "Which events occur in the new tale that do not occur in the original? How do the changes in plot and character behavior affect the overall meaning of the story?"

A Study of Perspective: Biographical and Historical Fiction

Biographies and histories enable gifted students to conceive imaginary versions of actual events from different viewpoints. It gives them an opportunity to critically and creatively debate points in history and politics based on their own revisions of events. By writing biographical and historical fiction, they can explore new and exciting perspectives.

Researching the facts. Use books, short films, and magazines to introduce students to the work of prominent men and women. Get students to research what influenced these individuals in their youth, how they overcame difficulties or obstacles in their lives, and what were the most significant contributions they made to society. As they write down this information, they should also note any questions they have about the person's life. Then ask them to find out the answers to these questions. One of the values of this activity is that it inspires further research and analysis of issues that appear in the story.

LANGUAGE ARTS STRATEGIES—Continued

Creating a point of view. Ask students to choose a person, animal, or object in this prominent person's life and describe an event from this perspective. Students often discover how individual points of view can create quite a different focus from that of the author who wrote the biography. For historical fiction, students can create a fictional character who, for example, fought in the Civil War. They could devise a fictional biography of this character and write an anecdote of an event that could have happened to this person in this time and place. This approach helps gifted students to see history in a different light, recognizing that within each daily news story, there are many individuals who see an event with slightly different perspectives.

These types of investigations with language arts engage the analytical minds and creative talents of gifted students. The strategies allow these students to expand their experiences with literature through their own creative designing and writing, and to gain a deeper insight into the people and events that have influenced our lives and shaped our world.

APPLICATIONS

USING CLASSICAL LITERATURE TO DEVELOP LANGUAGE ABILITY

Thompson (1999) makes a strong case for using classical literature to lure students away from the basal readers and to encounter new ideas that extend their capabilities in language. Here are some of this suggestions.

- *Identifying with a character.* Encourage students to read classics, such as those found in the Junior Great Books or Great Books programs. The characters in these literary masterpieces provide a powerful source of virtual mentors. Suggest that students talk about which characters they like and explain their reasons. Describe something the character did that they would like to do. What other choices can the character make, and what are their consequences?

- *Enriching vocabulary.* Classic literature offers a rich source of vocabulary not usually found in basal readers. Ask students to select words they found particularly interesting, to define them, and to speculate why the author might have chosen those words. What other words might the author have used? Thompson has compiled a word database, which includes a number of unusual items found in common classics. Here are the first ten books on his list, followed by the number of noteworthy words each contains:
  Uncle Tom's Cabin, Harriet Beecher Stowe, 714
  Ivanhoe, Sir Walter Scott, 519
  Gulliver's Travels, Jonathan Swift, 472
  The War of the Worlds, H. G. Wells, 379
  Dracula, Bram Stoker, 345
  Tom Sawyer, Mark Twain, 293
  Robinson Crusoe, Daniel Defoe, 279
  Treasure Island, Robert Louis Stevenson, 254
  Silas Marner, George Eliot (Mary Ann Evans), 216
  To Kill a Mockingbird, Harper Lee, 208

USING CLASSICAL LITERATURE—Continued

- *Classic ideas.* Classic literature exposes students to the divergent, complex, and conflicting ideas of heroes like Mark Twain, Martin Luther King, Henry David Thoreau, and Thomas Jefferson. These voices express all kinds of humanitarian and uplifting themes: be yourself, be free, be ethical, find happiness, and protect the people.

- *Quality and quantity.* Some of these books will need to be assigned as home reading because few schools can dedicate time for the amount of reading necessary for gifted students. Two classics per semester might be reasonable for middle and high school students. Teachers should also ensure that they assign books rich in vocabulary.

- *The power of ancient words.* Teachers should encourage students with high ability in language arts to study the structure of words, thereby enriching their own vocabulary and ensuring their success in tackling examinations (e.g., the SAT) that assess vocabulary development. Just studying the Greek and Latin stems, for example, can help a student gain understanding of over 5,000 new words. Some other advantages of learning these stems are

  Power learning - Because the stems appear in many words and combinations, this approach to learning vocabulary is more powerful than learning one word at a time.

  Spelling - Thousands of English words are nothing more than several stems in a row. By learning the stems, a student learns spelling for many words at the same time.

  Standardized tests - The final few, and most difficult, questions on the SAT analogies test contain vocabulary words that are almost always stem-based. Students who have studied these stems, therefore, are likely to do better.

  Sense of history - As students study the stems of words, they realize that language was not just invented in our time, but also reflects a historic development of many voices over eons.

  Advanced vocabulary - Many stem-based words are big words used by science and technology. The names of biological species and diseases are just two examples of how

USING CLASSICAL LITERATURE—Continued

new words are continually created from Latin and Greek roots.

● *The power of stems.* Greek and Latin stems form the basis for many words in English. Middle school students gifted in language arts may find the pursuit of these stems an enjoyable project. However, it is more important to learn the stem and its definition than the word example. Here are a few common stems for starters.

ante-, antecedent, anterior, anteroom
anti-, antibody, antitoxin, antithesis
circum-, circumnavigate, circumspect, circumvent
con-, contract, confine, conjunction
equi-, equivocate, equilateral, equinox
intra-, intramural, intravenous, intracoastal
mal-, malapropism, malodorous, malicious
non-, nonprofit, nonchalant, nonfeasance
pre-, presume, precede, premature
semi-, semifinal, semicircle, semiformal
super-, superb, supervise, superfluous
sym-, symbiosis, symbolic, symphony
un-, unfit, undeniable, unconventional

● *Pursuing grammar.* Grammar is often viewed by students as tedious and a waste of time. But students gifted in language arts may find studying grammar to be a useful method for critical thinking about language. Grammar provides a way for students to think about how they use language, how grammar can clarify or muddle, and how different authors use language in their own styles. This approach offers a deeper appreciation for literature and the enjoyment of crafting good sentences and compositions.

APPLICATIONS

AUTHOR'S CHAIR

This activity gives writers an opportunity to share their writing products with an audience. A special time and chair are designated for this activity, which provides the author with valuable feedback from classmates. It is appropriate for grades 3 and higher.

Purpose

- To provide students an audience for their writings and motivation to write more in the future.
- To promote listening skills for students in the audience.
- To develop the analyzing and critical thinking skills necessary to critique someone else's work. The critical reviews benefit the writings of both the presenter and the members of the audience.

Procedure

- Select a special chair, such as an overstuffed chair or an office executive's chair, as the Author's Chair. The author orally presents the written material.
- Audience members listen carefully, mentally noting what they like and do not like about the writing.
- The teacher may wish to model the types of responses that would be appropriate from the audience. For example: "The language you used to describe the sunrise at the beach was vivid." "I could really feel the sadness in the character's words when she responded to the bad news."
- Audience members then share only what they liked about the writing, and the author responds to these comments. The author or teacher may set a limit on the number of responses from each audience member or the entire group.
- Set a time limit for the activity. For grades 3 to 5, 15 to 20 minutes is usually sufficient. Longer sessions may be appropriate for the upper grades.

APPLICATIONS

STUDENT JOURNAL WRITING

Student journals are an effective means for integrating the components of language, and they benefit all students. They are particularly effective with gifted language arts students, who usually enjoy all forms of language expression. Here are some suggestions for using this strategy effectively (Cobine, 1995).

Format

The journal writing portion of a lesson can be structured in many different ways, depending on the grade level, purpose, and type of journal. For example, the teacher can start with an oral reading of a passage from literature and follow it with journal writing about the passage (Note: *both* teacher and students write their entries). To model a critical response and to set students at ease about sharing their entries, the teacher should read his or her entry first.

In another format, the teacher initiates a 15-minute focused pre-journal writing session about the day's reading. Afterwards, the teacher separates the class into small groups, appoints a leader, and assigns a focus task or question for discussion. The groups share the results of their discussions with each other and individually write a second version that will become part of their journals.

Types of Journals

Journal writing serves several useful purposes that can be combined into one student notebook. For example, a notebook in English class might be modeled after a book, containing a preface, a body of chapters, and a glossary. These divisions suggest three different types of journal entries, designed to achieve separate goals.

Dialogue journals. Dialogue journals foster communicativeness among students and can serve as the preface for the combined notebook. These journals are personal, informal, succinct, and direct. As a preface for the notebook, students could write about their perspective and respond to questions the teacher may have written alongside their entries. Later, the teacher could write comments about the students' responses. In this way, students have a real audience who helps to enhance their reflection and rhetorical awareness.

STUDENT JOURNAL WRITING—Continued

Literary journals. The literary journal can serve as the body of chapters for the combined notebook. In this type of journal, students maintain a record of their personal responses to passages from literature. Their writings may include predictions about plot, analyses of characters, and insights about themes. Whenever the plot or actions of a character are suggestive of real-life experiences, the students can also include those personal references in their entries.

Subject journals. The subject journal serves as the glossary for the student notebook. For an English-class notebook, there are several possible uses. One section could be reserved for student responses to the author's biography or about historic events mentioned in the literary work. Another section might represent a personalized dictionary of literary and linguistic terms for further study. A third section could be a personalized stylebook of grammatical, rhetorical, and mechanical concerns about their writings. Here, the students track the progress of their language usage throughout the course.

Journal writing promotes communication, clarity of thought, and investigation into language styles. At the same time, it connects the processes of reading, writing, and discourse. The different types of journals and the diverse student participation accommodate multiple learning styles and offer exciting challenges to gifted students.

APPLICATIONS

LITERATURE CIRCLES

In literature circles, small groups of students read and discuss the same book. The discussions are led by their reactions to the characters and events in the book. Collaboration is critical to the success of this activity because it forms the bridge by which students connect their understandings about the literary work with those of others in the real world.

Procedure

- Students choose their own reading material from a list provided by the teacher.
- Small temporary groups are formed, based upon the book choice of the student. Different groups read different books.
- Groups meet on a regular schedule to discuss their reading. The students use written (or sketched) notes to guide their discussions.
- Discussion topics come from the student but are cleared through the teacher.
- The group discussions should be open, so personal connections and open-ended questions are welcome.
- Students play a rotating assortment of task roles. For example, the roles and tasks might include

    Discussion director: This student develops a list of questions that the group wants to discuss about the book. The questions should focus on big ideas and stay away from small details.

    Literary presenter: This student selects a few special sections that the group would like to hear read aloud. This is to help students remember some powerful, mysterious, puzzling, humorous, or important sections of the text.

    Connector: This student looks for connections between the group's book and the real world. It may involve connecting the reading to students' lives, to happenings at school or in the community, or to similar events at other times and places.

LITERATURE CIRCLES—Continued

> *Illustrator*: This student draws a quality picture related to the reading. Other students should comment on the picture before the illustrator explains it.
>
> *Summarizer*: This student prepares a brief summary of the day's reading, which includes key points, main highlights, and the essential theme of the group's literary choice.

- The teacher serves as a facilitator, not as a group member or instructor.
- The group's work is evaluated by student self-evaluation and by teacher observation.
- When the books are finished, the groups share with each other and new groups are formed around new literary choices.

Guidelines

- Literature circles are *not* meant to be teacher- or text-centered activities.
- Groups should not be formed solely by ability. However, a group formed entirely of students who are gifted in the language arts may be appropriate.
- These circles are not the place to do skills work.
- The group's operating rules should encourage student responsibility, independence, and ownership.

APPLICATIONS

CONDUCTING A WRITER'S WORKSHOP

A writer's workshop is a sophisticated format that is particularly effective in reviewing, evaluating, and improving an author's literary descriptions and style. It was first used with adult writers who were interested in pursing writing as a career. The basic structure, however, can be modified to accommodate younger writers.

Because it is a labor- and time-intensive strategy, it should be used sparingly and only with more mature middle and high school students who are gifted in language arts, who have a strong self-image, and who can devote the required time and effort. During the workshop, a panel of peers examines the strengths and weaknesses of an author's paper, accentuating positive aspects and suggesting improvements in style and content.

Format

- A group of panel members (usually other student authors) reads the author's paper carefully before the workshop.

- In one format, the author is present but does *not* participate during most of the discussion. The author takes notes in order to respond later to the panelists' comments. (Another variation allows the written paper to be discussed by a group that includes the author, a moderator, and several reviewers who are familiar with the author's work. The author selects and reads a paragraph and expresses feelings about the selection. One or two reviewers then briefly summarize their viewpoint of the author's paper, but they should avoid debating inconsistencies between their interpretations of the work's content.)

- The panel then discusses and praises what they liked about the paper in terms of content and style.

- Following the discussion on positive aspects, the panel presents ways to improve the content and style of the paper, offering constructive suggestions on how to make the work better. The protocol is to first state the problem and then follow with a suggestion on how to solve the problem.

CONDUCTING A WRITER'S WORKSHOP—Continued

- During the discussion of both the positive aspects and the areas needing improvement, the author does not participate. Nor do the reviewers address the author directly. The reviewers should refer to the author in the third person and should not look at the author when making comments.
- After this discussion, the author may ask questions of the reviewers to clarify and better understand their comments.
- The audience thanks the author for writing the paper.

Guidelines

- The teacher's main duty during this process is to act as moderator and ensure that the students behave courteously towards each other and towards the author. People feel uneasy when being evaluated, even under the best of circumstances. The teacher needs to insist on an atmosphere that is constructive and conducive to insightful discussions, rather than allowing students to show off their intellect by attacking others.
- Panel reviewers are usually authors themselves, whose papers will also go through this process. In some situations, teachers may wish to include non-authors in the class as reviewers. Nonauthors may have good comments to contribute but may not be good writers.

APPLICATIONS

OUT-OF-SCHOOL ENRICHMENT ACTIVITIES FOR STUDENTS GIFTED IN LANGUAGE ARTS

The following activities offer students who are gifted in the language arts additional opportunities for enrichment in language and for extending their talents.

- *Local theater and drama groups.* Opportunities to participate in local theater and drama groups that include live performances can be a very enriching experience for these students. The pariticipation can be as passive as just watching rehearsals or involve being an actual member of the production.

- *Reading groups.* Exceptional readers may wish to participate in reading groups organized by older students or an interested parent. The Internet is a useful source of information about these groups and can also provide information on websites that show what students are reading in other schools and in other countries.

- *Creative writing and poetry societies.* Some communities have societies dedicated to creative writing or poetry, giving students the opportunity to write for pleasure (and for an audience) outside school.

- *Visiting the media.* Visits to the offices of radio and television stations, newspapers, and publishing companies can provide exciting insights into the world of journalism. Gifted students might even be able to contribute copy of their own.

- *Lectures and seminars.* Gifted students may be able to enroll in lectures and seminars on topics of special interest at local universities, galleries, and museums, as a way of extending the breadth and depth of their subject knowledge.

5

Mathematical Talent

Quick, how much is 37 times 489? What is the square root of 7,569? If you are like most people, you will need a few minutes along with pencil and paper to answer these questions. But people who are highly skilled at mathematics can solve these problems in a few seconds without a calculator or a pencil. How do they do it? Is it an inherited gift?

Mathematics is often viewed with such awe that those who understand and manipulate numbers with ease are usually considered gifted. Yet, studies show that infants demonstrate number sense very early in their development and begin to do addition and subtraction much earlier than previously thought. The notion that number sense is hard-wired into the brain makes sense in terms of our development as a species. Counting (e.g., determining how many animals in a pack represented a danger) and arithmetic operations (e.g., deciding how much to plant to feed the clan) were major contributors to our survival and, over time, became part of our genetic code.

Some researchers believe that number sense is hard-wired into the brain, and that human infants can do simple addition and subtraction.

Debates continue over the nature of the number sense that infants have and over whether addition and subtraction are actually innate or are arithmetic competencies that develop in the early years. Karen Wynn (1992, 1998), now at Yale University, believes that infants are genetically programmed to recognize discrete numbers of objects and to perform rudimentary addition and subtraction. Her studies also found that 8-month-old infants could reliably distinguish individual objects from collections and could discriminate among different objects within their visual field (Chiang and Wynn, 2000). Other researchers, such as Ann Wakeley at the University of California, Berkeley, believe that infants can distinguish general numbers of objects through contour and shape, but they cannot count discrete items and have weak or no innate ability to add or subtract (Wakeley, Rivera, and Langer, 2000).

Given the difficulty of carrying out these types of studies with infants and of trying to speculate on what the infants are thinking, the debate is likely to continue for some time. What is of greater importance, perhaps, is that regardless of whether mathematical abilities are innate or quickly acquired, they are important skills for success in a complex world.

MATHEMATICAL THINKING AND THE BRAIN ■

How does the brain process arithmetic and mathematical operations? Is the processing dependent on language or visual-spatial representations? What conditions affect an individual's mathematical competence? These and similar questions have been the focus of scientific investigations for decades. In the past, answers to these types of questions came from observing the behavior of mathematicians and from their own musings about what occurred in their minds while thinking about mathematics. Some mathematicians, including Albert Einstein, insisted that words and language had little or no role in their thought processes; others stressed that language played a vital role in their interpretation of symbol systems. Still others claimed that mathematical insights were opaque operations that did not emerge from conscious, explicit thought. Now brain imaging and stimulation techniques are studying cerebral activity during various types of mathematical operations and have produced some fascinating revelations.

Arithmetic Fact Retrieval and Processing

Several recent studies have focused on determining where simple arithmetic functions, such as addition and multiplication, are processed in the brain. One study showed that electrical stimulation of the cortex in the left parietal lobe (Figure 5.1) impaired performance on simple multiplication problems and disrupted the retrieval of arithmetic facts (Whalen, McCloskey, Lesser, and Gordon, 1997). This finding supported the observations of other researchers who noted that patients with left parietal lobe damage had difficulty with arithmetic operations (Hittmair-Delazer, Semenza, and Denes, 1994). However, the

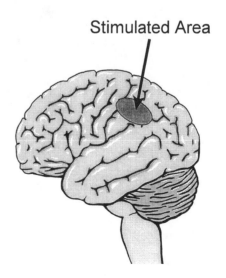

Figure 5.1 The shaded area shows the region of the left parietal lobe where arithmetic processing may occur.

results of these studies do not exclude the possibility that other regions of the brain may play a lesser role in arithmetic fact retrieval and processing.

The left parietal lobe is also the part of Albert Einstein's brain that was about 15 percent larger than normal. Because of the size of his related cortical structures, the researchers who examined Einstein's brain estimated that this extensive development of the parietal lobe probably occurred early in Einstein's lifetime, when he was already showing prowess at number manipulation and spatial abilities (Witelson, Kigar, and Harvey, 1999). The unanswered question, of course, is whether the larger parietal lobe is the cause or result of Einstein's intense work with mathematical operations.

Number Processing, Language, and Visual-Spatial Dependence

An area of considerable research interest has been the degree to which mathematical operations are dependent on other cerebral functions. If the ability to manipulate numbers is innate, as some researchers believe, then it would seem that mathematical processing would be associated with other innate human talents, such as language and visual-spatial representations.

Apparently, different brain regions are called into action when we change the way we process numbers. An fMRI study found that multiplication, subtraction, and number comparison activate different regions of the brain's left and right parietal lobes (Chocon, Cohen, van der Moortele, and Dehaene, 1999). The researchers hypothesized that although both parietal areas are involved in manipulating quantity information, only the left parietal region provides the connection between quantity information and the linguistic code stored in Broca's and Wernicke's areas.

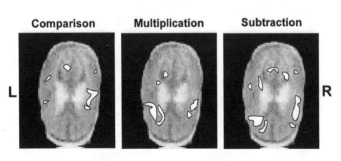

Figure 5.2 These representations of fMRI scans show that the right parietal lobe is most activated during number comparison but the left parietal lobe is most activated during multiplication. However, during subtraction, both lobes are highly activated (Chochon, et al., 1999).

Results from the study seemed to support this hypothesis. During number comparison, the right parietal region was the most activated region because comparison involves accessing the Arabic number system and does not require any linguistic translation (Figure 5.2). During multiplication, the left parietal lobe was more strongly activated because the brain monitors the results of the process through verbal computations (i.e., verbalized the results internally).

MATHEMATICAL TALENT **137**

Finally, during subtraction, both the left and right parietal lobes were activated because subtraction requires both the internal numbering system and the verbal naming of the resulting quantity.

A study by Stanislas Dehaene and his colleagues of bilingual adults used fMRI techniques to examine brain activity while the subjects performed exact and approximate arithmetic calculations (Dehaene, Spelke, Pinel, Stanescu, and Tsivkin, 1999). For example, in the tasks requiring *exact* addition, subjects were asked to give the sum of two numerically close numbers shown on a card (e.g., $5 + 4 = ?$), and to identify the answer on the following card (7 or 9?). Using the same problem, the exercise was repeated and subjects were asked to find an *approximate* calculation (3 or 8?).

The results of the study were quite surprising. First, with repetition, the performance of the subjects improved considerably (i.e., response times dropped about 45 percent), regardless of the language used to

> **Exact and approximate arithmetic calculations appear to be processed in different parts of the brain.**

present the problem. However, in exact calculations, the bilingual subjects responded significantly faster when the problem was presented in the same language in which they were given the original instructions for the study, but more slowly if the problem was presented in the other language. This was true regardless of the subjects' native language. Apparently, the instructions were stored in a language-specific format that accelerated the exact arithmetic calculations when the language of the problem and instructions were the same, but hindered the exact calculations when the languages were different. In contrast, no differences were noticed because of language changes in problems involving approximate calculations, indicating that those operations were independent of language.

In the second phase of the study, a different group of bilingual adults was asked to perform more complex exact and approximate arithmetic calculations. The fMRI results showed that different areas of the brain were used for exact calculations than were used for approximate calculations. Exact arithmetic calculations activated mainly the left frontal lobe and the left angular gyrus. Both of these areas have been associated with language tasks, indicating that this network is probably using language-dependent coding to carry out verbal processes needed to perform exact arithmetic calculations. In contrast, approximation tasks activated the left and right parietal lobes and portions of the right occipital lobe. These areas are outside the language processing regions and are usually associated with visual-spatial operations, such as mental rotation and guided hand movements (Figure 5.3).

Implications for Studying Mathematics

These several studies seem to confirm that there is no one area of the brain for mathematical computation. Different cerebral regions are activated to perform different calculations, some of which require input from the language areas located in the left hemisphere. This would suggest that people who have strong neural connections between the quantity and language centers are likely to be more proficient in mathematics than individuals whose connections are weaker.

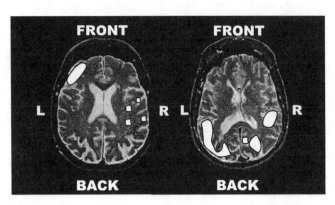

Figure 5.3 The illustration on the left is a representation of an fMRI image showing that the left frontal lobe was the area of main activation during exact calculations. The representation on the right shows that approximate calculations activated the left and right parietal lobes and portions of the occipital lobe (Dehaene, et al., 1999).

Even for simple arithmetic computations, multiple mental representations are used to perform different tasks. To some degree, they also help explain the diverse views that mathematicians have about their own thinking processes.

Exact computations seem to involve language-specific operations and rely on left-hemisphere circuits in the frontal lobe to complete their work. Thus, success in learning symbolic arithmetic and calculus may depend heavily on an individual's ability to process verbal language, which may affect the recognition and processing of mathematical language. In other words, good verbal language skills mean good exact computation skills.

Approximate arithmetic, on the other hand, shows no dependence on language and seems to rely more on visual-spatial representations in the left and right parietal lobes. This may be called the Einstein area (see Chapter 2), where complex spatial portrayals are created and enriched. It is possible that this language-independent representation of quantity is associated with our evolutionary history, whereby approximating the number of animals in a herd or pack was sufficient for our survival. This tendency toward approximation allowed neural networks the freedom to focus on holistic relationships and patterns rather than to get bogged down in handling discrete numbers.

> **Exact computation seems related to verbal language skills, while approximate computation is related to visual-spatial skills.**

Conceptual knowledge has a greater influence on procedural knowledge than the reverse.

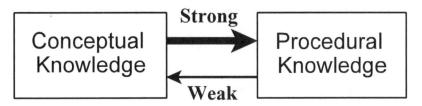

Figure 5.4 The diagram illustrates the different influences that conceptual and procedural knowledge have on each other.

Conceptual and Procedural Knowledge

Understanding mathematics, like most learning endeavors, requires acquiring the grand scheme of a topic, usually referred to as *conceptual knowledge*, as well as the steps and procedures needed to achieve a solution to a problem, known as *procedural knowledge*. Psychologists have long debated how these two components interact with each other during the acquisition of new learning, especially in the early years.

A study of 4th- and 5th-grade students examined the relationship between the students' conceptual understanding of mathematical equivalence and their procedures for solving problems involving equivalence (e.g., $4+5+7 = 4+ \underline{?}$). The students were pretested on their conceptual and procedural knowledge of equivalence. They were split into two groups and taught either the concept of equivalence or the steps needed to solve problems of equivalence. Posttests were given to determine how easily they could transfer their understanding to solve problems (Rittle-Johnson, and Alibali, 1999).

Those taught with conceptual knowledge had a good conceptual understanding of equivalence and could also devise the correct procedures for solving equivalence problems. In contrast, the students taught only the procedural knowledge had some conceptual understanding but only limited transfer of the procedure to a new problem. The findings seem to indicate that there is a causal relationship between conceptual and procedural knowledge, and that conceptual knowledge has a greater influence on the acquisition of procedural knowledge than the reverse (Figure 5.4).

Experienced teachers will not be surprised by the results of the preceding study. Most of us have experienced learning situations in which we were more or less following a series of steps without really understanding why we were doing it. Beginning cooks can carefully follow a written recipe and even produce a decent product, but they have no clue about how the ingredients came together to make the dish. Moreover, they would not know how to make modifications if they lacked one of the ingredients.

Implications for the Study of Mathematics

In most lessons, teachers should ensure that they find ways to present mathematics conceptually first and check for the students' conceptual understanding before moving on to any procedural steps involved in solving problems associated with the concept.

■ IDENTIFYING THE MATHEMATICALLY GIFTED

Mathematically promising students are not always easy to spot. They may feel self-conscious about their abilities and may prefer to remain in the background rather than have attention brought to them. As a result, their competence may not be identified at all, or they may be encouraged to skip classes or grades in the hope that their specific needs eventually will be met.

Some Attributes of Mathematical Giftedness

Students with high mathematical ability

- Learn and understand mathematical ideas very quickly.
- Display multiple strategies for solving problems. They prefer to approach the problem from different perspectives and at varying levels of difficulty. The more layers the problem has, the more involved these students become in seeking solutions.
- Engage other students in their activities. They tend to talk to themselves or others as they walk through various approaches to the problem. They make convincing arguments about their views and try to recruit others to their position.

- Sustain their concentration and show great tenacity in pursuing solutions.
- Switch approaches easily and avoid nonproductive approaches.
- Operate easily with symbols and spatial concepts.
- Quickly recognize similarities, differences, and patterns.
- Look at problems more analytically than holistically.
- Work systematically and accurately.
- Demonstrate mathematical abilities in other subject areas by using charts, tables, and graphs to make their points and illustrate their data.

Of course, not all the students who possess these attributes are willing to work hard at mathematics, or even to be very creative. We see potential, but students may put little effort into using their mathematical capabilities. Truly gifted students not only possess these attributes but are also creative, working hard to develop their abilities. The earlier that school personnel identify these students, the better. Whether mathematical ability is innate or acquired, however, the early years are an important time for developing the cerebral areas and establishing the neural networks that perform arithmetic computation as well as create and manipulate mathematical abstractions.

TEACHING THE MATHEMATICALLY GIFTED ■

Classroom Challenges

Providing Unique Opportunities

One reason that mathematically gifted students are not identified may be that the method of teaching mathematics in the classroom does not evoke the type of thinking processes associated with high mathematical ability. Instruction that focuses mainly on memorizing rules, formulas, and procedural steps will provide few opportunities for gifted students to demonstrate their higher-level competencies. In this environment, they are more likely to be bored, withdrawn, or even act out to show their displeasure with activities that offer little or no challenge. Teachers are more likely to spot gifted students when the instruction is differentiated so that the mathematically talented can pursue interesting and thought-provoking problems.

Some teachers of mathematics are not prepared to deal with highly-gifted students. Interviews of 12 middle and high school mathematics teachers found that some harbored resentment toward their gifted students. The teachers said that their own poor training in mathematics or lack of a strong mathematical background was the main source of these feelings. They felt intimidated by the questions gifted students asked and often responded by shifting to classroom activities that replaced creativity with routine. Some teachers who tried to impress these students with their own mathematical competence found that the bright students took that as a challenge. Ironically, interviews of the students revealed that they appreciated teachers who were honest about their own mathematical abilities and who were willing to be co-learners and explore mathematics along with the students (Mingus and Grassi, 1999).

> **Because of their own lack of knowledge, some mathematics teachers admit to feeling intimidated by, and even resenting, mathematically gifted students.**

Creating a learning environment that encourages and nurtures the talents of mathematically gifted students requires sustained effort and is no easy task. These students grasp information quickly and seek higher meaning and challenge in what they are learning. Because the mathematics curriculum in most schools today is designed for that school's average learner, the needs of students who are exceptionally talented in mathematics often go unmet. Thus, the teacher has to search for unique opportunities for gifted students, such as designing open-ended problems, setting up cooperative learning groups of high-ability students, and helping students become involved in the talent searches sponsored by nearly a dozen US universities.

Diversity in Homogeneity

Even among groups of mathematically gifted students, there can be a great deal of individual variability. Thus, engaging these students in diverse projects that allow them to use their strengths improves their achievement dramatically. Kalchman and Case (1999) conducted a study whereby the same teacher presented a curriculum unit on mathematical functions to two groups of highly motivated and gifted high school boys. For the control group, the unit centered around solving problems from the textbook plus compiling and applying definitions related to functions. The students engaged in activities that were largely procedural, such as creating tables and graphs and relating their solutions to prior problems. The sequential nature of the follow-up exercises in the textbook made individualization very difficult.

In the experimental group, however, the teacher used a technique called jigsaw learning. In this format, different groups of students acquired specialized knowledge about mathematical functions. They then reformed into new teams so that the expertise of all the group members had to be combined to solve a new problem. This approach promoted an environment whereby these high-ability students could feel part of a community of learners and could have the opportunity to display their unique talents. Although the experimental and control groups had similar scores on a pretest, the experimental group's scores on the posttest were significantly higher than the control group's scores (Figure 5.5). These findings, as in other studies, reaffirm that variations in degree of talent and ability exist in a seemingly homogeneous group of mathematically gifted students. Teachers, therefore, need to consider and recognize the individual needs and differences of gifted students, even within the same class.

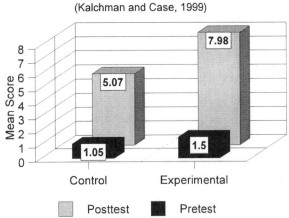

Pre- and Posttest Means

(Kalchman and Case, 1999)

Figure 5.5 This graph compares the pre- and posttest mean scores of the control and experimental groups.

Assessing Achievement in Mathematics

Assessing how well our students are doing in mathematics can be done by comparing their performances on tests to those of similar students in other countries. Started in the 1960s, the International Mathematics and Science Study was designed to do just that. In the first two mathematics studies, conducted in the mid-1960s and the early 1980s, US students did not fare well. Curriculum reform movements in the late 1980s and 1990s were supposed to improve achievement in several areas including mathematics and science. But, when the Third International Mathematics and Science Study (TIMSS) was completed, the American public was surprised to learn that in 1995, US 8th graders scored only 28th among the 41 countries whose students took the test (NCES, 1999). Four years later, the followup TIMSS report showed that in 1999, 8th graders had scored somewhat better: 19th among the 38 participating nations (NCES, 2001). (The US 8th graders' scores on the science portions of the TIMSS were only slightly better.)

Of particular concern in the 1995 study was the fact that US high school seniors in advanced mathematics classes (pre-calculus, calculus, and AP calculus) scored 15th among the 16 nations participating in this portion of the TIMSS. Coming in next to last prompted a national outcry for curriculum reform in K-12 mathematics. As a result, the 1995 report forced many districts to reexamine how secondary school teachers were delivering mathematics and science to advanced-ability students. Frances and Underhill (1996) proposed an integrated program of mathematics and science instruction on the basis of guidelines from the National Council of Teachers of Mathematics, the American Association for the Advancement of Science, and the National Research Council. The researchers' earlier studies had found that students achieved much better in classes where mathematics and science teachers had worked together to integrate their curriculum.

In practice, teachers of the gifted rarely have the resources or time to develop and implement an integrated mathematics-science curriculum, But when it does happen, studies show a significant improvement in student achievement. Here are a few examples of programs that have tried to improve mathematics instruction, especially for gifted students.

The Georgia GEMS Study

The Georgia program for Gifted Education in Math and Science (Ga-GEMS) was designed to give students with high potential in mathematics and science opportunities to study these two areas in an enriched environment (Tyler-Wood, Mortenson, Putney, and Cass, 2000). Sixty-four gifted high school students participated in a 2-year controlled study designed to determine whether a newly developed integrated mathematics and science curriculum would assist gifted students in their acquisition of higher-level mathematics and science. The students were divided into two matched groups of 32 each. During the academic year, the control group participated in their traditional tracked science and mathematics classes for high-ability

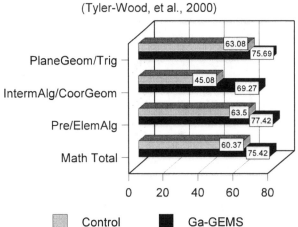

Comparison of ACT Mean Scores
(Tyler-Wood, et al., 2000)

Figure 5.6 A comparison of the ACT scores of the Ga-GEMS and a control group after 2 years in the study. Each group had 32 high-ability students.

students, while the Ga-GEMS students participated in the integrated mathematics and science curriculum.

Teachers implementing the Ga-GEMS curriculum used a team-teaching approach and engaged students in hands-on experiences, extended laboratory projects, and field trips. At the end of the 2-year program, both groups were administered the science and mathematics portions of the American College Test (ACT). Students participating in the Ga-GEMS project scored significantly higher on all the ACT subtests (Figure 5.6).

The researchers in this study were also interested in comparing the frequency of seven types of classroom activities that occurred in the two groups. To do this, they videotaped each group for 45 to 55 minutes on 10 occasions. The tapes were analyzed by three different individuals and their scores were averaged. Researchers found significant differences between the frequency of activities in the Ga-GEMS group and the control groups. Compared to the Ga-GEMS classes, teachers in the control classes spent more time on lecture and seat work, less time on group work, and no time on laboratory work (Table 5.1).

Table 5.1 Percentage of Occurrences of Classroom Activities (Tyler-Wood, et al., 2000)		
Activity	**Ga-GEMS %**	**Control %**
Lecture	27	45
Lab Work	22	0
Seat Work	5	14
Question and Answer	14	17
Group Work	23	8
Teacher Giving Directions	6	9
No Structured Activities	3	7

Developing the Ga-GEMS integrated curriculum took over 1,000 hours of teacher time. Many school districts cannot afford this type of investment in time and resources. Nonetheless, this effort offered gifted students an opportunity to continue their high school experience while pursuing interests in mathematics and science. Other school districts may want to consider undertaking a similar program that may require less time but still be as effective.

The Music Spatial-Temporal (MST) Math Program

Although not designed specifically for gifted students, this program evolved from the work of Gordon Shaw, the researcher whose work in 1993 led to the so-called "Mozart Effect." After retiring from the University of California, Irvine, he established the Music Intelligence Neural Development (M.I.N.D.) Institute in 1997 to conduct research on the influence of music on spatial-temporal reasoning—the ability to form a mental image and to think ahead in space and time. Shaw, himself a theoretical physicist, believed that training primary grade students in music would build the neural structures necessary to enhance spatial-temporal reasoning, which is crucial for understanding mathematics and science. Shaw and his colleagues at the Institute developed the Music Spatial-Temporal (MST) Math Program to teach mathematics by exploiting the brain's innate ability to do spatial-temporal reasoning. This program complements the typical language-analytical methods (symbols, word problems, equations) usually begun at home during the pre-school years as well as emphasized in the primary grades. Music training is also introduced, which includes a listening component, music theory skills, and piano keyboard instruction. The students use mathematics video game software to visualize and understand difficult concepts, and to integrate them with the regular language-based mathematics curriculum.

In a study designed to test the effectiveness of the MST program, nearly 1,100 2nd graders were taught difficult mathematical concepts using the video computer games. To assess their level of achievement, the MST students were first administered the 2nd-grade California standardized exams in advanced mathematics concepts (AMC). This test includes questions on fraction, proportions, symmetry, graphs, and pre-algebra. The students were then asked to answer relevant questions from the 3rd- through 5th-grade AMC tests, in which the heavily language-loaded presentations had been simplified. The 2nd-grade MST Math program students scored significantly higher than the 3rd-grade (13.51 vs. 12.1) and slightly higher than the 4th grade (13.51 vs. 13.24) students, at the same schools, who were not in the

2000-2001 AMC Test Average Scores

MST 2nd Graders vs. 3rd and 4th Graders

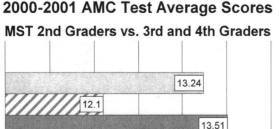
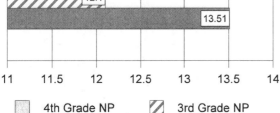

Figure 5.7 Comparison of the average scores of 2nd-grade MST Math Program students with 3rd- and 4th-grade students who were not in the program. (NP=Not in Program)

program but who had one to two years of additional mathematics training (Figure 5.7). It is also worth noting that 2nd-grade students at *all ability levels* benefitted from the MST program (M.I.N.D., 2002).

Gender Differences in Mathematics: Do They Really Exist?

Since the 1970s, gender differences in mathematics performance has been a controversial topic among educators and researchers. Statistical evidence that boys are smarter at mathematics than girls came from the Study of Mathematically Precocious Youth conducted in the early 1980s. Gifted 7th graders were administered the mathematics section of the Scholastic Aptitude Test (SAT-M). Four times as many boys scored above 600 as girls, and 13 times as many boys scored above 700 (Benbow and Stanley, 1983). Male college-bound students also displayed a

> **Gender differences in mathematics seem to be greater for high-ability students than for the general student population.**

mathematics advantage by consistently scoring higher on both the SAT-M and the mathematics section of the American College Test (ACT).

Ensuing studies found other differences between male and female performance on specific types of mathematical skills. For example, males seemed to have an advantage over females in mathematical operations involving visual-spatial ability, while females did better in mathematical computation. One possible explanation for these findings is that more male than female brains seem to have a visual-spatial preference (see Chapter 3) and would therefore perform better in solving these types of problems. In contrast, more females have analytic preferences and would tend to do better with computation problems.

Numerous other studies in the 1980s through the mid-1990s yielded conflicting results, especially with regard to the age at which the gender differences emerge. Some studies reported differences in the early elementary years, others by age 12, and still others argued that gender differences did not appear until high school. The discrepancies among these studies can be explained in part by the limited sample sizes and by the use of a select population, such as gifted or college-bound students. More recently, a major study by Leahey and Guo (2001) sought to overcome the deficiencies of previous studies by using large samples and data from the National Longitudinal Study of Youth (NLSY) and the National Educational Longitudinal Study (NELS). This approach not only reduced the bias due to small and select samples, but also allowed the researchers to examine mathematical performance from kindergarten to grade 12, rather than at one or two developmental stages. They were also able to separate out performance differences by mathematical skill and by selected student populations. Table 5.2 summarizes some of their findings.

Table 5.2 Gender Differences in Mathematics Summary of Findings from the Study by Leahy and Guo (2001)	

Major Findings (Elementary Students and NLSY data)
 	
No. of Students: 4,126
No. of Scores: 12,159
	General Mathematics Skill:
	  Almost no gender differences in mean scores among the general population. Boys' scores did have more *variance* than girls' scores, but it was not statistically significant.
	High-Scoring Students:
	  Boys and girls had similar overall *averages*.
	  Ages 4-7, high-ability girls did better than high-ability boys**.**
	  Ages 8-10, high-ability boys did better than high-ability girls.
	  Ages 11-13, no significant differences.
	Reasoning Skill:
	  Few differences in younger children; a slight advantage to female students among 11- to13-year-olds.

Major Findings (Secondary Students and NELS data)
 	
No. of Students: 9,787
No. of Scores: 26,253
	General Mathematics Skill:
	  In 8th grade, males scored an average of 0.5 points higher than females. This difference increased to 1.32 by 12th grade. The difference was *not significant* at the 5 percent level.
	High-Scoring Students:
	  High-ability boys did better than high-ability girls.
	Reasoning Skill:
	  In 8th grade, no gender differences. In high school, male scores were slightly higher than female, but not statistically significant.
	Geometry Skill:
	  In 8th grade, males held a very slight advantage, which increased to a statistically significant advantage in 12th grade.

In summary, Leahy and Guo found that there were a few and slight gender differences that did not appear until the end of high school. These differences also were greater for high-ability students than for the general population. Males seemed to have an advantage in geometry and females, in computation in the early grades. Differences in brain development and learning style preferences may account for these findings. But is it possible that there are societal and cultural factors at work as well? For example, more boys elect to take more mathematics and science courses, which could further develop their visual-spatial abilities and thereby improve their performance on certain tests, such as geometry. These skills are not really emphasized until high school, which could explain the emergence of the gender differences at that time.

Three important points need to be made at this time: First, there are gender differences in mathematics that are slight, develop late, and are subject specific. Second, the findings do *not* support the notion that males generally have a powerful innate superiority in mathematics over females. It may just be that the slight advantage they do have, especially in visual-spatial operations, are more obvious in the later high school years. Third, the fact that much of higher mathematics involves visual-spatial and abstract reasoning may explain why a large portion of top mathematicians are male.

APPLICATIONS

IDENTIFYING THE MATHEMATICALLY GIFTED

Students who are gifted in mathematics display certain attributes. Specific classroom activities (see the next application) can often reveal these attributes. Use the scale below to help decide if a particular student is gifted in mathematics. If you rate the student with scores of 4 or 5 on more than half of the characteristics, then further assessment is warranted.

The student....	A little	Some	A lot
1. Learns and understands mathematical ideas very quickly.	1 — 2 — 3 — 4 — 5		
2. Displays multiple strategies for solving problems.	1 — 2 — 3 — 4 — 5		
3. Engages others in problem solving.	1 — 2 — 3 — 4 — 5		
4. Sustains concentration and shows great tenacity in pursuing problems.	1 — 2 — 3 — 4 — 5		
5. Switches approaches easily and avoids nonproductive approaches.	1 — 2 — 3 — 4 — 5		
6. Operates easily with symbols and spatial concepts.	1 — 2 — 3 — 4 — 5		
7. Quickly recognizes similarities, differences, and patterns.	1 — 2 — 3 — 4 — 5		
8. Looks at problems more analytically than holistically.	1 — 2 — 3 — 4 — 5		
9. Works systematically and accurately.	1 — 2 — 3 — 4 — 5		
10. Demonstrates mathematical abilities in other subject areas.	1 — 2 — 3 — 4 — 5		
11. Prefers to present information through charts, tables, and graphs.	1 — 2 — 3 — 4 — 5		

APPLICATIONS

CLASSROOM ACTIVITIES TO HELP IDENTIFY MATHEMATICALLY GIFTED STUDENTS

When teaching mathematics at any grade level, offering classroom activities at varying levels of difficulty and complexity can help teachers identify mathematically gifted students. Here are a few suggestions for accomplishing this task (Hoeflinger, 1998).

- Offer open-ended problems that have an array of discrete levels and can be solved using multiple strategies. (A simple test to identify a problem of this type: If you are unsure how to proceed in order to solve the problem, then it most likely requires a multistep approach.)

- Provide thought-provoking and nonroutine problems about once a week. Look for the ways the students organize knowledge, argue their position, make conjectures, and clarify their thoughts. Are they looking for patterns and can they recognize and explain them? What type of reasoning and logic are they using? How quickly and accurately can they solve the problem? Make anecdotal notes on how students respond to specific problems, the types of strategies they use, and their progress.

- As problems are solved, raise the level of complexity for ensuing problems until the students are involved in a spirited debate about potential approaches to solutions. Be certain, however, that the students know and understand the necessary mathematics vocabulary in the event that they need to seek information from other sources.

- Mathematically gifted students often show their talents in other curriculum areas. They tend to view the world in mathematical ways and to use mathematical symbols and language in their other work. ➤ In writing, they often demonstrate a clarity of logic, precision, and sequencing, sometimes using tables and charts to organize information.

CLASSROOM ACTIVITIES—Continued

➤ Social Studies offers another area where they can apply their unique abilities to create models and design tables and graphs to illustrate data (e.g., population growth in an area using birth and death rates, etc.). Can they use this information to make and support predictions about future growth?

➤ Science experiments also provide many opportunities for these students to show their abilities, especially in collecting, organizing, and manipulating quantitative experimental data. Can they use the data to make predictions when other experimental variables are changed?

● Avoid giving textbooks to truly gifted students and allowing them to move at their own pace. Like other students, they also need nurturing and encouragement to move ahead faster.

● Cluster the gifted mathematics students in small cooperative groups and give them a complex problem to solve while you carry on instruction with the rest of the class. Ensure that group members have time to discuss their problem-solving strategies and to make connections to curriculum objectives.

● Look to other sources for mathematical problems, games, and ideas for these students to pursue. Those sources can include texts from higher grade levels, other teacher colleagues, journals published by the National Council of Teachers of Mathematics (NCTM), curriculum materials from the state Department of Education, local public and university libraries, and the Internet.

APPLICATIONS

TEACHING MATHEMATICALLY GIFTED STUDENTS IN MIXED-ABILITY CLASSROOMS

After identifying students who are mathematically gifted, working with them in a mixed-ability classroom can present problems unless the teacher finds ways to differentiate instruction. Mathematically gifted students still have educational needs, but they will be better than other students at handling and organizing data, formulating problems, and expressing and transferring ideas. Here are some suggestions for differentiating instruction for the mathematically gifted (Johnson, 2000).

Assessment

- Give pre-assessments to determine which students already know the material. In the elementary grades, gifted learners still need to know the facts necessary to complete their learning objectives. Work with those students who do not know the basics, and allow the gifted students to complete more complex learning tasks.

- Develop assessments that allow for differences in creativity, understanding, and accomplishment. Give students chances to express themselves orally and in writing to show what they have learned.

Curriculum Materials

- Select textbooks that offer enriched opportunities. Too many mathematics textbooks repeat topics every year prior to algebra. Most texts are written for average students and are not appropriate for the gifted.

- Use multiple resources, such as college textbooks and research reports, because no one textbook can meet the needs of these learners.

TEACHING IN MIXED-ABILITY CLASSROOMS—Continued

- Use technology as a tool, an inspiration, or as an independent learning environment that allows gifted students the opportunity to reach the depth and breadth they need to maintain their interest. Computer programming is a special skill. Using spreadsheets, databases, and graphic and scientific calculators can lead to powerful data analysis.

- The World Wide Web is a vast source of material, contests, student and teacher resources, and information about mathematical ideas usually not found in textbooks.

Instructional Techniques

- Flexibility in pacing is important. Some students may be mastering basic skills while others are working on advanced topics.

- Use inquiry-based, discovery learning approaches that emphasize open-ended problems with multiple paths to multiple solutions. Have students design their own methods for solving complex problems or answering complicated questions. You will be surprised at what gifted students can discover.

- Ask lots of higher-level questions that encourage students to discuss and justify their approaches to problem solving.

- Differentiate assignments so that gifted students do not get just more problems of the same type. Offer choices, such as a regular assignment, a more challenging one, or one that matches the students' interests.

- Offer AP level courses in statistics, calculus, and computer science. Students should also be encouraged to take classes at local colleges if they have exhausted all the high school possibilities.

- Provide units and problems that go beyond the normal curriculum and relate to the real world. Use concrete experiences that incorporate manipulatives or hands-on activities.

TEACHING IN MIXED-ABILITY CLASSROOMS—Continued

● Ensure that students realize that you expect their learning products to be of high quality.

● Offer opportunities to participate in contests, such as the Mathematical Olympiad. Give students feedback on their performance, and use some of the contest's problems for classroom discussion.

● Allow students access to mentors who represent diverse cultural and linguistic groups. Mentors can come from within the school, the community, or be available through teleconferencing or the Internet. Use guest speakers in the classroom to talk about how mathematics has benefitted their careers.

Grouping

● Provide some activities that can be done individually or in groups, based on student choice. Grouping is productive because gifted students working alone are learning no more than they would at home. Be sure to give them guidelines on their interactions with other group members and appropriate feedback afterward.

Using differentiated instruction in regular mathematics classrooms not only benefits gifted students but also has the potential for enriching the learning experience for all students, because some may also want to try the more challenging tasks. With this approach, all students will have the chance to work at their own level of challenge.

APPLICATIONS

CHOOSING CONTENT FOR ELEMENTARY SCHOOL MATHEMATICS

Mathematics textbooks and programs for elementary school abound. So how do educators decide which program has the best approach in light of what we know about how the human brain learns mathematics. Although the research is still in its early stages, it seems clear that the young mind is more likely to be successful in displaying mathematical talent if educators are aware of three characteristics:

Multi-Step Learning

Too often, elementary mathematics is presented in textbooks (and therefore taught) as a collection of separate one-step skill operations or routines. Genuine mathematical problems are typically multistep, however, requiring the learner to identify intermediate steps in order to move from what is known to what is sought. These steps should be discovered by students as the teacher guides them along. Some drill and practice are necessary, but too much of these will encourage the memorization of single-step routines, carried out procedurally with little understanding. Thus, a mathematical topic for gifted students should give rise to a rich source of problems that require the integration of several basic steps for analysis and for solving problems.

Making Connections

Gifted students should experience mathematics as a collection of relationships among distinct themes, and not as a body of unrelated methods and rules. The teacher's role here is to help students look for connections among seemingly unrelated ideas. Recognizing that new methods and problems are often more familiar than they seem at first is a basic insight that gifted students need to experience regularly.

ELEMENTARY SCHOOL MATHEMATICS—Continued

Logic and Proof

One important component of understanding the connections between different parts of elementary mathematics is the notion that these connections have a logical basis, and thus must be established by exact calculation. These calculations, or proofs, establish whether some mathematical relationship really is true. Teachers should cultivate in gifted students an understanding of the need for proof and help them recognize that, in mathematics, it is exact calculation (or proof) that determines correctness. By gaining this understanding, students realize that the solutions to mathematical problems can be determined objectively and are not subject to the arbitrary whim of any person.

APPLICATIONS

SELECTING TEACHING STRATEGIES FOR MATHEMATICS

Teaching strategies in mathematics for gifted students should aim to

- Develop deeper understanding
- Lay stronger foundations
- Foster a willingness to seek out the connections between different aspects of mathematics
- Involve higher-level thinking skills
- Cultivate a desire to understand why particular mathematical methods are correct.

The following points also need to be considered:

- Strategies should develop higher-level thinking by challenging students to observe, compare, hypothesize, criticize, classify, interpret, and summarize.
- Teachers should use open-ended problems and make clear what areas the students should pursue, what processes should be involved, and what outcomes are achievable and expected.
- Teachers should not expect gifted students to work in undirected and unsupported ways for extended periods of time.
- Strategies should have clear objectives and be designed to increase the students' ability to analyze and solve problems, to stimulate creativity, and to encourage initiative and self-direction.
- Care should be taken in selecting supplemental strategies so that students see their work as challenging and not as drudgery.
- Be sure to offer opportunities for extended research in areas of student interest.

APPLICATIONS

TALENT SEARCHES AVAILABLE
FOR THE MATHEMATICALLY GIFTED

Talent searches are valuable opportunities for meeting the needs of mathematically gifted elementary and secondary students. Rotigel and Lupkowski-Shoplik (1999) describe the process and benefits of these searches. Over 200,000 students nationwide take advantage of the programs offered annually by nearly a dozen sponsoring universities (see list in **Resources**). Through its selection process, the talent search can not only help teachers identify mathematically gifted students, but can also give guidance for designing educational experiences appropriate to the students' ability levels.

School personnel should realize that talent searches are not restricted to just the most highly gifted, nor just to mathematics. Students who score in the top 5 percent of their age group in just one area (e.g., mathematics) are eligible. Sometimes, these students have not been identified for the school's gifted program because their talent lies in just one area, or because they do not receive high scores in language arts.

The Testing Process

Students who score at or above the 95th percentile on the Composite or Math Total, Vocabulary, Reading, Language Total, or Science subtest on a nationally normed achievement test (e.g., Iowa Test of Basic Skills) are recommended for additional testing. An above-level test is administered next, usually two to five grade-levels above the grade placement of the student. This allows the student to demonstrate mastery of more advanced concepts and results in a greater spread of scores, which can be used by teachers for educational planning. Examples of above-level tests are the Scholastic Assessment Test (SAT), the American College Testing program (ACT), or the EXPLORE test.

Using the Test Results

The above-level test helps to identify the level of a student's mathematical ability. A student who scores in the 95th percentile on the grade-level test may have demonstrated all he or she knows. Consequently, this student's performance on the above-level test will be low. For another student, the

TALENT SEARCHES FOR THE MATHEMATICALLY GIFTED—Continued

above-level test may show high scores in some or all areas, indicating exceptional achievement and ability.

For example, let's say that two 3rd-graders, Student A and Student B, both scored in the 99th percentile on their grade-level test. However, on the above-level 8th-grade test, Student A scores at the 26th percentile and Student B, at the 96th percentile, compared to other 8th graders. Although the two students' abilities seemed similar on the grade-level test, the above-level results show a very different picture. Both students are in their school's gifted program (as they should be) and both need more challenging activities. Student A needs more enrichment in mathematics, participation in contests, group work with students of similar aptitude in mathematics, and curriculum compacting (perhaps, 2 years of mathematics in one). Student B needs all the same options as Student A, plus individually-paced instruction as well as course- and grade-skipping. Student B may also be an excellent candidate for a university-sponsored Elementary Student Talent Search.

Benefits of Talent Search Participation

Accuracy of Diagnosis. Because above-level tests have a higher ceiling than grade-level tests, they more accurately measure students' abilities, thereby allowing for the development of specific educational plans for each identified student.

Development of Specific Educational Plans. The scores that the students receive on the above-level assessment lead to the development of specific recommendations that best match the students' demonstrated achievement and abilities. Suggestions can range from enrichment to honors classes to acceleration (see Table 5.3).

Opportunities to Participate in University-Sponsored Talent Searches. Students who enter talent search programs have a broad range of options including summer, weekend, and online programs as well as correspondence courses. These opportunities offer students a chance to study topics that may not be available at their home schools. The summer programs offer the chance for like-minded students to live together for several weeks and to study subjects intensively at a pace consistent with their interests and capabilities.

Learning About Themselves. Students in talent searches gain more insight into their abilities and achievement, putting them in a better position to

TALENT SEARCHES FOR THE MATHEMATICALLY GIFTED—Continued

make important choices, such as which college to attend or which career to pursue.

Recognition of Their Abilities. Some talent search programs recognize students' outstanding abilities through scholarships, awards, and honors. Several colleges and universities that sponsor talent searches, for example, also offer scholarships for students to participate in college courses while still attending high school.

Continuing Information. Talent search programs continue to provide participants with newsletters and other printed information about research findings, scholarships, and other educational opportunities. Studies show that, when compared to gifted nonparticipants, talent search participants pursue more rigorous courses of study, accelerate their education to a greater extent, and participate in more extracurricular activities (Olszewski-Kubilius, 1998).

On the following page, Table 5.3 shows some guidelines for developing the educational plan for students who achieve different scores on the above-level tests (Rotigel and Lupkowski-Shoplik, 1999).

TALENT SEARCHES FOR THE MATHEMATICALLY GIFTED—Continued

Table 5.3 Educational Planning Guidelines for Students Who Have Taken Above-Level Tests			
Tests and Scores	EXPLORE-Mathematics Scale score 1-13 (taken in 4th grade) OR SAT-Mathematics Score of 200-500 (taken in 7th grade)	EXPLORE-Mathematics Scale score 14-20 (taken in 4th grade) OR SAT-Mathematics Score of 510-630 (taken in 7th grade)	EXPLORE-Mathematics Scale score 21-25 (taken in 4th grade) OR SAT-Mathematics Score of 640-800 (taken in 7th grade)
Components of the Plan	Academic counseling and development of an educational plan In-school enrichment; participation in competitions and contests Supplemental course work; Summer programs for enrichment Algebra I in 7th grade; AP calculus in 11th grade; College-level mathematics courses in 12th grade	Academic counseling and development of an educational plan Curriculum compacting (taking 2 years of mathematics in one year) Summer program of fast-paced classes in mathematics Algebra I in 6th grade; AP calculus in 10th grade; College-level mathematics courses in 11th and 12th grades	All of the options in the previous column, plus: An individualized program of study based on diagnostic testing in mathematics Consider grade skipping, early admission to high school, and taking college classes early Mentorships for advanced study in mathematics

6

Musical Talent

Most people view musical talent as a gift. But there is mounting scientific evidence that all of us have some musical capability, and that our recognition of music begins shortly after birth (if not before). A study in Japan used 2-day-old infants of congenitally deaf and homebound parents to ensure that the infants had not been exposed to music before birth (Masataka, 1999). The infants heard two types of songs: those that were recorded when sung to infants and those sung for adults. By measuring response times, the researchers found that the infants had a distinct preference for the songs directed toward infants. Because these infants had no pre-natal or post-natal exposure to music, these findings may indicate that infants are born with an innate preference for music—the type they are likely to hear from their parents.

Another study conducted experiments with 72 adults who had no musical training or education (nonmusicians) and used electroencephalography (EEG) to measure their responses to various musical chords (Koelsch, Gunter, and Friederici, 2000). The subjects listened to chord sequences that infrequently contained chords that did not fit their sound expectations. Brain activity increased when

> **Every normal brain is a musical brain.**

they heard the improper chord and decreased when the expected chord was played. When asked, the subjects could not explain their responses. Apparently, these subjects with no musical training still had an innate and subconscious expectation of which chords did or did not fit a musical sequence.

The study also showed that as the musical keys changed, the subjects could still identify which chord fit which key, and their brain activity increased when a chord did not fit the key. This occurred even though the subjects knew nothing about musical keys or the fit of chords to those keys. The researchers concluded that the subjects' brains were interpreting complex musical relationships, setting up musical expectations, and detecting violations of those expectations with no conscious realization or effort on the part of their owners. The results strengthen the notion that the human brain has innate musical ability. Music may become even more important to us as we age. Researchers have found that the debilitating effects of cognitive dementia and Alzheimer's disease often diminish when one learns to play a musical instrument.

Frankly, we really did not need science to tell us that the normal brain is a musical brain. Just think of how easily our brain takes a sequence of mixed tones presented at different tempos, groups the sounds, and perceives coherent music. We can detect a wrong note in a musical string, pick out melody and harmony, and respond to tempo and timbre. We can anticipate which note should complete a musical phrase. We can unwittingly memorize tunes and lyrics with no conscious effort and have that tune play incessantly in our head. Moreover, we do all this without conscious thought.

■ WHY ARE HUMANS MUSICAL?

Music *is* everywhere and everyone is musical. Anthropologists have never discovered a culture that did not have music. Although the styles of singing and the type of musical instruments very widely, some form of music exists in all cultures, from Eskimo villages to the tropical rainforests. Of course, the notion that music is innate to all humans raises an interesting question: Why? Some psychologists think music is a useless frill that developed when our neural circuits became more sophisticated. But others feel that the importance of music goes much deeper, given the role it has played in the development of our diverse cultures over thousand of years. The oldest musical instrument found to date is a crude bone flute, discovered in southern Germany with human remains that are about 36,000 years old.

Charles Darwin speculated in 1871 that music evolved as part of courtship. Just as birds sing to attract mates, Darwin suggested that early humans used music to attract and retain sexual partners. Subsequent psychologists support Darwin's ideas but propose that the power of music began at the cradle. Because young humans take so long to develop, anything that bonded mother and infant, such as music, would have immediate survival benefit and genetic staying power. In nearly all cultures today, adults carry on sing-song conversations with babies, often with both ending up in duets and rhythmic movements. Music is also used to bond groups of families into tribes. Listening to the same music, or singing and dancing together, can unite teams, villages, and cultures into a productive cluster or a dangerous mob. Music can also be a catharsis, allowing rage or grief to be channeled to public release, as in the case of those singing the national anthem in the days following the collapse of the World Trade Center towers (Milius, 2001).

Although no one knows for sure why humans are musical animals, several theories abound. But, based on historical and evolutionary records as well as the increasingly convincing evidence from neuroscience, the best explanation seems to be that, just as in other primates, singing helped primitive humans find mates, communicate and care for their young, and bond with others in the tribe. All the other benefits of music are secondary but no less enjoyable.

> **Music helped primitive humans find mates, communicate, and care for their young as well as bond with others in the tribe.**

The idea that all human beings are musical has tremendous implications for the teaching of music. Music education should be available to all members of the school community and not just for students with obvious musical talent or whose parents deem it important.

WHAT IS MUSICAL TALENT? ■

Listening to music is one thing, but being able to *create* music is something else. Most people can process musical input and detect complex rhythm and phrases, as well as produce passable vocal music. But far fewer people seem to possess the capacity to master a musical instrument. Why is that? If music is innate, shouldn't most of us be able to learn how to play musical instruments almost as quickly as running or singing? Is it possible that the skills necessary to play a musical instrument require different brain structures? In other words, is the brain's ability to create music a distinct talent whose development is directed by genetic predispositions not found in most people? The question of how much influence genes have on talent of any kind is currently being questioned by scientists.

An extensive study by Richard Howe at the University of Exeter in England has stirred debate over how much of talent is the result of genetic predisposition and how much is a matter of sustained and rigorous practice (Howe, Davidson, and Sloboda, 1998). According to Howe and his colleagues, popular belief in Western cultures holds that talent has four components:

- People are born with the capacity to attain high levels of achievement in various activities, such as mathematics, music, literatures, and sports.
- These talents will be exhibited to some extent early in life.
- Only a small minority of people are born with these talents.
- Talent comes in different amounts, so that the "talented" are only those who achieve the highest levels of expertise or success.

Nature or Nurture?

This "either you are born with it or not" approach to explaining talent is often supported by circular reasoning: "He plays so well because he is talented. How do we know he is talented? Because he plays so well." Music is especially rich in folklore that supposedly substantiates the genetic source of musical achievement. The examples of child prodigies, such as Mozart and Artur Rubenstein, are often used to support the idea that talents appear early in life. Adding to the notion that these children are born with special capabilities, these people cite that perfect pitch (more accurately, absolute pitch) also is innate in these high achievers. Still others refer to the discovery that some parts of the brain in great achievers are larger than normal, suggesting that the talent resulted from prenatal changes in brain development.

Table 6.1 Is Musical Talent Genetic?	
Pros	**Alternative Possibilities**
Child prodigies are evidence that innate talent appears early.	Child prodigies are rare; many professional musicians were not prodigies.
Perfect pitch is innate and a sign of special capability.	Perfect pitch may be acquired early through extensive musical training.
Larger brain areas cause musical talent.	Musical experience and practice cause larger brain areas.

Howe suggests that these arguments are weak evidence to support talent as purely genetic and that there may be alternative explanations (Table 6.1). First, he notes that much of what is written about child prodigies is anecdotal, and there are very few musical prodigies compared to the larger number of highly successful professional musicians who did not display early signs of talent. Mozart's father, Leopold, was a musician. Would the young Wolfgang have become such a musical wonder had he not been exposed to music from birth? Second, there is evidence that perfect pitch appears in young children who have been given extensive musical training. Consequently, it is just as likely that perfect pitch may be acquired early in life rather than be innate. Third, because brain growth can be affected by experience, increased brain size could be the *result* of musical experiences and practice, rather than being the cause of musical achievement.

Accordingly, is seems that activities, such as practice, accomplished *after* birth may have a significant effect on musical achievement. To examine the power of practice, John Sloboda and his colleagues interviewed 257 young musicians between the ages of eight and 18 about their performance history from the start of playing a musical instrument (Sloboda, Davidson, Howe, and Moore, 1996). Ninety-four of these students kept a diary for a period of 42 weeks to record the

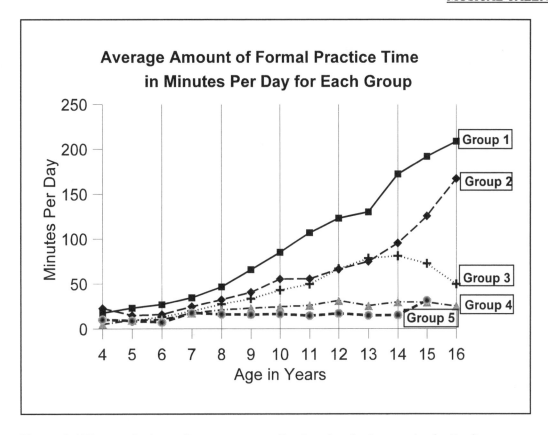

Figure 6.1 The graph shows the average practice time in minutes per day for the five groups (Sloboda, et al., 1996).

amount of time devoted to practice and other activities. The sample included participants with a broad range of musical achievement, from students who were attending a highly selective music school to individuals who had abandoned their playing after a year or less of formal instruction. Music achievement was measured by their degree of skill in playing their musical instruments through an externally validated performance examination.

Participants were divided into five groups on the basis of their level of musical competence. Group 1 was the target group, comprising students enrolled in a highly selective music school. Group 2 were students who had applied for but had not been accepted to the music school. Students in Group 3 had expressed interest in attending a music school but had not followed through with a formal application. Group 4 consisted of students who were learning a musical instrument at a nonspecialist school. Students who had been unsuccessful at instrumental music were in Group 5, having not played for at least one year prior to the study.

Not surprisingly, the researchers found a strong relationship between musical achievement and the amount of formal practice undertaken (Figure 6.1). High achievers practiced the most (Groups 1 and 2), moderate achievers practiced a moderate amount of time (Group 3), and low achievers barely practiced at all (Groups 4 and 5). Furthermore, the researchers found that high achievers who practiced less were *no more successful than low achievers*. Another important finding was that differences in practice patterns began very early in age and from the time of starting to learn an instrument. Those who practiced a lot when they were young also practiced a lot when they were older, and vice versa. These results support the premise that formal, intense practice is a major determinant of musical achievement.

What Has Science Discovered?

As the nature versus nurture debate over musical achievement continues, scientists have been making some interesting observations about music and the human brain. Table 6.2 shows some of their findings. At first glance, getting involved with music, especially at an early age, seems to have significant impact on the growing brain. That may be true. But it is important to point out that probably anything we do at an early age affects brain organization and development. For example, a comparison of the brains of mathematicians to nonmathematicians, of professional dancers to non-dancers, would likely also show structural, and perhaps functional, differences.

> **Formal, intense practice is a major determinant of musical achievement.**

Table 6.2 Some Findings from Science on Musical Ability	
Study	Findings
Elbert, et al., 1995; using PET	Compared to nonplayers, string players had greater cerebral activity and a larger area of the right motor cortex that controls the fingers of the left hand. The effects were greater for those who began playing at an early age.
Pascual-Leone, et al., 1995; using MEG	The area of the motor cortex controlling the fingers increased in size in response to piano exercises.
Schlaug, Jancke, Huang, and Steinmetz, 1995; using PET	(1) Musicians had greater activity in left temporal lobes than nonmusicians. (2) Musicians with perfect (absolute) pitch had greater activity in left temporal lobe than musicians without perfect pitch.
Pantev, et al., 1998; using PET	The auditory cortex was 25 percent larger in experienced musicians than in nonmusicians, and the effect was greater for those who started studying music at an early age.

Table 6.2 (Continued) Some Findings from Science on Musical Ability	
Study	Findings
Gregersen, 1998	In-depth reviews of genetic data showed evidence of a genetic predisposition to perfect (absolute) pitch, which could be expressed as a result of childhood exposure to music. Some children with perfect pitch also demonstrated exceptional mathematical ability.
Glassman, 1999	Harmonic relationships in music may account for the dynamics and limitations of working memory.
Ohnishi, et al., 2001; using fMRI	(1) Musicians processed music in brain areas that were different from the brain areas of nonmusicians. Musicians showed more activation in the left temporal lobe but nonmusicians had more brain activity in the right temporal lobe. (2) The degree of activation for musicians was correlated with the age at which the individual started musical training; the younger the starting age, the greater the activation. (3) Trained musicians with perfect pitch had greater activation than those without this ability. These findings suggest that early music training influences the brain to organize networks in the left hemisphere to process the analytical data needed to create music.
Itoh, Fujii, Suzuki, and Nakada, 2001; using fMRI	These colleagues reaffirmed the role of the left hemisphere when playing an instrument. The left parietal lobe was more highly activated than the right when musically trained subjects played the piano, regardless of whether they used their left or right hand separately, or used both hands.
Schlaug and Christian, 2001; using MRI	Musicians trained at an early age showed larger gray matter volumes in the left and right sensory and motor cortex regions and the left parietal lobe.

So, Where Are We?

Researchers have to speculate on possible explanations for their findings. At this time, these explanations do not resolve the nature versus nurture debate and may not for the foreseeable future. Even musically talented students have mixed views on the heritability of their own musical achievement. Tremblay and Gagné (2001) asked 80 musically talented students to use a 100-point Likert-type scale to rate the extent to which they believed seven components of musical ability could be inherited. The heritability scale ranged from *Not at all* to *Completely*. The seven components were as follows: auditory (ability to recognize and discriminate sounds), creativity (ability to improvise or compose melody), interpretation (ability

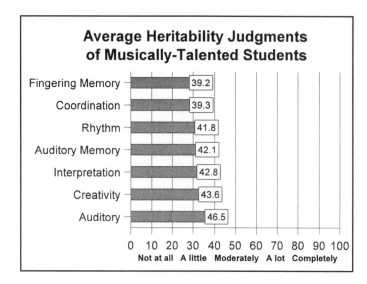

Figure 6.2   The average scores of musically-talented students on their beliefs that these musical abilities are inherited (Tremblay and Gagné, 2001).

to play a musical piece with feeling), auditory memory (ability to memorize a melody quickly), rhythm (ability to reproduce beats, duration of sounds, pauses, and tempo of a melody), coordination (ability to move hands on the instrument and to synchronize both hands), and fingering memory (ability to memorize fingering). Most students' scores fell in the moderate portion of the scale, ranging from 39.2 to 46.5 (Figure 6.2). Apparently, the music students believed that musical ability is inherited to a moderate degree and that practice and experience did not account totally for their musical achievement.

Ironically, the judgments of these talented musicians may be closer than the scientific studies to explaining what really accounts for musical achievement. On the one hand, the belief that talent is entirely innate has been overworked and, unfortunately, has led people to avoid the challenge of playing a musical instrument altogether. Too often, students invoke the absence of innate talent as the excuse for their failure and readiness to abandon their efforts. "It's not my fault. No one in my family is any good at (fill in the blank, here)," is not an uncommon excuse heard in today's classrooms. However, many accomplished musicians who displayed no early musical talent have become successful through their efforts at regular and determined practice. Granted, they may not be concert virtuosos, but their music can still provide enjoyment for themselves and others.

On the other hand, science cannot discount the possibility of a genetic predisposition to music. This genetic influence, for example, could be in the form of a larger auditory cortex capable of greater sensitivity to, and discrimination of, patterns of sounds. Another possibility is the development of a strong voice box and enhanced breathing musculature to produce powerful and melodic vocal music. Whatever the genetic contribution, such individuals, especially in a strong musical environment, will likely reach exceptionally high levels of musical achievement.

Although our understanding of how music affects the human brain is still far from complete, some of the following points can still be made:

- In most people, the brain has an innate ability to process music from birth.
- When listening to music, the processing may affect and enhance other cerebral functions, such as mathematical operations, kinesthetic performance, and memory recall.
- In most people, musical achievement may result more from efforts at regular and sustained practice than from genetic influences.
- A few people may be born with genetic predispositions which, in the right environment, will allow them to become extraordinary musical performers.
- The musical brain is highly resilient and persists even in people with profound mental and emotional disabilities.

READING AND MEMORIZING MUSIC ■

Reading Music

Highly successful musicians need to read musical notes and lyrics rapidly in order to produce fluent vocal and instrumental sound. Yet, some of these musically talented individuals have only average abilities in the reading of text.

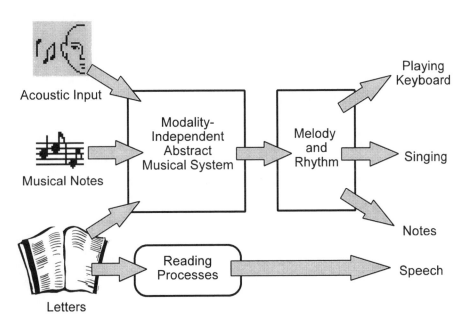

Figure 6.3 This diagram shows that the processing of musical notes and letters (lyrics) is functionally distinct from reading text and requires different cognitive operations (Stewart and Walsh, 2001).

How can this be? Should not the ability to read music with incredible speed also apply to reading text or vice versa? Apparently, this is not the case. A series of brain imaging studies on how the brain processes music in normal and brain-damaged musicians revealed that the ability to read or write music is a functionally distinct process from reading or writing text (Cappelletti, Waley-Cohen, Butterworth, and Kopelman, 2000; Stewart and Walsh, 2001). When the musicians read music, the notes and letters were integrated in the brain along with the acoustic input of what had just been played or sung. A network of brain regions, which Cappelletti and his colleagues called the *abstract musical system*, converted the input into melody and rhythm to produce the playing, singing, or writing of the next musical notes (Figure 6.3). During this process, the PET studies showed that the lower occipital and the rear part of the parietal lobes were the most activated areas (Figure 6.4). Damage to these regions resulted in the loss of the ability to read music, but not text. Apparently, different cerebral areas process text that is not related to music, but used instead for the production of speech. These findings may also suggest that there are different memory systems for storing music and nonmusical text. If so, it would explain why some patients with Alzheimer's disease, who have lost their ability to speak, are still able to sing songs and their lyrics with few or no errors.

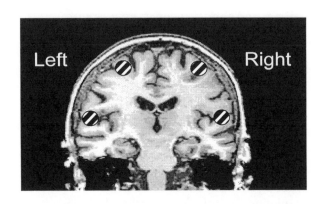

Figure 6.4 The circles in this representation of a PET scan show the areas of the occipital and parietal lobes that were most activated while a musician was reading music (Cappelletti, et al., 2000).

The results of the latest studies seem to be leading away from the earlier theory that music was essentially a right hemisphere function. It seems that music processing is spread throughout the brain and that selectively changing the focus of attention dramatically alters the patterns and intensity of cerebral activation.

Memorizing Music

Professional vocal and instrumental musicians often need to memorize large amounts of music if they want to perform publically. Although musical performance involves recall mainly from long-term memory, working memory is employed whenever the performers begin to improvise on the stored music. Yet, working memory is thought to have a functional limit of about seven chunks in most adults (Sousa, 2001a)—a capacity that would seem far too small to explain the rapid and varied modifications that some musicians display during a performance.

To do this, they must have some means of binding more items within the chunks, thereby increasing the total item count in working memory. (Although working memory has a functional capacity of only so many chunks it can process at one time,

> **Musicians brains may be much better at chunking information than the brains of nonmusicians.**

there appears to be no functional limit to the number of items that can be combined into a chunk.)

Some researchers now speculate that harmonic frequencies of brain waves may be the binding medium. This hypothesis holds that (1) items bond into a chunk because some specific property synchronizes and unifies them, and (2) harmonic frequencies within an octave band of brain waves are the synchronizing mechanisms (Glassman, 1999). This theory also suggests that because trained musicians are more attuned and responsive to harmonics, their brains are much better at increasing chunk size than the brains of nonmusicians, thereby raising the item count in working memory and significantly improving the efficiency of the transfer of chunks between working and long-term memories.

Music As Another Way of Knowing

Neuroscience research into music supports the notion that music is disassociated from linguistic and other types of cognitive processing. Thus, processing music offers a unique way of acquiring nonverbal information. By studying how the brain processes music, scientists can learn things about the brain that they cannot get from other cognitive processes. Moreover, music allows us to know, discover, express, and share aspects of the human condition that we cannot

> **Music allows us to know, discover, express, and share aspects of the human condition that we cannot experience through any other means.**

experience through any other means. For that reason alone, we should be grateful for the music that talented performers create to help us all get a deeper understanding of what it means to be human.

■ DEVELOPING MUSICALLY TALENTED STUDENTS

The Identification Process

Identifying musically talented students requires a set of effective criteria and procedures deemed valid by professionals who work with these types of students. Haroutounian (2000) surveyed over 140 teachers, musicians, and arts specialists who work with musically talented students. The following are the most common criteria for identifying musical talent:

Musical Awareness and Discrimination

▸   Perceptual awareness of sound: internally senses sound and listens discriminately

▸   Rhythmic sense: fluidly responds to rhythm and maintains a steady pulse

▸   Sense of pitch: discriminates pitches; remembers and repeats melodies

Creative Interpretation

▸   Experiments with and manipulates sound

▸   Performs and reacts to music with personal expression and involvement

▸   Is aware of the aesthetic qualities of sound

Commitment

▸   Perseveres in musical activities

▸   Works with focused concentration and internal motivation

▸   Refines ideas, constructively critiques musical work of others and self

The identification process should also reach beyond the school to include recommendations from peers, private teachers, music directors, and other community members familiar with the student's musical abilities. An audition would also be appropriate.

The Nature of Practice

The extensive practice required of most musically talented students requires continuing encouragement by parents and teachers. Parents are there at the beginning and establish the routine and habits of practice from the onset. These routines set the work ethic, which can make the difference between the student reaching high or only moderate levels of mastery.

The teacher's role is critical to progressive musical development. As a tutor, the teacher provides a one-on-one environment where there are no limits to the student's progress. Being part of a performance group, such as a band, orchestra, or chorus, can greatly motivate student musicians to try more challenging musical pieces. To do so necessitates a form of practice that requires the student to work at optimal intensity. This is called *deliberate practice*, and teachers often provide the direction and encouragement that will help students recognize its value. As we discussed earlier in this chapter, the amount of practice time per week needed to produce high levels of mastery depends on the intensity of practice done in the student's early years. Musically talented teenagers who have learned the strategies of deliberate practice can achieve maximum results in less time.

Music teaching in the elementary grades is designed to reach all students. However, in the secondary schools, music classes are elective courses attracting students who have some degree of interest in vocal and instrumental music. They may represent a wide range of musical abilities, from passing interest to extraordinary talent. Given this mix, the music teacher may opt for a performance-based approach, hoping that it will appeal to a majority of the students. Furthermore, public performance helps to highlight the music curriculum and perhaps to garner community support during times when budgets are tight. This single-minded approach, however, is usually not sufficient to meet the needs of students who have already discovered their musical ability, nor will it entice those who have yet to realize their potential in music.

Looking for New Approaches to Teaching Music

Some music educators are examining the research findings in cognitive science and suggesting newer approaches to teaching music in secondary schools. Specifically, attention is focused on three factors that are influencing classroom instruction (Haroutounian, 2000; Webster, 2000):

(1) *Shifting from a teacher-centered, didactic format to a student-centered, constructivist approach.* The performance-oriented approach requires that the teacher constantly play the role of director, preparing for the next competition, festival, or concert. As a result, performance takes precedence over sharing the process of making musical decisions with students. Constructivism is an instructional format that emphasizes the importance of keeping the learner as an active participant rather than a passive receiver. Guided by the teacher, the students are engaged in creative activities that allow them to show mastery of music through their actions.

(2) *Expanding the use of technology and the Internet.* Computer software and the Internet provide many new resources for students to deal with music creatively rather than just practicing a musical piece to the teacher's specifications. With project-centered learning, teachers can encourage students to use computers and synthesizers to experiment creatively with sound.

(3) *Using creative thinking skills and metaperception.* One of the major goals of music education is to engage students' imaginations. This is more likely to occur in classrooms where teachers regularly involve students in divergent experiences that require creative thinking. Teachers will help students see music as an art form when they encourage them to create music thoughtfully through composition, performance, improvisation, and active listening. As students absorb abstract musical concepts, they learn to make creative decisions to solve musical problems. In essence, they are combining fine-tuned discrimination of the senses with high cognitive functioning to solve artistic problems. This process, sometimes called *metaperception*, is the artistic equivalent of metacognition. It includes sensing sound internally, remembering this sound, and manipulating the sound to communicate an emotional interpretation to others.

Academic Achievement Versus Musical Study

As musically talented students in secondary schools reach higher levels of performance, they begin to think about the possibility of a career in music. They crave practice time, expand their playing ability to additional instruments, and get involved in more musical performances. Parents, meanwhile, who had been so supportive when the student was younger, may not now welcome the notion of music as their child's career choice. Ironically, the student is then torn between coping with the demands of additional practice and performance time, while simultaneously trying to satisfy parental desires for more intense academic studies to keep career options open. Although it is true that many musically talented students are also gifted academically, this combined pressure can sometimes be too much. As a result, some musically talented students end their music lessons to relieve the pressure.

Working with parents, music teachers may be able to help their talented students deal with this difficult situation by looking at flexible scheduling that allows the student to pursue music lessons at other times. Programs such as MusicLink help schools develop individualized curriculums for talented students.

Implications for Teaching Music in Secondary Schools

Musically talented secondary school students have reached the intermediate to advanced level of talent development. Curriculum programs should be independently developed to meet the needs of these students (Haroutounian, 2000).

Intermediate Level: Lessons should develop the technical skills needed for advancing repertoire and exploring musical structure and style. Students seek opportunities to perform outside the school and wish to do so with technical skill and accuracy. Intermediate level students
♫   Acquire more refined practice techniques
♫   Enjoy opportunities for performing both in and outside of school
♫   Develop technical proficiency
♫   Desire accuracy and precision in performance
♫   Experience a cognitive shift in musical thinking from active to interpretive understanding
♫   Expand performing opportunities to include occasional judged competitions
♫   Prefer instruction on musical understanding and technical development
♫   Delicately balance input from teachers, parents, and other students on competition, practice, and performance

Advanced Level: Lessons should be designed to hone already-developed technical skills and to enhance personal interpretations appropriate to the style, dynamic qualities, and aesthetic nature of the music. These students are usually already engaged in competition-level performances. Advanced level students
♫   Analyze musical history, theory, and structure
♫   Understand stylistic differences along with various interpretations that reflect these styles
♫   Develop creative interpretation and artistic reasoning
♫   Fine-tune practice techniques and make maximum use of time for musical problem solving
♫   Use technical skills to create subtle qualities of tonal color
♫   Develop confidence through performances in professional-type settings
♫   Demonstrate subtlety and sensitivity in the critique of music performed by themselves and others

Differentiated Curriculum

Different levels of musical talent development in secondary schools can be addressed though differentiated curriculum. For a variety of reasons, the musical talents of some students do not emerge until they reach high school. Many vocal musicians, for example, do not begin taking singing lessons until adolescence, usually at the urging of a school choral director. Potential composers emerge when they start using computers to manipulate music in creative ways. Wind or brass instrument players often do not get serious about their musical studies until high school. And then there are the self-taught musicians, who are more likely to be discovered displaying their skills outside the school setting. Because these students are at varying levels of development, the music curriculum must be sufficiently flexible to meet their different needs. Haroutounian (2000) separates these students into five categories and suggests different curriculum options for each.

Advanced students who are conservatory-bound. Maximum practice time should be allotted to exceptionally talented students who are serious about pursuing a musical career. If they plan to attend a conservatory, the entrance audition is likely to be the major determinant for admissions. Consequently, the demands of intense practice may result in less time devoted to other academic studies. Guidance counselors can be helpful in developing curricular options for these exceptional talents. Although some of these students attend Saturday classes and lessons at conservatories, those who remain in a normal high school setting need independent study options to allow sufficient flexibility for practice.

Advanced students not yet committed to a career. Advanced musically talented students who have not yet committed to a performance career should have curricular options that extend beyond performance. These options could include creative work in composition, improvisation, and even collaborative projects with other art forms. The goal is to move these students out of a performance-based focus from time to time, getting them involved in creative ventures rarely offered in the traditional high school music curriculum.

Self-taught students. The talents of self-trained students lie outside the traditional secondary school music program. They have learned to develop their skills in a haphazard way, rather than through formal training. Offering instruction in the traditional studio setting may not be successful. The differentiated curriculum for self-taught students should investigate topics such as creative composition exploration, which can also include instruction in basic musical notation.

The critical listener. Critical listeners translate musical ideas into words. Their written or verbal critiques demonstrate astute musical awareness and creative verbal talents. Differentiated curriculum for critical listeners should offer comparative listening and critique of professional recordings, mentoring with a professional music critic, and opportunities for writing music reviews for the school paper.

The musical history student. Outstanding history students with musical training may be fascinated with the musical significance of historical eras, musical styles emerging from cultural influences, or other musicological connections. The curricular framework for these students should aim to link music and history in independent study or projects located within the regular gifted education program.

Conclusion

All students can develop their knowledge, understanding, and skills in music. Some may need more help than others, but that is true in any subject. Students who are generally gifted will need challenging musical contexts that will enable them to extend and apply their more general abilities. Music provides a context in which generally gifted students can deal with a range of complex factors and bring them together when making and responding to music. Generally gifted students already have the ability to think quickly and assimilate information, so these talents will also be evident when engaging in music. Furthermore, because music is abstract, it provides a means of identifying and developing skills that are not dependent on language skills. Thus, music can help teachers recognize giftedness in students who are not yet strong in language, especially those students whose first language is not English. Students who display strong musical interest and are vocally or instrumentally accomplished will need special attention so that the school environment continues to develop their talents.

> **Music can help teachers recognize giftedness in students who are not yet strong in language, especially those students whose first language is not English.**

Musically talented students should have every opportunity to complete their talent development through high school, regardless of their future career decisions. They should be allowed to engage in challenging curricular experiences in their specialized field of interest. Schools can offer differentiated curriculum through student-developed interdisciplinary and independent study options, accelerated learning in performance classes, and courses in musical theory, composition, and music history. Teachers working with these students can serve as liaisons between the school and community to ensure student access to community resources related to music.

APPLICATIONS

IDENTIFYING YOUNG STUDENTS WITH MUSICAL TALENT

Identifying musical capabilities in young students is not easy because most children enjoy making music, especially when listening to it. But there are some general characteristics that are likely to identify those individuals who have a greater than average interest in music. When trying to determine if a specific student has musical talent, rate the individual on the degree to which they possess the characteristics listed below. This instrument works best with elementary school children. The list is by no means exhaustive. But if the child rates high on most of the items, talk with the parents and other professional for their input.

The student...	A little	Some	A lot
1. Is captivated by sound and engages fully with music.	1 — 2 — 3 — 4 — 5		
2. Selects an instrument with care and is unwilling to relinquish it.	1 — 2 — 3 — 4 — 5		
3. Memorizes music quickly without any apparent effort.	1 — 2 — 3 — 4 — 5		
4. Can repeat, usually after just one hearing, complex melodic phrases given by the teacher.	1 — 2 — 3 — 4 — 5		
5. Can sing and/or play music with a natural awareness of musical phrasing.	1 — 2 — 3 — 4 — 5		
6. Often responds physically to music.	1 — 2 — 3 — 4 — 5		
7. Demonstrates the ability to communicate through music.	1 — 2 — 3 — 4 — 5		
8. Shows a sustained inner drive to make music.	1 — 2 — 3 — 4 — 5		

APPLICATIONS

SUGGESTIONS FOR ENCOURAGING MUSICALLY TALENTED STUDENTS

Research studies indicate that the earlier individuals begin to use their musical talents, the more likely they are to continue their practice through their adolescence and young adulthood. Although musical talent generally appears in the younger years, there may be secondary school students whose talents have not yet been recognized. One of the goals of working with students who have already developed skills playing an instrument is to develop broader musical skills, as well as inspiring a deeper knowledge and understanding of music. This can occur in nearly all elementary classrooms whenever teachers feel comfortable addressing the skills of musically talented children.

The teacher helps build these skills and talent by

- Setting up challenging musical tasks and expecting a high-quality response. Students tend to meet the expectations that are set for them.

- Allowing students to take the lead in a class activity, such as starting a song or conducting the class.

- Including quick recall activities whereby students echo increasingly complex patterns given by the teacher. This choral response approach should be used sparingly, but it does encourage participation by those young students who may be shy.

- Encouraging special instruction in voice or on an instrument.

- Providing open-ended tasks or new contexts in which students can apply previously learned skills. Musically talented students usually seek out ways to apply their musical interests to classroom projects.

- Allowing opportunities in the classroom for students to use skills, such as instrumental skills, that they have learned outside the classroom.

MUSICALLY TALENTED STUDENTS—Continued

- Enabling students to use improvisation in their work, within certain limits identified by the teacher. Improvisation is an important component of creativity in music.

- Asking students, when appropriate, to analyze and evaluate music in relation to how it is constructed and produced. Further discussions can include identifying how music can be affected by different influences and the various ways that music can affect us.

- Encouraging students to participate in school choirs, bands, and orchestras.

- Providing opportunities for students to perform outside of school at public events throughout the community.

- Ensuring that students experience live professional musical presentations at regular intervals, followed by an analysis and constructive critique of the performances.

The Importance of In-School and Out-of-School Musical Activities

Teachers can often be a positive force in convincing students to get involved with musical groups. Participation by musically talented students in both in-school and out-of-school activities involving music contributes significantly to their musical achievement, especially in the elementary and early secondary grades. In 1997, the National Assessment of Educational Progress (NAEP) conducted a major study of the arts in the schools, using the 8th grade as the benchmark (Persky, Sandene, and Askew, 1999). The study assessed the students' ability to perform three processes: creating, performing, and responding. Responding refers to observing, describing, analyzing, and evaluating works of art.

MUSICALLY TALENTED STUDENTS—Continued

Figures 6.5 and 6.6 show the percentage of 8th grade students who scored at the three levels of a scale of music achievement relating their in-school and out-of-school activities in music. Clearly, participating in musical activities seems closely aligned with student achievement in music. However, the study did not specifically identify highly gifted musical students as a separate population.

In-School Music Activities (Figure 6.5). Students who participated in music activities within the school community were much more likely to score in the upper level of the responding scale in music achievement. The greatest gains were by students who owned a musical instrument, sang in school vocal groups, or played in a school band.

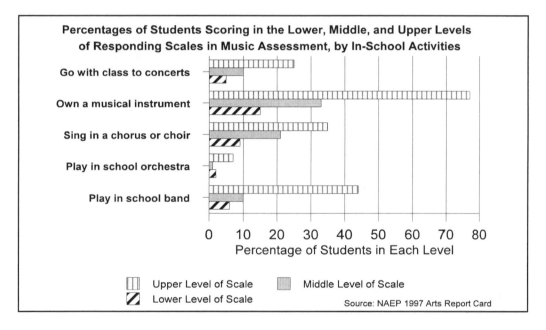

Figure 6.5 This graph shows the percentage of 8th grade students who scored in the lower, middle, and upper levels of the responding scale in music assessment, listed by their in-school activities in music.

Out-of-School Music Activities (Figure 6.6). Students who participated in out-of-school music activities were also more likely to score in the upper level of the responding scale in music achievement. The greatest gains were by students who played a musical instrument and took private music lessons.

MUSICALLY TALENTED STUDENTS—Continued

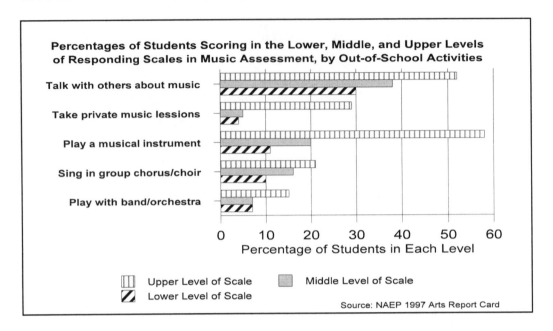

Figure 6.6 This graph shows the percentage of 8th grade students who scored in the lower, middle, and upper levels of the responding scale in music assessment, listed by their out-of-school activities in music.

APPLICATIONS

TEACHING MUSICALLY TALENTED STUDENTS IN SECONDARY SCHOOLS

Music educators are suggesting that discoveries in cognitive science should have an impact on the teaching of music in today's schools. Webster (2000) suggests that the following three factors need to be considered by music teachers in designing their lessons for musically talented students in secondary schools.

♫   **Constructivism.** This instructional approach focuses lesson design on activities that engage students in creative experiences so that they can construct their own understanding of the learning with the teacher's guidance. For example, instead of teaching music reading, listening, and movement through a teacher-centered approach with fact- and skill-oriented content, use small, interactive groups where students can discuss and create ways of including composition and improvisation. Other strategies might include asking students to write reports about the music they are playing, discussing the music content ("Why did the composer use this key?"), or even using student conductors on the podium.

♫   **Technology and the Internet.** Computers, software, synthesizers, and the Internet are just some of the new ways that students can manipulate musical sounds. Music sequencing notation and digital audio software allow students to compose music in ways that were not possible just a few years ago. For example, a software program available on the Internet, known as *Making More Music* (http://voyager.learntech.com), permits student groups to use a painting metaphor to draw layers with musical gestures. The program translates the drawings into musical notation and allows students to experiment with tempo, dynamics, and choice of timbre. As the students become more familiar with revision and

TEACHING STUDENTS IN SECONDARY SCHOOLS—Continued

other musical ideas, the program allows them to manipulate motives and phrases. Another source of real-world examples of technological applications to music can be found at the Music Teachers and Technology web page sponsored by George Reese, School of Education, the University of Illinois at Urbana-Champaign (*http://www-camil.music.uiuc.edu/mtt/default.htm*).

♫ **Creative Thinking Skills.** When teachers resort to problem-centered learning, students are able to pursue tasks that have more than one correct answer. Working alone or in groups, students are allowed to create their own examples of musical structures rather than be limited just to the teacher's example. This balance of convergent and divergent activities can be especially effective in performance venues by encouraging students to give their opinions about interpretations, by asking probing questions about the musical works they are performing, and by requiring them to practice music that creates solutions to various problems of performance. Internet resources, such as *HyperStudio*, can extend these activities further. With this approach, students of all ability levels get a deeper understanding of the learning because they are directly involved in solving problems. Moreover, these types of projects allow students to make judgments about musical content and context, use their creative thinking skills, constructively criticize others' works, and develop with other students a collective understanding of the music being studied. Although all students benefit, divergent activities such as these are particularly meaningful for the more musically talented students.

7

Underachieving Gifted Students

The phrase "underachieving gifted students" may sound like an oxymoron. But they do exist, and some educators and critics of education see underachievement as a major crisis in our nation's schools, not just for the gifted, but for all children. Underachievement can result when a gifted student acquires—for whatever reasons—some complex behaviors that erode academic performance. Whether it occurs quickly or slowly, underachievement prevents gifted students from reaching their potential. Consequently, it is an issue that must be addressed and remedied as much as any other obstacle to learning.

WHAT IS UNDERACHIEVEMENT? ■

Defining underachievement is not easy, especially among gifted students. Part of the problem lies in the definition of giftedness. Each school district has its own definition, although most rely on the use of an intelligence or achievement test score and teacher recommendations. These measures are not always reliable because few mentally gifted students truly excel in all subjects and on all academic tasks. Another problem is the definition of *underachievement*. Most commonly, it is a discrepancy between performance and an ability index, usually an IQ score. Ford (1996) reviewed over 100 studies and noted that many different instruments and criteria were used to measure underachievement, further thwarting attempts to establish a common definition.

Gifted underachievers generally display any of three behavioral responses to the school setting: noncommunicative and withdrawn, passively compliant, and aggressive/disruptive. Behaviors in all three groups reflect a belief in their inability to influence outcomes in school, a low or unrealistic self-concept, and negative attitudes toward school in general. They also tend to be easily distracted, supersensitive, and socially isolated (Achor and Tarr, 1996).

Underachievement is a pattern as complicated as the children to whom this label is applied. Consequently, some researchers believe that a more accurate way to define underachievement is to consider its various components (Delisle and Berger, 1990):

- *Underachievement Is a Behavior.* Underachievement is a behavior, not an attitude or set of work habits. Behaviors change over time and can be more directly modified than attitudes or habits. By referring to underachieving behaviors, we help these students recognize those aspects of their lives that they can change.

- *Underachievement Is Content and Situation Specific.* Gifted students can succeed in some situations and not in others. Those who may not be successful in school, for example, are often successful in outside activities, such as sports, music, or after-school jobs. Labeling a student as an underachiever ignores the positive outcomes of those areas in which the student *does* succeed. It makes more sense to label the area of underachievement, not the student (e.g., the student is underachieving in mathematics or social studies).

- *Underachievement Is Defined Differently by Different People.* As long as a student is passing, some students, parents, or teachers will not see underachievement. To others, getting a lower grade than expected is considered underachievement. Understanding the erratic nature of what constitutes success and failure is necessary to recognizing why some students underachieve.

- *Underachievement Is Tied to Self-Concept.* Self-concept can become a self-fulfilling prophesy. If students see themselves as failures, they eventually place self-imposed limits on what is possible. Good grades are dismissed as accidents or luck, but poor grades serve to reinforce a negative self-concept. Students with this attitude often give up trying because they assume that failure is inevitable. The results are low self-concept and limited incentive to change.

SOME CAUSES OF UNDERACHIEVEMENT ▪

A combination of factors, both in the home and at school, can cause underachievement. Of all the possible causes, the following seem most prevalent.

- *Lack of Nurturing of Intellectual Potential.* Families with low socioeconomic status often fail to provide the environment that develops and stimulates high-level thinking. Enriching experiences, such as educational activities, travel, and shared problem solving, are few. Low-income students may come from specific ethnic or cultural groups that do not encourage intellectual development, from economically disadvantaged urban sites, or from isolated rural areas.

- ***Over-Empowerment and Over-Expectation.*** Giving children too much power too soon can lead to underachievement. Children from single-parent households, and first and only children, are the most likely candidates. Parents may also have overly exaggerated or misplaced expectations of their child's abilities, causing the child to become withdrawn in school participation. By labeling their children as the athlete, the social one, or the creative one, parents can add to competitive pressures.

- *Conflict in Values.* Students may withdraw from participating in school if they sense a conflict between the values of the school and the gifted program and those of the culture from which they come. For example, female students may underachieve because their culture may not value or expect females to pursue a college education or career. Other gifted students may underachieve because they do not want to be perceived as bookworms or nerds by their peers.

- *Lack of Motivation.* Prevailing instructional methods may not be compatible with the learning style of highly gifted students. The level of instruction may be below these students' capabilities, and classroom rules and restrictions may discourage their full participation. Classrooms that are over-competitive or under-competitive may also lead to achievement problems.

- *Learning Disabilities.* It is possible that underachieving gifted students may have psychological or physical problems that can interfere with learning. Developmental delays (physical, social, and emotional), neurological impairments (brain injury), and deficits in specific academic skills can all lead to poor academic performance. (See Chapter 8 on the twice-exceptional student.)

Adjusting to Giftedness

Some gifted students, especially adolescents between the ages of 11 and 15, may underachieve because they have serious problems adjusting to their giftedness. Perfectionism, urealistic appraisal of their gifts, rejection from peers, competitiveness, and confusion over mixed messages about their talents can all erode their achievement in school. Buescher (1990) identifies seven obstacles that can interfere with an adolescent's adjustment to giftedness.

- *Ownership of Talents.* It is not unusual for some talented adolescents to deny their talent, often because of peer pressure to conform and the adolescent's sense of being predictable. These individuals lack self-esteem and have doubts about the objectivity of their parents or teachers in identifying their gifts.

- *Giving of Themselves.* Because they have received gifts in abundance, talented adolescents sometimes feel that they must give of themselves in abundance and that their abilities belong to their teachers, parents and society.

- *Dissonance.* Gifted adolescents have learned to set high standards, to expect to do more, and to be more than their abilities might allow. In this drive toward perfection, these students experience real dissonance between how well they expect to accomplish something and how well it is actually done. This dissonance can be far greater than teachers or parents may realize.

- *Taking Risks.* Gifted adolescents are less likely to take the risks they took at an earlier age because they are more aware of the repercussions of their activities. Thus, they tend to be more cautious in weighing the advantages and disadvantages of possible choices, and in examining alternatives. They may even reject all risk taking, such as enrolling in advanced courses, competitions, or public presentations.

- *Competing Expectations.* The expectations of others (parents, teachers, peers, siblings, and friends) may compete with the gifted adolescent's own plans and goals. In effect, the adolescent's own expectations must face the onrush of the demands and desires of others. The greater the talent, the greater the expectations of others and outside interference. Trying to meet these expectations can drain energy and dampen the desire to succeed.

- *Impatience.* Gifted students can be just as impatient as other adolescents when looking for quick solutions to difficult questions or trying to develop social relationships. The impulsiveness makes them intolerant of ambiguity and unresolved situations. They can get angry if their hasty solutions fail, especially if other less capable students gloat over these failures. A string of such failures may prompt these students to withdraw.

- *Premature Identity.* For gifted adolescents, the weight of competing expectations, a low tolerance for ambiguity, and the pressure of multiple options all contribute to very early attempts to achieve an adult-like identity, even while in their early to middle teens. In an attempt to complete this identity, they may reach out for career choices that are inappropriate for their true age and that may interfere with the normal processes of identity resolution and acceptance.

IDENTIFYING GIFTED UNDERACHIEVERS ■

The problem of unidentified gifted underachievers has become more evident in recent years. Typical changes in school systems include the following:

- ▸ Use of more sophisticated and varied measures of intelligence and achievement
- ▸ A jump in the number of teacher referrals for special education services because of behavioral and learning problems
- ▸ Increase in efforts to recognize and develop the potential abilities of culturally different and minority children

▸ More reports by parents of out-of-school behaviors that demonstrate advanced interests and skills.

General Characteristics

Some of the most common characteristics and patterns of underachievement in gifted—as well as other—students are shown in the box to the left. Because gifted underachievers continue to fail in some areas, they tend to exhibit two general behavior patterns: *aggressive* or *withdrawn*. Aggressive behavior is characterized by stubbornly refusing to comply with requests, disrupting others, rejecting drill activities, alienating peers, and lack of self-direction in decision making. In contrast, withdrawn behavior patterns include lack of communication, working alone, little attempt to justify behavior, and little participation in classroom activities.

> **Characteristics of
> Gifted Underachievers**
> (Not all characteristics may be present in the same person.)
>
> • high IQ score
> • lack of effort
> • a skill deficit in at least one subject area
> • frequently unfinished work
> • inattentiveness to current task
> • low self-esteem
> • poor work and study habits
> • intense interest in one area
> • seeming inability to concentrate
> • failure to respond to usual motivating techniques

Studies classify underachieving gifted students into five types. The first type has low grades in general but high test scores (often on both criterion- and norm-referenced tests). In contrast, the second type displays low test scores but high course grades. The third type performs consistently below the level of capability in all subjects, and the fourth type underachieves only in certain subjects. Students whose underachievement goes unnoticed while in school comprise the fifth type. The existence of this type is most disconcerting because it means that these students will go through school seldom experiencing the educational opportunities that could have challenged them to reach their true potential.

> **Five Types of Gifted Underachievers**
>
> 1. Low grades, high test scores
> 2. Low test scores, high grades
> 3. Low performance in all subjects
> 4. Low performance in certain subjects
> 5. Unnoticed

Dependence and Dominance

Underachieving gifted students often protect themselves by developing defense mechanisms. These temporary adaptations use dependency and domination patterns. Sylvia Rimm (1996) is a pediatric psychologist who suggests that underachievers can adopt patterns of behavior that fall on one spectrum that describes their dependence or dominance and another spectrum that represents their degree of conformity. The interaction of these elements results in a chart of quadrants (see Figure 7.1).

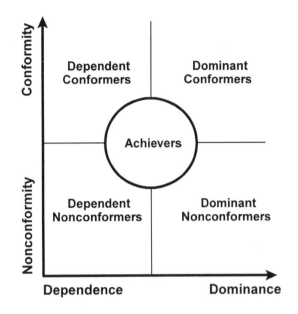

Figure 7.1 The quadrants represent different types of underachievers. (Adapted from Rimm, 1996).

According to Rimm, dependent children (left side of figure) have learned how to manipulate adults and get so much help from adults that they lose self-confidence. Because they do less, parents and teachers expect less. As a result, they can become overly sensitive, anxious, and even depressed. These children often go unnoticed.

In contrast, the dominant children (right side of figure) select only those activities they feel they can master. They manipulate adults by trapping them into arguments which can be about almost anything. Rimm maintains that if these children lose arguments, they develop enmity toward adults and use that as an excuse not to do their work or take on responsibilities. When the adults respond negatively to the manipulation, these dominant children complain that the adults do not like or understand them.

The upper and lower portions of the figure (conformity to nonconformity) represent the degree of severity of these children's problems. Those in the upper quadrants have minor problems and are likely to outgrow them. If they do not, however, then they may slip into the lower quadrants and their problems become more severe. Most dependent children will change to dominant by adolescence, although some retain a dependent-dominant mix, varying their response according to the situation.

Rimm believes that teachers and parents are often frustrated by these underachievers and inadvertently reinforce the undesirable patterns. Although children should be encouraged to be independent and creative, they should not be over-empowered so that adult guidance becomes impossible. Underachievement can be reversed, and in Rimm's model, that means adopting strategies that move the underachievers into the central circle of achievers—those children who are not dependent on defense mechanisms but who have confidence, an internal locus of control and who are resilient.

Spatially Gifted Students

Because language skills remain the most frequently used measure of academic giftedness, students who are strong in visual-spatial skills are often perceived as underachievers. Consequently, if they are poor in language skills, their teachers are more likely to focus on remediation and overlook any hint of giftedness. One major study at the University of Illinois in Urbana-Champaign found that, compared with other gifted students, students gifted in spatial ability were performing below their capabilities. Furthermore, this group had interests that were less compatible with traditional course work and received less college guidance from school counselors. The students were also less motivated by their educational experience and generally aspired to, and achieved, lower levels of academic and occupational success (Gohm, Humphreys, and Yao, 1998).

Despite the increased awareness of underachievement in gifted students, educators need to work harder to insure that these students are identified as early as possible for several reasons. The most obvious one is the potential loss of their contributions to society. The second—and less obvious reason—is the underachiever's vulnerability to significant social and mental health problems. It is not uncommon for the gifted underachiever to become a major behavioral problem at school and at home. This behavior results from the conflict between the individual's personal psychological needs and the lack of appropriate learning opportunities in the school. Additionally, having a better chance at reversing the patterns of underachievement is another reason for early identification of these students.

Underachievement: A Case Study
(Reis, Hébert, Díaz, Maxfield, and Ratley, 1995)

A 3-year study of 35 high-ability and underachieving students in an urban high school found the following:
- No relationship between underachievement and poverty, parental divorce, or family size.
- Underachievement began in elementary school due to lack of challenge.
- Underachievers were often not resilient enough to overcome urban problems, such as gangs and drugs.
- Abilities of underachievers were often not recognized by their parents, teachers, and guidance counselors during their elementary years.

UNDERACHIEVEMENT AMONG GIFTED MINORITY STUDENTS ■

Many studies have found an under-representation of minority students in gifted programs. As efforts continue to identify more minority gifted students, attention must also be focused on underachievement among the minority student population, especially African American as well as culturally and linguistically different students. Estimates of the number of gifted African American students who underachieve vary. One study of 149 middle and high school African American students found that almost 40 percent of gifted and potentially gifted students were underachievers (Ford, 1995). The study also revealed that the most effective variables for discriminating between the achievers and underachievers were: (1) attitudes of the students toward science, reading, and mathematics; (2) the perceptions that students had of their parents' desire for school success; and (3) the students' feelings about their own achievement.

Bernal (2002) maintains that no national data are available on the number of culturally and linguistically different students who underachieve or fail to get into gifted programs. But, on the basis of a sampling during the 1999-2000 school year of Texas school districts along the Mexican border, Bernal suggests that about 60 percent of these potentially gifted students were excluded from gifted programs and could be considered underachievers.

Several factors must be explored to understand why minority students underachieve. Ford and Thomas (1997) suggest that these factors fall into three categories: sociopsychological, family-related, and school-related.

- *Sociopsychological Factors.* Low academic self-concept and poor self-esteem are major contributors to underachievement. Racial identity must also be explored as a possible contributor. For example, How do students feel about their racial and ethnic heritage? Do they have a strong positive racial identity? If not, they may be especially vulnerable to negative comments by peers, such as "acting white" or "selling out," which contributes to low effort and low achievement. Specifically, many of these students must choose between their need for achievement and the need for peer affiliation. Too often, the need for affiliation wins.

> **Minority students need to choose between their need for achievement and the need for peer affiliation. Too often, the need for affiliation wins.**

    Minority students can attribute their outcomes to external factors, such as discrimination, and may thus put forth less effort than students who attribute outcomes to internal factors, such as ability and effort. Those minority students who substitute their belief in the power of work with their beliefs in glass ceilings and social injustices are not likely to reach their potential in school.

● *Family-Related Factors.* Numerous studies of gifted programs have found that family variables can influence the success of gifted students in school. The few studies that have examined the family influence on underachieving Black students found that the parents
  ▸ expressed feelings of helplessness and hopelessness
  ▸ were less involved and assertive in their children's education
  ▸ set unclear and unrealistic expectations for their children
  ▸ were less confident of their parenting skills.

● *School-Related Factors.* Factors in schools can influence the achievement of gifted minority students. Underachieving Black students often report
  ▸ less positive student-teacher relations
  ▸ too little time to understand the material
  ▸ less supportive classroom climate
  ▸ being disinterested and unmotivated in school.

Teacher expectations pay a big role in student achievement. Teachers who lack objectivity or training in gifted education and multicultural education may have different views of giftedness and underachievement, and thus are less likely to refer minority students for gifted education programs. Some teachers may have lower expectations for minority and low-income students than for other students. Consequently, minority students may not be identified as either gifted or underachieving. Eventually, these students underachieve due to frustration, disinterest, and lack of challenge.

Some research studies have identified key attributes of minority students' learning styles. For example, Black students tend to be field-dependent, concrete, and visual learners, but schools often emphasize abstract and verbal approaches. This mismatch between learning and teaching styles can result in confusion, frustration, and underachievement.

REVERSING PATTERNS OF UNDERACHIEVEMENT ■

Approaches to reversing patterns of underachievement are successful if they are based on the view that the poor performance has been shaped by forces within the school that can be changed. These forces include the social messages communicated by the teacher and peers that invite or discourage the student to participate, and the degree to which the curriculum and instructional strategies are compatible with the learning style of the underachiever. Thus, successful interventions will create positive forces that shape achievement behavior. These interventions must address three critical questions.

(1) What does it mean to be gifted and what are the associated problems?

(2) What are constructive ways of coping with the inevitable conflict that arises by the significant gap between performance level and cognitive ability?

(3) How can a student develop a healthier, more realistic self-concept?

Despite the frustration of working with students who are performing below their potential, strategies do exist that are effective in reversing underachievement. Three types of strategies are worth considering (Delisle and Berger, 1990).

● *Supportive Strategies.* These strategies focus on allowing students to feel that they are part of a group where problems and concerns can be discussed, and where curriculum activities can be chosen based on student needs and interests. Students may also be allowed to omit assignments for which they have already shown competency.

● *Intrinsic Strategies.* By accepting the notion that students' desires to achieve academically are closely linked to their self-concepts as learners, teachers use this type of strategy to encourage attempts, not just successes. Teachers also invite students to provide input on classroom rules and responsibilities. Students may also be allowed to evaluate their own work before submitting it to the teacher.

● *Remedial Strategies.* Underachievement is more likely to be reversed when teachers recognize that students make mistakes, and students can have individual strengths and weaknesses in addition to their intellectual, social, and emotional needs. Remedial strategies, therefore, are designed to allow students to excel in their areas of strength and interest. At the same time, teachers provide opportunities in the specific areas of each student's learning deficiencies. The classroom climate is one in which mistakes are considered part of the learning process for teacher and student alike.

Reversing Underachievement in Minority Students

Ford and Thomas (1997) suggest than additional efforts need to be made to reverse or prevent underachievement in gifted minority students. These interventions should

- ▸ Use valid and reliable measures for determining underachievement in minority populations
- ▸ Improve students' skills in organization, studying, time management, and taking tests
- ▸ Build self-esteem, social and academic self-concept, and racial identity
- ▸ Involve family members as partners in the educational process
- ▸ Provide appropriate school staff with training in gifted and multicultural education, which includes strategies for improving classroom climate and teacher expectations.

Bernal (2002) maintains that an effective way to improve achievement in gifted culturally and linguistically different (CLD) students is to change the nature of traditional gifted programs so that more of these students will qualify. He proposes the following remedies to address this problem of underrepresentation:

- ● *Evaluation:* Districts that have already had success in admitting and retaining CLD students need to evaluate their programs and share their data. The evaluation should focus on questions, such as
  - ▸ Who are the students that the program currently admits?
  - ▸ What are the students like who succeeded, and who failed?
  - ▸ What modifications have been made to the gifted program to accommodate these students and what have been the outcomes?

- ● *Multicultural Curriculum:* For CLD students to be successful in a gifted program, the curriculum must be multicultural. Districts need to train teachers in multicultural methodologies. This training should show teachers how to
  - ▸ Use examples from different cultures to make learning more

interesting to a wider group of students

▸ Demonstrate how new knowledge is influenced by ethnicity, history, and individual perspectives

▸ Use cooperative learning groups to promote positive interaction among students of diverse backgrounds, and

▸ Establish a classroom climate that makes CLD students feel wanted.

● *Recruitment:* Schools need to recruit authentic representatives of their respective minority groups into the gifted program's teaching staff. These individuals model some of the intellectual content and values of their cultural traditions for the benefit of all gifted students.

Other researchers have suggested using a variety of assessment approaches to enhance the identification of gifted minority students. Adams (1990) and Rhodes (1992) advocated the case study approach to the identification of gifted minority students. This approach uses a variety of information sources including rating scales, checklists, referrals, and peer nominations. Both Adams and Rhodes maintained that peer nomination forms are valuable because children can often identify their bright peers, and that they may be less biased toward cultural differences than their teachers.

Peer nomination instruments are often criticized for their lack of reliability and validity. However, a study involving 670 students in grades four through six did show that a peer nomination form designed to identify gifted Hispanic students had sufficient reliability and validity to warrant its use (Cunningham, Callahan, Plucker, Roberson, and Rapkin, 1998). The researchers recommended that the instrument be used with other minority groups, e.g., African Americans, Native Americans, and Asian Americans. A copy of the form used in this study can be found in **Applications** at the end of this chapter.

There is no simple answer to the problem of underachievement among gifted students. Some gifted students are high achievers in a highly-structured environment, but are underachievers if they have low self-esteem and cannot focus on a selected number of activities, establish priorities, and set long-term goals. Teachers and parents must remember that achievement and resilience can be taught. By doing so, they build the competencies and confidence that students will need as they grow and mature.

APPLICATIONS

PROGRAMMING COMPONENTS FOR REVERSING UNDERACHIEVEMENT IN GIFTED STUDENTS

Programs designed specifically to reverse underachievement in gifted students can occur in the regular classroom, in resource rooms, or through the development of a plan that involves a mentor in the school or community. Achor and Tarr (1996) suggest that the program should contain at least the following five elements.

Teacher | The teacher's perception of the student's problem is critical to the program's success. Consequently, the teachers must accept the fact that the student is gifted, does not want to underachieve or fail, needs to develop constructive coping skills, and has low self-esteem. To be successful, the teacher should be skilled in guidance techniques, have an accurate understanding of the nature of giftedness, and possess a positive attitude toward the challenge of working with this type of student.

Curriculum | Program success is more likely if the curriculum is challenging, relevant, and rewarding to the student. The curriculum should have a balance between basic skill development and more advanced exploration of the arts and sciences. Critical elements also include the development of personal interests and career possibilities. There should be plenty of opportunities for challenge and success.

PROGRAMMING COMPONENTS—Continued

Instruction	Instructional techniques should include minimal memorization and drill/practice activities and maximal opportunities for inquiry, creative production, and scientific inquiry. Nurturing the student's self-discipline is important, as well as encouraging self-directed learning activities. The instructional climate should foster anticipation, excitement, low pressure, and personal satisfaction.
Peer Group	The peer group should include at least a few other gifted students, possibly underachievers, who can become good friends. The group must be accepting of individual differences and diversity. Their interactions can help develop needed social skills.
Special Services	Appropriate special services should be provided for gifted underachievers who are also handicapped, for those requiring remedial instruction, and for group counseling. These students sometimes require family counseling as well as supplemental medical and psychological services.

APPLICATIONS

STRATEGIES FOR UNDERACHIEVING GIFTED STUDENTS

The following types of strategies are effective in preventing and reversing underachievement behavior in gifted students. They can be used by both teachers and parents (Delisle and Berger, 1990).

- **Supportive Strategies**
    - ▶ Do not assume that advanced intellectual ability also means advanced social and emotional skills.
    - ▶ Provide an atmosphere that is non-authoritarian, flexible, mutually respectful and questioning.
    - ▶ Establish reasonable rules and guidelines for behavior.
    - ▶ Give consistently positive feedback.
    - ▶ Provide strong support and encouragement.
    - ▶ Help them to accept their limitations as well as those of others, and to help others as a means of developing tolerance, understanding, empathy, and acceptance of human limitations.
    - ▶ Be a sounding board and listen to their questions without comment.
    - ▶ When it is time for solving problems, suggest possible solutions and encourage students to come up with their own solutions and strategies for choosing the best one.
    - ▶ Show enthusiasm for students' interests, observations, goals, and activities.
    - ▶ Avoid solving problems that the student is capable of managing.
    - ▶ Avoid establishing unrealistic expectations.
    - ▶ Provide a wide variety of opportunities for the students to experience success and to gain confidence in themselves.
    - ▶ Reserve time to have fun and to share daily activities.

UNDERACHIEVING GIFTED STUDENTS—Continued

- **Intrinsic Strategies**
  - ▸ Recognize that intellectual growth and development is a requirement for these children, and not merely an interest or a temporary phase that they are going through.
  - ▸ Avoid giving assignments that are too easy or too difficult.
  - ▸ Because learning style can affect achievement, ensure that these students are placed in programs that are sufficiently flexible and that have teachers who can address various learning style strengths and weaknesses. For example, gifted children are often strong in visual-spatial ability and weak in sequencing skills. They may also not do well in spelling, foreign languages, and mathematics, especially if they are taught in the traditional way.
  - ▸ Look for opportunities that allow students to explore topics in-depth, to participate in hands-on learning, and to develop adult expert-mentor relationships.
  - ▸ Encourage students to pursue their interests, recognizing, however, that some students will spend hours on a project and fail to submit required work. They need to be reminded that others may not be sympathetic to tardy or incomplete work.
  - ▸ Early career guidance can help these students set short- and long-term goals, complete required assignments, and plan for college.
  - ▸ Be aware of the fine line between encouragement and pressure. Encouragement emphasizes the process, steps, and effort used to achieve a goal; appraisal and evaluation are left to the student (intrinsic rewards). In contrast, pressure to perform focuses on outcomes and grades for which the student receives praise (extrinsic reward). Underachieving gifted students often reject praise as artificial and not authentic.

UNDERACHIEVING GIFTED STUDENTS—Continued

- **Remedial Strategies**
  - ▸ Be cautious about statements that may discourage the student, such as "Why did you get a C? You know you are gifted." Statements like these are rarely effective.
  - ▸ Avoid putting these students in situations where they are either winner or losers, and avoid comparing them to others. Rather, show them how to function in competition and how to deal with losing.
  - ▸ Special tutoring may help concerned students who are experiencing short-term academic difficulties. The tutor should be carefully selected to match the interests and learning style of the student.
  - ▸ Long-term underachievers rarely benefit from special tutoring or from study skills and time management courses. Other interventions that more directly address the *causes* of the underachievement need to be explored.

APPLICATIONS

ADDITIONAL STRATEGIES FOR
UNDERACHIEVING MINORITY STUDENTS

In addition to the strategies suggested in the previous pages, Ford (1996) offers some other considerations for enhancing achievement in minority students.

Supportive: Provide opportunities for these students to discuss their concerns with teachers and counselors who are trained in gifted and multicultural education. Classroom activities should focus more on cooperation than competition, and these students should get genuine positive reinforcement and praise when appropriate. Use activities that include multicultural components, mentors, and role models (such as teachers) from different ethnic and racial groups. Find substantive ways to involve family members and suggest ways that they can encourage the student at home.

Intrinsic: Allow students to have choices in selecting projects and in areas of interest. Vary teaching style to accommodate different learning styles. Use biographies of minority role models when appropriate. Include curriculum components that are multicultural, relevant, and personally meaningful to students.

Remedial: Implement academic counseling as soon as needed. Include tutoring and the teaching of study, time-management, organizational, and test-taking skills. Individual learning contracts and learning journals are also helpful.

APPLICATIONS

USING PEER NOMINATION FORMS
TO IDENTIFY GIFTED MINORITY STUDENTS

Cunningham, et al. (1998) used the following peer nomination form in a major study to help identify gifted Hispanic students in grades four through six. Because of the instrument's high reliability and validity in their study, the researchers recommend that the instrument also be used with other minority groups, e.g., African Americans, Native Americans, and Asian Americans.

The 10 questions address intellectual abilities (questions 1, 2, 3, 9, and 10) and creative and artistic abilities (questions 4, 5, 6, 7, and 8). The directions on the form ask students to consider all of the peers in their classes, and the instructions ensure the confidentiality of their responses. The form gathers different information from that provided by standardized tests and should be just one part of a multiple assessment process.

The researchers suggest that the items on the form be used independently or in appropriate clusters to nominate students. Therefore, rather than using an overall cut-off score, students should be considered for selection on the basis of the proportion of nominations (i.e., the number of nominations divided by the class size) in the area of giftedness—intellectual abilities or creative and artistic abilities.

USING PEER NOMINATION FORMS—Continued

Peer Referral Form
Cunningham, Callahan, Plucker, Roberson, and Rapkin, 1998
(Reprinted With Permission)

Teacher's Name_____

I am going to ask you to think of your classmates in a different way than you usually do. Read the questions below and try to think of which child in your class best fits each question. Think of the boys and girls, quiet kids and noisy kids, best friends and those with whom you don't usually play. You may only put down one name for each question. You may leave a space blank. You can use the same name for more than one question. You may not use your teacher's name or names of other adults. Please use first and last names. You do not have to put your name down on this form, so you can be completely honest.

---

1. What boy OR girl learns quickly, but doesn't speak up in class very often?

---

2. What girl OR boy will get interested in a project and spend extra time and take pride in his or her work?

---

3. What boy OR girl is smart in school, but doesn't show off about it?

---

4. What girl OR boy is really good at making up dances?

---

5. What boy OR girl is really good at making up games?

---

6. What girl OR boy is really good at making up music?

---

7. What boy OR girl is really good at making up stories?

---

8. What girl OR boy is really good at making up pictures?

---

9. What boy OR girl would you ask first if you needed any kind of help at school?

---

10. What girl OR boy would you ask to come to your house to help you work on a project? (Pretend that there would be someone to drive that person to your house.)

Note: Adapted from *Peer Referral as a Process for Locating Hispanic Students Who May Be Gifted* (unpublished doctoral dissertation, University of Arizona), by A. J. Udall, 1987.

8

The Twice-Exceptional Brain

The notion that a gifted child can have learning disabilities seems bizarre. As a result, many children who are gifted in some ways and deficient in others go undetected and unserved by our schools. Only in recent years have educators begun to recognize that high abilities and learning problems can coexist in the same person. But even with this recognition, many school districts still do not have procedures in place to screen, identify, and serve the needs of children with dual exceptionalities. What makes dual exceptionalities even possible is that the individual's strengths and weaknesses lie in different areas. Early observations of these students led to the term *paradoxical learners*, due to the many discrepancies in their school performance. Today, they are more commonly referred to as the twice-exceptional student.

■ IDENTIFYING TWICE-EXCEPTIONAL STUDENTS

Toll (1993) and Baum (1994) have suggested that gifted children who display learning problems fall into three distinct groups:

1. *Identified gifted, but also learning disabled.* The first group includes students identified as gifted but who exhibit learning difficulties in school. They often have poor spelling and handwriting and may appear disorganized or sloppy in their work. Through low motivation, laziness, or low self-esteem, they perform poorly and are often labeled as underachievers. Teachers expect them to achieve because they are labeled as gifted. As a result, their learning disabilities remain unrecognized until they lag behind their peers.

2. *No identification.* The second—and perhaps largest—group represents those children whose abilities and disabilities mask each other. They often function at grade level, are considered average students, and do not seem to have problems or any special needs. A majority of these students are unassertive, doing what is expected of them but not volunteering information about their abilities or interests. Although they may be seem to be performing well, they are in fact functioning well below their potential. In later high school years, as course work becomes more difficult, learning difficulties may become apparent, but their true potential will not be realized. Because neither exceptionality is identified, students in this group will not receive the educational programs necessary to meet their needs.

3. *Identified learning disabled, but also gifted.* The third group includes students who have already been diagnosed with learning disabilities but whose high abilities have never been recognized. This may be a larger group than one might believe at first. They are often placed in a learning-disabilities classroom where their difficulties suppress their intellectual performance. Little attention is given to their interests and strengths. Over time, they may become disruptive and find ways to use their creative abilities to avoid tasks. If their high ability remains unrecognized, then it never becomes part of their educational program, and these children never benefit from services to gifted children.

Children in all three groups are at risk for social and emotional problems when either their potential or learning disabilities go unrecognized. The problem is further compounded by the identification process because the activities used to select students for either learning disability or gifted services tend to be mutually exclusive. Consequently, these students often fail to meet the criteria for either type of service.

The Difficulties of Identification

Conservative estimates are that about 2 to 10 percent of students enrolled in gifted programs have learning disabilities (Dix and Schafer, 1996). The number of possible combinations of intellectual giftedness and learning disabilities is so great that any attempt to devise a single set of reliable measures is probably futile.

For example, gifted children with language or speech impairments cannot respond to tests requiring verbal answers. Children with hearing problems may neither be able to respond to oral directions nor possess the vocabulary necessary to express complex thoughts. Vision problems could prevent some children from understanding written vocabulary words. Learning disabilities could prevent some children from expressing themselves through speech or in writing. Moreover, dual exceptionality children often use their gifts to hide their disabilities, further complicating the identification process.

Nonetheless, researchers agree that a battery of measurements should be developed to assess these students. Assessment should include an achievement battery, an intelligence test, indicators of cognitive processing, and behavioral observations. Teachers should be given lists of characteristics (e.g., the "Characteristics of Gifted Children with Learning Disabilities" at the end of this chapter) to increase their awareness of behaviors displayed by students who are gifted and learning disabled. Parent interviews, self-concept scales, and talent checklists are just some of the tools that can be used to assess whether a child is gifted. The goal is early identification and intervention for gifted students with learning disabilities so that their needs and talents are recognized and appropriately addressed by the school staff.

Cline and Hegeman (2001) propose that the identification of gifted students with disabilities is particularly difficult for the following reasons:

> *Focus on Assessing the Disability.* Assessment of the disability should include looking for particular strengths, such as superior mental or artistic ability, and creativity. Besides medical information, test administrators should look at participation in extracurricular activities and performance in music, visual arts, drama, or dance.

> *Stereotypic Expectations.* The long-held perception that gifted children are motivated and mature while learning disabled children are unmotivated and sluggish needs to be overcome if we are to successfully identify this population.

> *Developmental Delays.* Delays in a student's cognitive development may result in disabilities that mask talents. Students with visual impairments, for example, will have difficulty with any abstract thinking that requires visual representation, but may have high capabilities in other areas of language expression.

> *Experiential Deficits.* Children in families with limited resources may not have had many opportunities for a variety of learning experiences (e.g., travel), thus inhibiting the expression of their unique abilities.

Narrow Views of Giftedness. Too many educators still hold a narrow view of giftedness as intellectual potential in mathematics and language. However, the works of Howard Gardner, Robert Sternberg (see Chapter 2), and others have provided broader conceptions of intelligence that may help in the identification of gifted students with learning disabilities.

Disability-Specific Concerns. Because a specific disability may affect a student's performance in certain parts of the testing process, test administrators may need to make adaptations or accommodations to the testing procedures. These alterations should be appropriate to the specific disability and could include omitting certain questions or extending the time for taking the test.

The Potential for Misdiagnosis

As psychologists and educators become more aware of the behaviors that suggest learning disabilities, concerns are now being raised that gifted students may be misdiagnosed as having psychological disorders as a result of the very behaviors that make them gifted. For example, many gifted children are intense in their work, engage in power struggles with adults, and are extremely sensitive to emotional situations. They are often impatient with themselves and others, displaying an intense idealism and concern for moral and social issues,

> Gifted students may be misdiagnosed as having psychological disorders as a result of the very behaviors that make them gifted.

which can create depression and anxiety. Further, gifted children are often bored in the regular classroom and their peer relations can be difficult. These problems, which can be associated with the characteristic strengths of gifted students, can be mislabeled and ultimately lead to misdiagnosis.

Psychologist James Webb has long been interested in the misdiagnosis of gifted students. Table 8.1 lists a few of the possible problems that he suggests may be linked to the typical strengths of gifted children (Webb, 2000). Webb contends that inexperienced health professionals are misreading the problems and mistakenly diagnosing some gifted children with attention-deficit hyperactivity disorder (ADHD), oppositional defiant disorder, bipolar disorder, and obsessive-compulsive disorder. No doubt, giftedness can coexist in students who have psychological disorders, but Webb believes that number is far smaller than currently diagnosed.

Table 8.1 Possible Problems Linked to the Typical Strengths of Gifted Children	
Strengths	**Possible Problems**
Quickly acquires and retains information.	Looks bored; gets impatient with slowness of others.
Enjoys intellectual activities and can conceptualize and synthesize abstract concepts.	May question teachers' procedures; resists practice and drill; omits details.
Seeks to organize things and people.	May be seen as rude or domineering.
Is self-critical and evaluates other critically.	Intolerant toward others; may become depressed.
Enjoys inventing new ways of doing things.	May reject what is already known; seen by others as different.
Strong desire to be accepted by others; has empathy for others.	Expects others to have similar values; sensitive to peer criticism; may feel alienated.
Has diverse interests and abilities.	Frustrated over lack of time; may appear disorganized.
Strong sense of humor.	Often sees the absurdities of situation; humor may not be understood by others; becomes class clown to get attention.
Displays intense efforts, high energy, eagerness, and alertness.	Eagerness may disrupt others; frustrated with inactivity; may be seen as hyperactive.

Similarly, some gifted students are being misdiagnosed with learning disabilities. According to Webb (2000) and Winner (2000), this can happen when health professionals misinterpret any of the following as a sign of learning dysfunction:

- large differences between the verbal IQ and performance IQ on the Wechsler intelligence tests
- large differences between the individual subscales on the intelligence and achievement sections of the Wechsler Intelligence Scale for Children
- poor handwriting
- poor sleep habits
- parental reports that the child is strong-willed, impertinent, weird, argumentative, and intense

Misdiagnosing Giftedness as Attention-Deficit Hyperactivity Disorder (ADHD)

In looking at Table 8.1, it is apparent that many of the possible problem behaviors linked to gifted students can readily be associated with the characteristics of attention-deficit hyperactivity disorder (ADHD). Specifically, the gifted characteristics of high motor activity, sensitivity, intensity, and impatience can easily be mistaken for ADHD. Surely, some gifted children suffer from ADHD, but many do not. So how do health and education professionals determine whether a child's behavior is merely the expression of giftedness or the sign of a gifted child with ADHD? Answering this question requires considering the settings and situations in which the child displays the problem behavior, as well as other potential explanations.

- *Consider the Setting and the Situation.* Gifted children do not exhibit the problem behaviors in all settings. For example, they may appear ADHD-like in one class, but not in another; or they may have problems on the ball field, but not at their music lessons. By contrast, children with ADHD exhibit their problem behaviors in all settings, although the intensity of their display may vary from one situation to another.

  Gifted children may be perceived as being off-task when their behavior might be related to boredom, mismatched learning style, lack of challenge in the curriculum, or other environmental factors. Providing more challenge will usually get them back to work. ADHD children have a difficult time focusing on their work no matter how interesting it may be.

  Hyperactivity is a common characteristic of gifted and ADHD children. However, for the gifted, their activity is highly focused and usually results in productive work or achievement of a specific goal. For ADHD children, their hyperactivity is found across all different types of situations and is often unfocused and unproductive.

- *Consider Other Sources.* Clinical studies report that a small percentage of gifted students suffer from borderline hypoglycemia (low blood sugar) and from various kinds of allergies (Webb, 2000; Silverman, 1993). Physical reactions in these conditions, coupled with the sensitivity and intensity characteristics of gifted children, can result in behavior that mimics ADHD. Once again, the intensity of their display will vary with diet, time of day, and other environmental factors.

One recent study found that highly gifted boys exhibit levels of behavior problems similar to boys who are learning disabled (Shaywitz, Holahan, Fletcher, Freudenheim, Makuch, Shaywitz, 2001). Surely, some gifted children have true learning disabilities, and their dual exceptionality should be addressed. However, health care professionals need to become more familiar with aspects of giftedness so that they are less likely to conclude that certain inherent characteristics of gifted children are signs of pathology.

> **Some highly gifted boys exhibit levels of behavior problems similar to boys who are learning disabled.**

Guidance and Counseling Interventions

School counselors can provide guidance and counseling services that benefit gifted students with learning disabilities. These services can often help students develop positive social relationships, raise their self-esteem, and improve their overall behavior. Furthermore, counselors can advocate on behalf of these students by raising awareness of their unique needs. By assisting in the identification process, using individual and group counseling, consulting with parents, and sharing academic strategies, counselors become important collaborators and facilitators in ensuring the academic success of gifted students with learning disabilities (McEachern and Bornot, 2001).

Because of the difficulties of accurately identifying and diagnosing gifted children with learning disabilities, no reliable data are currently available on the number of gifted children who are also diagnosed with specific learning deficits. Nevertheless, the following sections examine some of the more common combinations of giftedness and associated learning disabilities.

■ GIFTEDNESS AND ATTENTION-DEFICIT HYPERACTIVITY DISORDER (ADHD)

Some gifted children do have ADHD. Unfortunately, this dual exceptionality often means that such children are not recognized as having either exceptionality. Therefore, their needs for an appropriate education often go unmet.

What Is ADHD?

Attention-deficit hyperactivity disorder (ADHD) is a syndrome that interferes with an individual's ability to focus (inattention), regulate activity level (hyperactivity), and inhibit behavior (impulsivity). It is one of the most common learning disorders in children and adolescents. About 2 to 3 times more boys than girls are affected. ADHD usually becomes evident in preschool or early elementary years, frequently persisting into adolescence and occasionally into adulthood.

Although most children have some symptoms of hyperactivity, impulsivity, and inattention, there are those in whom these behaviors persist and become the rule rather than the exception. These individuals need to be assessed by health care professionals with input from parents and teachers. No specific test exists for ADHD. The diagnosis results from a thorough review of a physical examination, a variety of psychological tests, and the observable behaviors in

> **About 2 to 3 times more boys than girls are affected by ADHD.**

the child's everyday settings. A diagnosis of ADHD requires that six or more of the symptoms for inattention or for hyperactivity-impulsivity be present for at least 6 months, appear before the age of 7, and be evident across at least two of the child's environments (e.g., at home, in school, on the playground, etc.). Recently, ADHD has been classified into three subtypes: predominantly inattentive, predominantly hyperactive-impulsive, and the combined type (Sousa, 2001b).

What Causes ADHD?

The exact causes of ADHD are unknown. Scientific evidence indicates that this is a neurologically based medical problem for which there may be several causes. Some research studies suggest that the disorder results from an imbalance in certain neurotransmitters (most likely dopamine and serotonin) that help the brain regulate focus and behavior. ADHD has been associated with symptoms in children after difficult pregnancies and problem deliveries. Maternal smoking as well as exposure to environmental toxins, such as dioxins, during pregnancy also increase the risk of an ADHD child. Other studies indicate that the ADHD brain consumes less glucose—its main fuel source—than the non-ADHD brain, especially in the frontal lobe regions. Brain imaging studies have revealed structural differences in adults with ADHD, suggesting that the disorder may have a genetic component (Sousa, 2001b).

The Attention Loop

Because one of the main characteristics of ADHD (as well as attention deficit disorder, ADD) is the inability to control attention, recent research has focused on how the brain attends to incoming and internal stimuli. Attention seems to be the result of a loop-like process that involves the brain stem, the posterior (rear) cortex, and the prefrontal cortex (Figure 8.1). The brain stem collects the incoming data and sends it to the posterior cortex which integrates the data. Interpreting the data is the job of the prefrontal cortex, and its interpretation can modify what the brain stem transmits, thus completing the loop. Any breakdown in this loop will interfere with attention, and the degree of breakdown will affect the nature of the attention deficit, some with and others without hyperactivity (Goldberg, 2001).

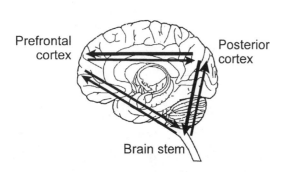

Figure 8.1 The attention loop involves the brain stem, the prefrontal cortex, and the posterior cortex.

Because gifted children have a higher functioning prefrontal cortex than their average peers, breakdowns in the attention loop are more likely to occur in the posterior cortex (sensory integration and emotional input) and in the brain stem. This may explain why gifted children with ADHD are more prone to have social and emotional problems rather than cognitive ones.

Characteristics of Gifted Children With ADHD

Assuming proper diagnosis, gifted children with ADHD do differ from *average* children with ADHD in the following ways (Lovecky, 1999).

- *Testing.* Gifted children with ADHD show great variability on tests of achievement and intelligence. Their performance is scattered and they miss many easy items while answering the difficult items correctly. Because of their excellent memory, they tend to score high on the subtests involving mathematics. They also tend to score high in abstract reasoning ability.

- *Study Skills.* These children often learn more rapidly and exhibit more mature metacognitive strategies (e.g., using of mnemonics;

grouping by category, patterns, or spatial characteristics; and recalling by association) than their age peers. However, they sometimes forget to use the strategies or may not use them efficiently. They tend to have more problems with study skills, such as note taking, organizing ideas, and outlining.

- *Developmental Issues*. Gifted children with ADHD show greater differences in their degree of social and emotional development than their average peers. They may behave less maturely than their peers in some situations and more maturely in others. They form friendships with those who will share their complex interests with the same intensity. However, they often misread social cues and show poor understanding of group dynamics and goals. They tend to be more emotional and show greater sensitivity than their age peers.

- *Interests*. Compared to their age peers, these children usually have more specialized interests and seek out activities that have greater complexity. Their interests are generally intense and last for years.

Gifted children with ADHD differ from other *gifted* children in that they

- ▸ Show greater degrees of differences in development across cognitive, social, and emotional areas and in their ability to act maturely.
- ▸ Have less ability to think sequentially and to use working memory adequately.
- ▸ Experience greater difficulty solving problems that use part-to-whole relationships because they have trouble selecting the main points among data.
- ▸ Tend to complete less work, hurry through it, take too long to complete simple things, and often change topics on projects.
- ▸ Find it difficult to work in groups, even with groups of gifted children.
- ▸ Do not feel a high degree of satisfaction or intrinsic reward for completing a project.

■ GIFTEDNESS AND AUTISM

To understand this twice-exceptional population, let us first examine the nature of autism and then look at some unique characteristics of individuals who are both gifted and autistic.

What Is Autism?

In autistic disorder (or autism), neurological problems develop that make it difficult for a person to communicate and form relationships with others. It is a spectrum disorder that runs the gamut from mild to severe. About 10 percent of people with autism are relatively high functioning (called high-functioning autism, or autistic savants), while others are mentally retarded or have serious language delays.

> **Approximately 10 percent of people with autism are high functioning and display savant skills.**

Autism affects about one person in 500, and 4 out of 5 of those affected are males. Although it may appear that the incidence of autism is increasing in American children, the medical community believes it is more likely that the prevalence of autism has been underestimated in the past.

The symptoms of autism usually appear before the age of 3. Children with autism do not interact well with others and may avoid eye contact. They may resist attention and affection, and they rarely seem upset when a parent leaves or show pleasure when the parent returns. Understanding the cues of others—such as a smile, wink, or grimace—is difficult for them as well. Some children with autism also tend to be physically aggressive at times, particularly when they are in a strange or overwhelming environment. At times they will break things, attack others, or harm themselves. There is no general agreement on the causes of autism, and given that this is a spectrum disorder, it is likely that there are multiple causes. Researchers have found that autism may be associated with genetic defects (autistic characteristics tend to run in families), with structural abnormalities in the frontal lobes and brain stem, or with low concentrations of serotonin (Sousa, 2001b).

Types of Autism

Although autism is officially classified in the Fourth Edition of the Diagnostic and Statistical Manual of Mental Disorders (commonly referred to as the DSM-IV, 2000) as only one type of pervasive developmental disorder, there is no clear consensus on this view. Other researchers believe that autism may be more closely related to social, sensory, or cognitive deficits. Despite the controversy, four types or autism have been identified on the basis of differences in behaviors:

- *Kanner-Type:* Sometimes called classic autism or early infantile autism, this type is characterized by the early onset of symptoms, lack of eye contact, late speech, repetitive behaviors, and possible mental retardation.

- *Asperger's Syndrome:* A pervasive developmental disorder on the autism spectrum characterized by social deficits, relatively normal cognitive and language development, and the presence of intense, idiosyncratic interests.

- *Pervasive Developmental Disorder–Not Otherwise Specified.* This classification is used when a child does not meet the defining criteria before the age of 3 years. Sometimes this classification is used when the condition appears less severe or inconsistent with the general criteria. It is usually more closely aligned with Kanner- Type autism than with Asperger's Syndrome.

- *Regressive/Epileptic Type.* This type is characterized by the inability to understand others, mixing of sensory inputs, abnormal EEG readings, mental retardation, and high anxiety levels.

For the purposes of this book, we will focus on Kanner-type autism and Asperger's syndrome because these are the two types that are most likely to coexist with giftedness.

Impact of Giftedness on Individuals With Classic (Kanner-Type) Autism

Giftedness also runs on a spectrum from mildly gifted to genius. It is sometimes difficult to separate high functioning individuals with mild autism from those who are gifted because they can share many similar traits. For example, both the gifted and autistic tend to focus intently on objects, behaviors, and activities. They display similar negative behaviors, such as stubbornness, indifference to socialization and dress, discourteousness, and resistance to teacher authority. Both groups are powerful visual thinkers and have keen senses. Individuals who are *both* gifted and autistic are difficult to identify because their strengths and weaknesses can mask each other. Nonetheless, they have to manage and adjust to their environment. Having these dual exceptionalities brings with it positive and negative impacts (Cash, 1999).

- *Positive Impacts*. The key to the success of gifted/autistic individuals often starts in school where they can learn compensatory strategies to manipulate their autistic weaknesses and tendencies. Through behavior modification programs and by using metacognitive strategies, they can gain acceptance and credibility, and be more easily accepted by society.

- *Negative Impacts*. Gifted/autistic individuals frequently move from one environment that praises their strengths to another that misunderstands and fears their unusual and perplexing characteristics. In school, gifted/autistic students may be placed in classes where their seemingly contradictory behaviors and non-traditional social interactions often confuse uninformed teachers and peers. As a result, the gifted/autistic students may be criticized and suffer social rejection. Although some of these dual-exceptional students are insensitive to the lack of connectedness (a typical autistic characteristic), others are frustrated by the ostracism.

Too often, gifted/autistic individuals do not receive intellectual opportunities and are frequently placed in classes with mentally-challenged students. The school focuses on addressing only their weaknesses and remediation becomes the sole educational goal. Consequently, these students can suffer from depression, low self-esteem, and lack of motivation. On the other hand, more educators are becoming aware that some autistic children may also be gifted, and are exploring interventions, such as early identification and screening, the use of diagnostic instruments, coordinated teacher and parent training, parent support networks, behavior modification programs, and learning theory reform. If prompt identification and appropriate interventions begin in school, there is a greater likelihood that gifted/autistic individuals can develop into important and contributing adults (Cash, 1999).

> **Too often, gifted/autistic individuals do not receive intellectual opportunities and are frequently placed in classes with mentally-challenged students.**

Asperger's Syndrome

Identified in 1944 by Austrian physician Hans Asperger, this syndrome is a developmental disorder with many of the same symptoms of autism. Asperger's syndrome (AS) may occur in as many as 26 out of 10,000 children (Note: Classic autism occurs in about 4 out of every 10,000 children.). The number of occurrences is changing as AS becomes better known and as the number of professionals diagnosing it increases. AS is usually referred to as *high-functioning autism* because people with the disorder generally display higher mental performance than those with typical autism.

Like autism, AS is a lifelong condition. The condition usually appears after the age of 18 months and is characterized by poor motor coordination and late mobility. As the child develops, other symptoms appear,

> **In classic autism, the male to female ratio is 4:1. In high-functioning Asperger's syndrome, that ratio is 9:1.**

such as routinized obsessive-compulsive behaviors, poor motor coordination with clumsy gait, strong attachments to places, poor eye contact, difficulty in relating to people, lack of empathy for others, and depression. Speech is often repetitive and pedantic, with monotone intonation and the absence of first person pronouns.

Savant skills are not present in all AS individuals. But they are common and usually involve extraordinary memory and preoccupation with the mastery of one or two subjects, such as history trivia, sports statistics, weather, and train schedules, often at the exclusion of learning in all other areas. Although their general language abilities are limited, they can carry on extensive discourse in their areas of special expertise but may have little grasp of the meaning of the words they are using. Some AS individuals have a history of *hyperlexia*, which is rote reading at a precocious age.

That AS individuals have problems with social interaction can be a particularly burdensome characteristic because it carries into adulthood, causing social isolation and frustration. AS children are often unable to understand the social customs associated with dating or to pick up on nonverbal social cues, such as eye contact, voice intonation, or gesturing. As a result, AS individuals often devise a set of rules to cope with social interactions. The rules are generally inflexible and serve only to further isolate these individuals rather than help them succeed in social situations. Several programs have been devised to help AS students enhance their social skills.

Genetic Components

There is growing evidence that both autism and AS have genetic components. First, in classic autism, the male to female ratio is 4:1; in high functioning AS, that ratio is 9:1. These gender differences are far too great to be explained entirely by differences in socialization. They more likely reflect developmental differences between the two sexes regulated by genetic information. Second, there is an increased incidence of AS profiles among relatives of children with AS. Third, there is an increased incidence of other developmental disorders among the siblings of AS children. One study investigated the genetic connection through a series of cognitive performance tasks to test whether the parents of children diagnosed with AS displayed similar cognitive traits (Baron-Cohen and Hammer, 1997). Mothers and fathers of AS children performed better than the control subjects on those tasks associated with AS strengths, but worse on the tasks associated as weakness in AS profiles. This finding lent support to the notion that parents of AS children carry mild forms of the disorder. Another finding was that male parents performed lower on all tasks than female parents, suggesting that the genetic factors that contribute to AS are more closely linked to males. However, it is likely that AS results from many contributing factors, including genetic ones.

Brain Imaging

Only a handful of studies have used brain imaging techniques to examine differences in cerebral functions of AS children compared to non-AS children. Using fMRI, one study found some differences in frontal lobe activity of AS and non-AS children during a task involving social judgment (Oktem, Diren, Karaagaoglu, and Anlar, 2001). However, more studies are needed to understand the sources and implications of these differences in activity levels.

General Characteristics of AS

More studies on AS have been undertaken in recent years as researchers try to further understand this exceptionality. A survey of these studies found that children and adolescents with AS tended to have the following characteristics (Barnhill, 2001; Henderson, 2001):

- An IQ range similar to the general public
- High oral language skills; low written language skills
- Fluent verbalization but poor problem-solving skills
- Knowledge of simple vocabulary but difficulty with inferences and abstract language

▸ Pronounced emotional difficulties recognized by others but not by themselves

▸ An approach to new learning that resembles a learned helplessness

▸ Low sensory thresholds causing a sensory overload that may be overwhelming

▸ Low ability to plan use of time or estimate time passage

▸ Difficulty with social/emotional cues

▸ Difficulty acknowledging that a perspective different from their own can exist

Direct and specific skill strategies can be used to help AS individuals cope with the challenges posed by these characteristics, especially in school and social situations.

Identification of Gifted Students with AS

Until recently, AS was generally diagnosed later than classic autism, most likely because AS individuals had relatively normal early development. As practitioners become more familiar with AS, earlier diagnosis means earlier intervention and appropriate services. Early diagnosis becomes even more important for gifted AS individuals so that programs can be devised to address their gifts as well as their disabilities. Finding the measure to accurately identify gifted AS students has not been easy. However, Henderson (2001) reports that the behavioral patterns, motor skills, gifted and talented characteristics, and leadership can be measured reliably by various instruments.

To parents and teachers, AS appears a serious disability, especially because it inhibits social interaction. Yet, individuals with AS develop deep interests in narrow topics and can often succeed in areas where attention to detail is critical and social discourse minimal. When given educational support and appropriate opportunities, many AS students are academically successful and attend college. Many AS persons are drawn to science, inventions,

> **When given educational support and appropriate opportunities, many students with Asperger's syndrome are academically successful and attend college.**

mathematics, and computers and can have successful careers in these areas. The December 2001 issue of *Wired* magazine, for instance, reported on the high number of AS people who are gainfully employed in computer or related industries in the Silicon Valley area of California. Areas of focused research also provide AS individuals with opportunities for career success.

Misdiagnosis of AS

> **Someone not familiar with the asynchronous development of gifted children could mistake these characteristics as signs of Asperger's syndrome.**

Just as the characteristics of giftedness can be misread as signs of psychological disorders and learning disabilities, so can they lead to a misdiagnosis of Asperger's syndrome (Amend, 2000). Intense fascination with a specific subject, an uneven profile of abilities, original problem-solving methods, and exceptional concentration are not only components of AS, but of giftedness as well. Someone not familiar with the asynchronous development of gifted children could mistake these characteristics as signs of AS.

Programs for the Troubled Gifted

Because of the complexities and possible combinations of dual exceptionalities, planning a program of instruction for these students can be complicated. But all of these students require programs that will nurture their gifts, address their disability, and provide the emotional support necessary to deal with any inconsistent abilities (Baum, 1994).

One common programming approach is for students to receive primary instruction in the regular classroom and also to attend a resource pullout program, a gifted pullout class, or a combination of both. In a study conducted by Nielsen and Morton-Albert (1989), the self-concepts of gifted students with learning disabilities varied with the type of educational services they were receiving. Not surprisingly, students had a lower self-concept when they primarily received learning disability services. In contrast, when these students also received gifted services that focused on their strengths, their self-concept scores closely matched the scores of gifted students without handicaps.

The researchers did find an exception to these findings: The self-concept scores of gifted students with learning disabilities and who were in self-contained learning disabled/gifted classes more closely matched those of students with learning disabilities than those of gifted students. Apparently, the self-concept of these students is influenced by their perceptions of how they are compared to other students by their parents and their peers.

SAVANT SYNDROME ■

In the 1880s, J. Langdon Down (known for naming Down's syndrome) described individuals he called "idiot savants," who were mentally retarded yet displayed extraordinary talents far beyond their handicaps. Now called Savant syndrome, it is a rare condition in which persons with various developmental disabilities have abilities that are remarkable considering their handicap (called *talented savants*) to those rarer individuals whose brilliance would be spectacular even in a normal person (called *prodigious savants*). About 10 percent of persons with autism have some savant abilities. This group represents about one-half of the savant population; the other half have some other form of developmental disability, such as mental retardation.

Treffert (2000a) describes their skills as falling within a narrow range including music (they have perfect pitch and usually play the piano), spatial skills, high-speed calculating and mathematical ability, calendar calculating, art (sculpture and drawing), and mechanical abilities. Other rare abilities occasionally emerge, such as unusual language skills, map memorization, and enhanced sense of touch and smell. The skills tend to be associated with right cerebral hemisphere activities (nonsymbolic, directly perceived) rather than the left hemisphere (sequential, logical, and language specialization (see Chapter 2). Regardless of the nature of the special skills, they are always linked to a phenomenal memory system that is very narrow but deep. This system, according to Treffert, is at the automatic level of procedural memory rather than at the higher level of cognitive memory common in normal individuals.

What Causes Savant Syndrome?

Because many savants display skills associated with right hemisphere lateralization, researchers speculated that the syndrome could be the result of injury to the left brain, either before, during, or shortly after birth. Recent CT and MRI imaging studies do reveal left hemisphere damage in savants, especially in areas near the frontal lobe (Treffert, 2000b). These findings suggest that savant syndrome is caused by damage to the left frontal hemisphere, which stimulates right hemisphere compensation. The damage also causes memory circuits to compensate by shifting from high-level, frontal lobe cognitive memory to low-level procedural memory (Figure 8.2). In prodigious savants, genetic factors may also be involved because practice alone cannot account for the extraordinary mastery of their savant skills.

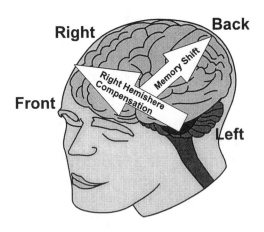

Figure 8.2 Damage to the left frontal hemisphere results in right hemisphere compensation and the shifting of memory circuits to low-level procedural memory.

One of the explanations offered for pre-natal brain injury lies in the potentially toxic effects of circulating testosterone in the fetus. Because the left hemisphere of the brain is slower in development than the right hemisphere, it is more vulnerable to testosterone's toxicity, which may explain the high male-to-female ratio in savant syndrome, autism, and other learning disabilities. As for injuries occurring after birth, Carter (1999) reported on one 9-year-old boy who was transformed from an average student to a mechanical genius after part of this left brain was destroyed by a bullet.

Dealing With Autistic Savants

As with most people who have dual exceptionalities, the question becomes: Do we train the talent or eliminate the deficit? But appropriate therapies do not have to take an either/or approach. Training the talent can lessen the effects of the deficits. With properly trained educators leading the way, a greater number of autistic savants are succeeding in the classroom and in the workplace.

■ HYPERLEXIA

Hyperlexia is a term applied to children who exhibit precocious reading skills but have significant problems with learning and language as well as impaired social skills. Hyperlexic children may also be diagnosed with autism, pervasive development disorder, attention deficit disorder, or Asperger's syndrome. Others receive no diagnosis and are considered just precocious. Controversy currently exists as to whether hyperlexia is a form of autism or a separate and distinct language disorder.

> **Controversy currently exists as to whether hyperlexia is a form of autism or a separate and distinct language disorder.**

Identification of Hyperlexia

Children are suspected of having hyperlexia if they exhibit the following three characteristics (Kupperman, Bligh, Barouski, 2002):

- *Precocious Reading Ability.* By the age of 18 to 24 months, parents are amazed by the child's ability to name letters and numbers. This skill was not taught to the child by parents. By 3 years of age, these children see printed words and read them, sometimes before they have really learned to talk. They are fascinated by the printed word.

- *Peculiar Language Learning Disorders.* Of those children who talk (there are also nonverbal hyperlexics), nearly all display echolalic speech (repeating what others have said) and good auditory memory for songs learned by rote, the alphabet, and numbers. They also show impairment in the ability to initiate or sustain a conversation, despite adequate speech.

- *Problems in Social Development.* The behaviors that may be observed include the following: noncompliance, extreme need for sameness, difficulty with transitions, difficulty in socializing with peers, and impaired ability to make peer friendships.

Types of Hyperlexia

Because behavioral symptoms subside in many children as their language comprehension and expression improve, identification of true hyperlexia is difficult. The studies on hyperlexia seem to indicate that there are three types (Treffert, 2000a; Kupperman, et al., 2002):

- *Just Precocious.* These are children who have very precocious reading skills and who are normal in all other aspects of development. They do not display any long-lasting autistic behaviors. Rather, these are normal children who just enjoy reading and whose brains are considerably more active when reading (Figure 8.3).

- *Precocious Reading/Autistic-Like Behaviors.* These children display exceptional reading skills coupled with autistic-like behaviors, such as echolalia, and impaired social skills. But these children are *not* autistic and may represent the group where a specific diagnosis of hyperlexia is most appropriate. The long-term outlook for this group is good.

- *Savant Behavior.* These children have such extraordinary reading skills that they display savant skills, associated with autism or some other developmental disorder. In this case, the hyperlexia is but one symptom of a more serious spectrum disorder.

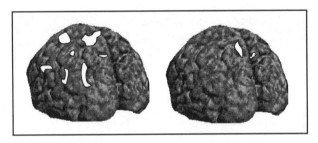

Figure 8.3 This representation of PET scans shows how the brain of a young hyperlexic reader (left) is much more active (white areas) than that of an age-matched control (Restak, 2001).

Dealing With Hyperlexia

Because of the various types of hyperlexia, a comprehensive assessment by a knowledgeable team is essential for proper diagnosis. For instance, it is important to differentiate these children from those whose language disorders may be related to a hearing loss, autism mental retardation, or emotional disturbance. Although hyperlexic children are like other children with language learning disorders, they are more fortunate in that they have the reading skill to use as a supportive resource. Nonetheless, hyperlexia is puzzling because it raises questions about the relationship between reading and language. A child may display exceptional reading ability while also presenting a collection of linguistic, behavioral, and social deficits.

Kupperman and her colleagues (2002) report that most of the children with hyperlexia show remarkable improvement from the time they are first diagnosed at the age of 2 or 3 until they enter 2nd grade. At first, their behavior looks autistic (i.e., they are echolalic and not able to understand much language). However, as their language comprehension and expressive language improve, these children emerge out of their autism. By the time they reach 1st or 2nd grade, they lose most of their autistic characteristics but may still

> **Most children with hyperlexia lose their autistic-like characteristics by 2nd or 3rd grade.**

remain aloof from other children. At this point, they can be taught social skills. Emphasis should be placed on intensive speech and language therapy because the success of these children depends on the development of their comprehension and use of language.

APPLICATIONS

CHARACTERISTICS OF GIFTED CHILDREN WITH DISABILITIES

Although recognizing giftedness in children with disabilities is no easy task, some characteristics do emerge that can help educators (and parents) in this process. Tables 8.1 and 8.2 on the following pages are adapted from the work of Colleen Willard-Holt (1999) who surveyed the research literature and collected characteristics of children with dual exceptionalities.

Table 8.1 shows the characteristics of gifted students who also have physical, hearing, and vision impairments. Table 8.2 describes the characteristics of gifted students who also have learning disabilities and attention problems. It is important to note that some students are misdiagnosed with attention-deficit hyperactivity disorder (ADHD) when in fact they are gifted and are reacting to an inappropriate learning environment (Sousa, 2001b, p. 51).

One way to distinguish between the two is to examine the persistence and pervasiveness of the problem behavior. Gifted children are more likely to act out in specific situations where they are not challenged. Students who display problem behavior in all situations may have ADHD. It is also possible for a child to be both gifted and have ADHD.

GIFTED CHILDREN WITH DISABILITIES—Continued

Table 8.1 Characteristics of Gifted Students with Physical, Hearing, and Vision Impairments (Adapted from C. Willard-Holt, 1999, *Dual Exceptionalities*, ERIC Clearinghouse on Disabilities and Gifted Education, Arlington, VA)		
Gifted with Physical Disabilities	Gifted with Hearing Impairments	Gifted with Vision Impairments
❏ Development of compensatory skills ❏ Creative in finding alternative ways of communicating and accomplishing tasks ❏ Impressive store of knowledge ❏ Good sense of humor ❏ Superior memory ❏ Insightful ❏ Ability to set and strive for long-term goals ❏ Advanced academic skills ❏ Good problem-solving skills ❏ Persistence and patience ❏ Greater maturity than age mates ❏ High motivation to achieve ❏ Self-criticism and perfectionism ❏ Possible difficulty with abstractions ❏ Possible limited achievement due to pace of work	❏ Development of speech and reading skills without instruction ❏ Early reading ability ❏ Function in regular school setting ❏ High reasoning ability ❏ Rapid grasp of ideas ❏ Excellent memory ❏ Nontraditional ways of getting information ❏ Self-starter ❏ Intuitive ❏ Ingenuity in problem solving ❏ Delays in concept attainment ❏ Symbolic language abilities ❏ Wide range of interests ❏ Good sense of humor ❏ Enjoys manipulating the environment	❏ Fast rate of learning ❏ Excellent memory ❏ Superior verbal communication skills and vocabulary ❏ Advanced problem-solving skills ❏ Motivation to know ❏ Excellent ability to concentrate ❏ Creative production of thought that progresses more slowly than sighted students ❏ Slower rate of cognitive development than sighted students

GIFTED CHILDREN WITH DISABILITIES—Continued

Table 8.2 Characteristics of Gifted Students with Learning Disabilities and Attention Problems (Adapted from C. Willard-Holt, 1999, *Dual Exceptionalities,* ERIC Clearinghouse on Disabilities and Gifted Education, Arlington, VA)		
Gifted With Learning Disabilities	**Gifted Who Are Bored**	**Gifted With ADHD**
❑ High abstract reasoning ❑ Advanced vocabulary ❑ Good mathematical skills ❑ Sophisticated sense of humor ❑ Keen visual memory and spatial skills ❑ Insightful ❑ Creative ❑ Imaginative ❑ Good problem-solving skills ❑ High performance in science, music, arts ❑ Difficulty with memorization, computation, phonics, spelling ❑ Grasp of metaphors and satire ❑ Understanding of complex systems and models ❑ Often fails to complete assignments ❑ Difficulties with sequential tasks	❑ Poor attention and daydreaming ❑ Low tolerance with tasks that seem irrelevant ❑ Question school customs, rules and traditions ❑ High activity level ❑ May need less sleep ❑ Begin many projects but take few to completion ❑ Lose or forget homework ❑ Disorganized ❑ Judgment lags behind intellectual growth ❑ Intensity may lead to power struggle with authorities ❑ May appear careless ❑ Difficulty restraining desire to talk ❑ High sensitivity to criticism ❑ Do not exhibit problem behavior in all settings	❑ Poor sustained attention ❑ Shift from one uncompleted activity to another ❑ Diminished persistence on tasks not having immediate consequences ❑ Impulsive ❑ Poor delay of gratification ❑ More active and more restless than other children ❑ Often talk excessively ❑ Poor adherence to requests to regulate behavior in social settings ❑ Inattentive to details ❑ Often interrupt or intrude on others ❑ Highly sensitive to criticism ❑ Often lose things required for tasks at school or at home ❑ Problem behaviors exist in *all* settings, but are more severe in some ❑ High variability in task performance and in time used to accomplish tasks

APPLICATIONS

SOME TEACHING STRATEGIES FOR GIFTED/LEARNING DISABLED STUDENTS

Several successful teaching strategies and practices have been suggested in the literature. These should be considered in addition to providing supplemental gifted services for students who are both gifted and learning disabled (Dix and Schafer,1996; Rivera, Murdock, and Sexton,1995; Silverman, 1989a).

Instruction:

- *Staff Development.* Ongoing staff development is necessary to ensure that educators have the information they need to screen, identify, and successfully teach gifted/learning disabled students.

- *Basic Skills.* Teachers should continue with their instruction in basic skills because these students often have learning problems in these areas.

- *Technology.* Incorporate technology into lessons whenever possible. Equipment such as cameras, calculators, computers, and audio and video recorders can help students reach their potential and produce quality work.

- *Student Strengths and Weaknesses.* Students already know their weaknesses; help them find, appreciate, and use their strengths. Offer options that allow students to use their strengths and preferred ways of learning.

- *Classroom Materials.* When possible, students need to select from a variety of classroom materials to show mastery of the learning in a manner that matches their strengths. A variety of assessment tools, such as performance measures and portfolios, should also be available.

SOME TEACHING STRATEGIES FOR
GIFTED/LEARNING DISABLED STUDENTS—Continued

- *Compensation Strategies.* Teachers should neither focus on students' weaknesses nor ignore them. Students need to be taught compensation strategies to address their weaknesses. For example, they can learn calculator skills to do math computation or learn to use a computer and a spell checker to compensate for poor spelling.

- *Instructional Approaches.* Emphasize higher-order abstract thinking, creativity, and a problem-solving approach. Promote active inquiry, discussion, and experimentation.

- *Teaching Strategy and Learning Disability.* Whenever possible, match the teaching strategy to address the learning disability. For example, if a student has auditory processing difficulties, avoid a quick-response format as these students will need more time to respond to verbal inquiries.

- *Number of Instructions.* Remember the capacity limits of working memory and limit the number of instructions given at any one time.

- *Chalkboard.* Many of these students need visual tools to help them remember directions or steps in a procedure.

- *Modeling.* Allow students to observe others who are successfully performing a task before they try it themselves. Develop models that demonstrate different ways of thinking and communicating.

- *Visual and Hands-On Procedures.* Classroom strategies that include visual and hands-on activities take advantage of these students' learning strengths.

- *Self-Concept.* Find opportunities to assist in strengthening the students' self-concept.

- *Time.* Provide for individual pacing in areas of the students' strengths and disabilities.

SOME TEACHING STRATEGIES FOR
GIFTED/LEARNING DISABLED STUDENTS—Continued

Classroom Dynamics:

- *Proximity and Quiet.* Place students with attention problems near the teacher, and provide for them a quiet space with a minimum of distractions.

- *Eye Contact.* These students often have short attention spans and are easily distracted. Before giving individual instructions, make eye contact with the student to ensure that attention is focused on you.

- *Expectations.* Expect students to participate in all activities and strive for normal peer interactions whenever possible. Facilitate acceptance and demand respect for all members of the class. Treat a student with a disability the same way you would treat a student without that disability.

- *Differences.* Model ways to celebrate individual differences. Discuss the implications of talents and disabilities with the class.

APPLICATIONS

SOME COUNSELING STRATEGIES FOR GIFTED/LEARNING-DISABLED STUDENTS

School counselors can play an important role in helping gifted/learning-disabled students adjust and succeed in school. McEachern and Bornot (2001) suggest that counselors can contribute in the following ways.

- *Consulting With Parents.* Parents seek answers as to why their child can exhibit intellectual abilities while having difficulty in school performance. Counselors can do the following:

  — Provide parents with information on the diagnosis and suggest strategies that support the education of their child when at home.

  — Reduce tension between parents, teachers, and students and suggest appropriate emotional responses.

  — Set up support groups among parents so they can share similar concerns, discuss strategies for change, and gain confidence in parenting.

- *Sharing Academic Strategies With Teachers.* Counselors can work with teachers to design curriculum and instruction activities that are more likely to keep gifted/learning-disabled students engaged and successful. Here are some ways that counselors can help:

  — Urge that the curriculum focus on exploratory, discovery, and investigative learning, including provisions for the various learning styles of these students. Activities that involve art, photography, drama, and other self-directed and unconventional methods should be encouraged.

  — Include technology in the curriculum, such as using computers for word processing, to improve language and writing skills, and for individualized instruction and introducing calculators and tape recorders (audio and video) as instructional tools.

  — Advise teachers to develop student strengths as well as to remedy student weaknesses. Overemphasis on student weaknesses will lower their self-esteem and confidence. Advise teachers, too, on the importance of providing emotional encouragement and assurance

SOME COUNSELING STRATEGIES FOR
GIFTED/LEARNING-DISABLED STUDENTS—Continued

that tell students they can be successful.

— Use film, videos, books, and guest speakers to expose these students to local and nationally known role models of gifted individuals with learning disabilities who have been successful.

— Collaborate with teachers of the gifted to discuss ways of supporting the social and psychological needs of these students. These teachers may also agree to conduct small-group counseling sessions and behavior modification interventions in the classroom, so that students do not have to be taken out of class for such activities.

— Increase teachers' understanding of gifted/learning-disabled students by facilitating and coordinating workshops that offer guest speakers who can give expert information and resources. Counselors can prepare special materials that will help teachers identify these students for referral as well as select and incorporate learning strategies that are likely to be successful.

● *Individual and Group Counseling With Students.* Gifted/learning-disabled students often have difficulty facing the fact that they have some areas of high performance and others in which they are less capable than their peers. Teachers sometimes tell these students that they are bright but lazy and that they are not living up to their potential. The pressure to excel and meet others' expectations often puts these students at greater risk for stress, self-blame, depression, and suicide. Counselor interventions—individual or group, as appropriate—can include the following:

— Helping these students understand that inadequacy in one area or skill does not mean inadequacy in all areas. Offer ideas on ways to use their strengths to build up their weaknesses.

— Discouraging negative thinking by helping students rephrase the negativism into positive expressions. Suggest both stress-reduction strategies and healthy coping behaviors.

— Using art therapy as a creative and symbolic way for relieving the pressure these students feel and for discussing problems and setting goals.

— Conducting sessions on the use of problem-solving strategies to identify and address areas of strengths and weakness. Also helpful

SOME COUNSELING STRATEGIES FOR
GIFTED/LEARNING-DISABLED STUDENTS—Continued

are sessions to teach about constructive peer interactions, goal-setting, and positive study habits, such as note taking, summarizing, and preparing for tests.

- *Advocacy*. Counselors can become effective advocates for gifted/learning-disabled students by
  — Discussing with other school personnel the problems and general needs of these students.
  — Monitoring the progress of these students through their school experiences, assuring that their courses are consistent with their career goals, and encouraging that they are participating in appropriate extracurricular activities.
  — Using peers as tutors in the academic areas for which the gifted/learning-disabled students need assistance.
  — Assuring, as members of the child study team, that these students receive appropriate services, including referrals to outside agencies, if necessary.

School counselors are in a unique position to serve as facilitators, teachers, and advocates for the under-served population of gifted students with learning disabilities.

APPLICATIONS

WORKING WITH GIFTED CHILDREN WITH ADHD

Interventions for gifted children with ADHD have to be somewhat different from those recommended for average children with ADHD. Here are some items to consider when developing the Individualized Education Plan (IEP) for these children (Lovecky, 1999):

- *Acceleration.* These children may need acceleration while being taught the metacognitive skills to support the higher level of thinking required for more challenging work. This suggests a differentiated program rather than just being placed in an advanced class.

- *Enhance Strengths, Build on Weaknesses.* Gifted children with ADHD need academic programs that will allow them to enhance their strengths while building on their weaker areas. For example, they may need to be taught organizational and study skills in the context of their high-level work—learnings that their gifted peers without ADHD usually acquire without difficulty. Their program should also provide mentors in their areas of strength to maintain the stimulation and complexity needed to enhance their cognitive development.

- *Team Approach.* Without a comprehensive educational plan that includes addressing their cognitive, social, and emotional needs, these children will not enhance their ability to focus and sustain attention. Further, they may develop ineffective work habits and achieve less. If they lose their interest in learning, emotional and behavioral problems may emerge that can further affect their achievement. A team of specialists with expertise in both giftedness and ADHD is an effective approach for meeting the unique needs of these children.

APPLICATIONS

MANAGING STUDENTS WITH ASPERGER'S SYNDROME

Although students with Asperger's syndrome (AS) can be managed in the regular classroom, they often need educational support services. Occasionally, the resource room or tutoring can be helpful by providing individualized instruction and review. However, some students with high-functioning AS are able to adapt and function in school with educators who are understanding, knowledgeable, and flexible. Here are some suggestions for managing AS students in an instructional setting (Bauer, 1996).

- Keep classroom routines as consistent, predictable, and structured as possible because AS students do not like surprises.
- Prepare students in advance for any changes or transitions, such as vacation days and holiday breaks.
- Apply rules carefully. Rules should be clearly expressed and written down. However, they should be applied with some flexibility. That is, instructions do not need to be exactly the same for AS students as for the rest of the class. This approach also models tolerance for student peers.
- Use visuals (e.g., charts, schedules, lists, and pictures) and emphasize the visual cues that can be used for retention. Although many AS students have strong visual preferences as part of their learning-style profile, they also have poor visual memory.
- Take full advantage of the student's special area of interest when teaching. Allowing the student access to special interest areas can also be used as a reward for completing other tasks or for displaying appropriate behavior.
- Protect the student from bullying. One approach is to educate peers about learning differences so that the class becomes a supportive social as well as educational environment.
- Look for ways to take advantage of the special interest areas of AS students, such as using them occasionally to help other students. This technique can help the AS student gain acceptance from peers, who begin to recognize the value of the AS students' capabilities.

MANAGING STUDENTS WITH ASPERGER'S SYNDROME—Continued

- Help the student gain proficiency in frontal lobe executive functions by teaching strategies to improve their organizational skills and study habits.

- Avoid escalating power struggles. Displays of authority may cause these students to become rigid and stubborn, and their behavior can rapidly get out of control. If that occurs, it is often better to back away and let the situation cool down. Of course, preventative measures, such as negotiating and offering choices at the outset may avoid the confrontation entirely.

- Keep the teaching on a concrete level because AS students have difficulty understanding abstract language forms, such as metaphors, idioms, figurative speech, and sarcasm. When possible, try to recast abstract concepts into simpler and more concrete components.

- Ensure that other members of the school staff who come in contact with AS students are properly trained in management approaches and are aware of their needs.

- Work closely with the student's parents because they are usually familiar with the management and instructional strategies that have worked in the past. Frequent communication regarding challenges and areas of progress is more likely to result in parents and educators working toward similar and productive solutions.

APPLICATIONS

ENHANCING THE SOCIAL INTERACTION SKILLS OF ASPERGER'S SYNDROME STUDENTS

Students with Asperger's syndrome (AS) usually have difficulty engaging in the social interactions expected for their age. This often leads to social isolation and frustration. Marjorie Bock (2001) has developed a social behavioral learning strategy for AS students to guide their social interactions. The strategy is composed of four components and is called SODA, an acronym for <u>S</u>top, <u>O</u>bserve, <u>D</u>eliberate, and <u>A</u>ct. Each component contains three to five questions or statements that can be individualized to meet the specific needs and age level of students.

STOP

This component helps the student understand the social setting, determine the sequence of events that will occur, and select a low-traffic area to complete the rest of the tasks. The typical questions are

What is the room arrangement?
What is the activity schedule or routine?
Where should I go to observe?

OBSERVE

The second component helps students note social cues by observing what the people are doing. If they can hear what people are saying, they should listen for similarities across conversations, note the length of a typical conversation, as well as what the people do when the conversation ends. The typical questions are

What are the people doing?
What are the people saying?
What is the length of a typical conversation?
What do the people do after they have visited?

ENHANCING THE SOCIAL INTERACTION SKILLS OF ASPERGER'S SYNDROME STUDENTS—Continued

DELIBERATE

The third component helps the students decide what they would like to do and say as well as look for cues to let them know if the people would like to visit longer or end the visit. The typical questions are

What would I like to do?

What would I like to say?

How will I know when others would like to visit longer or would like to end this conversation?

ACT

The last component helps students interact with others. They select the person with whom they would like to converse and present a greeting. They then listen to the speaker and decide what they would like to learn more about. They share some of their own related experiences and then look for cues to decide if the person wants to continue talking or end the visit. The typical statements are

Approach person(s) with whom I like to visit.

Say, "Hello, how are you?"

Listen to person(s) and ask related questions.

Look for cues that this person would like to end or continue the visit.

This is the basic SODA format. Other questions can be added to each component as needed. Bock suggests that teaching SODA should involve at least one session to present and explain the model, and at least three sessions to demonstrate each component. Students then practice the strategy in class for three sessions, followed by at least three out-of-class situations. The goal here is to get AS students to replace their inflexible and ineffective social interaction rules with SODA so that they can recognize and attend to social cues, selecting the appropriate response to various social situations.

APPLICATIONS

HELPING STUDENTS WITH HYPERLEXIA

Educators are just beginning to recognize that children who enter school diagnosed with hyperlexia need some special attention. Early intervention seems to be the best remedy for improving their comprehension and use of language as well as their social skills. The American Hyperlexia Association recommends the following considerations in designing school programs for hyperlexic children (Kupperman, et al., 2002).

Placement	Although hyperlexic children can spell, decode, and write at much higher levels than their peers, their language comprehension and socialization may preclude them from regular school programs. However, their verbal language skills are the reverse of normal development, and special education teachers need to be adequately trained for this unusual developmental situation.
Educational Goals	Instruction should aim to • Facilitate accommodation to school structure and group learning • Develop language comprehension and expression • Improve social interaction with peers • Develop alternative learning strategies • Address behavioral issues
Classroom Conditions	Classrooms (regular or special) that include hyperlexic students should • Be small so that these students are not overwhelmed with too much peer input • Contain a strong language development component that includes expressive, receptive, and written and oral language activities • Have a structured but not rigid class routine. These children do best when they can anticipate what is happening next and when they get help for schedule changes. • Use a variety of behavioral interventions. Too rigid a behavioral modification system may be frustrating, and these children may not accept behavioral rewards. • Use visual and manipulative materials • Provide opportunities for social interactions with an appropriate peer group • Include opportunities for mainstreaming in areas such as arts, music, athletics, recess, and lunch • Offer the services of speech/language pathologists

HELPING STUDENTS WITH HYPERLEXIA—Continued

Types of Classrooms

KINDERGARTEN

Regular kindergarten: Some hyperlexic children adjust easily to regular kindergarten with supportive services, such as an aide. Adjustment is easier if these students are given both written and verbal instructions, and given individual as well as group directions. Large class size is often a problem.

Developmental kindergarten: Although the smaller class size and more individualized program can be helpful, other children in the class may have difficulties in areas that are strengths for the hyperlexic child (e.g., working on letter recognition or shapes). There also may be too much emphasis on the development of pre-reading skills.

PRIMARY GRADES

Regular Education: This format can work for hyperlexic children who have had early intervention on language and behavioral skills. The regular education teacher and the class need to be prepared for the hyperlexic child. Support services and parent involvement may be necessary.

Communication Disorders Classroom: Because of their strong emphasis on language intervention and academic orientation, these classes are usually appropriate for hyperlexic children. Mainstreaming into regular education is possible, and generally there is enough variety in the peer group to include hyperlexic children with age-appropriate social skills.

Learning Disabilities Classes: Some hyperlexic children succeed in these classes where the academic work is highly individualized. However, because hyperlexic children are quite different from the typical learning-disabled child who has trouble reading, the focus should be on language and socialization issues.

Behavior Disorders and Emotionally Handicapped Classes: These classes are generally inappropriate for hyperlexic children because their behavioral issues are related to their language disorder. As language skills improve, so does the behavior.

9

Putting It All Together

In the preceding chapters, we have discussed the nature of the gifted brain and suggested strategies that can help gifted students succeed in school. We have looked at general giftedness as well as at some of the specific types of giftedness in the areas of language, mathematics, and music. The problem of underachieving and twice-exceptional students was also examined, including specific strategies to meet their atypical needs.

As educators reflect on how to best meet the needs of gifted students, they must do so at a time when changes are occurring in the structure and organization of schools and classrooms. Inclusion policies are returning more students with special needs to the regular education program, and budget cuts are trimming pull-out programs targeted for identified gifted and talented students. Consequently, teachers are now faced with trying to address curriculum standards while dealing with a range of student abilities that is broader than ever. Although resources are available both in and outside the school for gifted students, the regular classroom teacher is most likely to be their primary educator. With that reality in mind, this chapter suggests how teachers can identify gifted students, establish an effective learning environment to meet their needs, and incorporate relevant teaching strategies within the context of the inclusive classroom.

> In today's schools, the regular classroom teacher is likely to be the primary educator of gifted students.

■ IDENTIFYING GIFTED STUDENTS

Because some students do not begin to show their gifts until after entering school, teachers may be the first to recognize potential areas of giftedness. As teachers observe their students, they begin to assess intellectual potential along with other factors, such as emotional and social needs.

Preliminary Assessment for Giftedness

The first indications that a student may be gifted will most likely come from observations of high performance in one or more of the following areas:

- ▸ *General intellectual ability:* Students who have high intelligence test scores, usually two standard deviations above the mean, on individual and group measures.
- ▸ *Specific academic aptitude:* Students who show outstanding performance in a specific area (e.g., language arts, science, or mathematics) and who score above the 95th percentile in achievement tests.
- ▸ *Leadership ability:* Students who can direct individuals or groups to a common decision or action. They can negotiate and adapt in difficult situations.
- ▸ *Creative and productive thinking:* Students who can produce new ideas by bringing together dissimilar or independent elements, and who have the aptitude for developing new meanings that have social value.
- ▸ *Psychomotor ability:* Students who have outstanding motor abilities such as practical, mechanical, spatial, and physical skills.
- ▸ *Visual and performing arts:* Students who demonstrate talent in visual art, dance, music, drama, or related studies.

Follow-Up Assessments

If there is evidence of high intellectual or performance ability, the teacher must determine whether the student is truly gifted. Before submitting the student to a barrage of tests, the teacher should assess the student's capabilities on a number of characteristics that the research literature associates with giftedness.

The Characteristics of Giftedness Scale in the **Applications** section at the end of this chapter identifies 25 characteristics that are common among gifted students. Using this scale may help the teacher make a more valid preliminary judgment about a specific student's abilities (Silverman, Chitwood, and Waters, 1986).

Students who are gifted in the performing arts usually display many of the characteristics of giftedness in addition to their advanced skills in the main area of competence. Thus, the scale can be used to identify students who are talented in different domains. Although these characteristics can distinguish between gifted and average students, they have not been shown to distinguish different levels of giftedness.

Some students who score high on the characteristics scale do not get high scores on tests of achievement. These students may have other problems, such as hearing and vision deficits that impair their classroom participation and depress scores on standardized tests. In this event, it helps to look at the subtest scores to determine areas of strength and weakness. Gifted children often score high on subtests that measure abstract reasoning.

Identifying Minority Students

Minority students continue to be underrepresented in gifted programs. One reason for this situation is not that they are less talented than the other classmates, but that their different experiences, values, and beliefs have prevented them from demonstrating their abilities through the assessment instruments that are commonly used for selection into gifted education programs. These students often do better on nontraditional assessments.

Because the goal of gifted education is inclusivity, not exclusivity, Schwartz (1997) suggests that the following methods be used to identify giftedness so that all students receive fair consideration for gifted education opportunities.

Standardized Tests. More recent standardized tests are designed to reduce cultural bias. They include Mercer's System of Multicultural Pluralistic Assessment, Renzulli and Hartman's Scale for Rating Behavioral Characteristics of Superior Students, and Bruch's Abbreviated Binet for the Disadvantaged.

Observation. Information from parents, educators, and classmates can draw attention to the talents of others. Parents can notice their child's degree of interest in intellectual tasks. Teacher observations allow for the evaluation of a child's development over time. How students use their time, how they solve problems, and what interests them can all be indicators of giftedness. Also, just asking students who is the most helpful among them can turn a teacher's attention to an otherwise unnoticed child.

Self-Identification. Students can sometimes reveal through interest inventories the talents they display in nonschool settings, such as participation in community theater or music groups. They may also describe the type of role they play in the family at home.

Portfolios. Materials in student portfolios often show the learning, progress, and applications of knowledge that these students have made. Also, unlike standardized tests, portfolios permit the assessment of students' creativity. An assessment rubric that has been mutually developed by student and teacher can help to make the evaluation of portfolios easier and more objective.

Educators should ensure that procedures are in place to identify the special talents of students from diverse backgrounds. Moreover, the gifted education programs should reflect and respect their culture and learning styles. Doing so will help these students obtain the enriching educational experiences and materials they need to fully reach their potential.

DEVELOPING THE LEARNING ENVIRONMENT ■

Some teachers deal with a widely heterogeneous class by establishing greater control, reducing flexibility of assignments, and presenting more teacher-centered lessons. Although this approach may work for some students, gifted students need to develop their knowledge and practice their skills in a flexible and secure learning environment that

- Encourages students to use a variety of resources, ideas, tasks, and methods as they pursue learning goals. By having these options, the gifted students can continue to pursue learning objectives on their own while the teacher attends to other students who may need more help in the inclusive classroom.

- Is student-centered and that values and accepts the variety of student interests and learning styles. The more heterogeneous the class, the greater the variety of learning styles among students.

- Encourages students to be open to ideas and initiatives offered by others.

- Allows students to work in a variety of interactive settings, such as individually, in pairs, in small groups, or with students in other classes, as appropriate. Also, using gifted students as mentors for other students can enhance the spirit of learning as a cooperative venture.

● Supports student independence and autonomy within reasonable limits that are mutually set by the students and teacher, where appropriate.

● Is not constrained by subject boundaries or other conventional curricular limitations. Gifted students often have strong interests in specific areas. Look for ways to connect the curriculum to their interests.

● Encourages students to reflect on the processes they use to learn and on the factors that help them to make progress.

■ STRATEGIES FOR THE GIFTED IN THE INCLUSIVE CLASSROOM

Although much research is available on meeting the needs of gifted students in the inclusive classroom, few studies examine the effects of instructional strategies on both gifted and non-gifted students. However, Johnsen and Ryser (1996) describe five areas of differentiation and six strategies that do emerge from those studies that affect the performance of gifted students in regular classrooms. They suggest that teachers need to differentiate by

▸ Modifying curriculum content
▸ Allowing for student preferences
▸ Altering the pace of instruction
▸ Creating a flexible classroom environment
▸ Using specific instructional strategies

The following six strategies have shown to increase critical thinking, creativity, and problem solving abilities:

▸ Posing open-ended questions that require higher-level thinking
▸ Modeling thinking strategies, such as decision making and evaluation
▸ Accepting ideas and suggestions from students and expanding on them
▸ Facilitating independent and original problems and solutions
▸ Helping student identify rules, principles, and relationships
▸ Taking time to explain the nature of errors

Westberg and Archambault (1998) conducted an extensive study on teaching elementary gifted students in inclusive settings and identified the themes and common approaches used by these teachers. The following strategies occurred most frequently:

▶ Establishing high standards for all students in the classroom
▶ Making curriculum modifications to increase the level of challenge
▶ Finding mentors for students in their areas of intense interest
▶ Encouraging independent investigations and projects as often as possible
▶ Creating flexible instructional groups to maintain interest and to keep students engaged

More strategies on specific curriculum topics will be found in the **Application** sections of previous chapters.

WHERE DO WE GO FROM HERE? ■

Researchers and practitioners in gifted education are concerned that gifted students are not being adequately identified or challenged in our schools (Winner, 1996). Parents complain that their children are usually bored and unengaged in school. These students are often underachievers and tend to be highly critical of their teachers, who they feel know less than they do. In many instances, teachers fail to recognize a student as gifted and may think the student is unmotivated or learning disabled. If the student is recognized as gifted, the teacher may have few opportunities to offer curriculum at the appropriate level, and the student may have to learn independently. Surely, we can do better than this.

Why Are We Not Doing More for Gifted Students?

Why are schools not doing more for our most gifted students? In my opinion, several major factors are contributing to the lack of progress.

Budget Constraints

Although some school districts are making valiant efforts to maintain high quality programs for gifted and talented students, the reality is that budget constraints are forcing cutbacks on programs already in place or preventing new programs from getting off the ground. As the number of students with learning disabilities grows, more funds must be shifted to that area, often reducing the amount available for other programs. This "rob Peter to pay Paul" approach is lamentable, but it is still the way most school districts allocate budgetary resources when expenses are rising faster than revenues.

The Egalitarian Compromise

Shifting funds from gifted programs to special education needs is sometimes justified by our need to maintain an egalitarian society. However, we too often see little reason for helping the gifted—presuming that they already have an advantage—and turn our attention primarily to students at the other end of the ability spectrum.

> **The obstacles to doing more for our gifted students are**
> ▸   **Budget constraints**
> ▸   **Egalitarianism**
> ▸   **Anti-intellectualism**

But the truth is that many potentially gifted students come from families who do not have the financial means to provide all the resources necessary to fulfill their child's potential. These parents must rely on the public schools to perform that important task. The notion that "those bright kids don't need more money" is not only wrong, but it undermines the mission of public schools: to help all children fully develop into learned citizens.

Anti-intellectualism

Students with different gifts and talents get a different slice of the educational dollar. Talented athletes and musicians usually have their sports and music activities fully funded and often have plenty of additional opportunities outside of school. Students who are intellectually gifted, on the other hand, usually get placed in a pull-out enrichment program that meets once or twice a week. This is a weak program compared to the opportunities available to the athletically or musically gifted.

Some Considerations for Helping Gifted Students

Intellectual giftedness, of course, runs on a spectrum from mildly to moderately to profoundly gifted. The mildly gifted stay in regular classes because they often fail to meet the minimum scores necessary for selection into the gifted programs. The moderately gifted (usually IQ scores of around 130) can become candidates for gifted programs if other conditions (e.g., teacher recommendations) are met. This group represents the vast majority of the gifted students who participate in gifted education programs. Students who are profoundly gifted (generally with IQ scores of 160 and higher) are not challenged by current public education gifted programs and probably will not find appropriate educational experiences until they reach college.

Are Pull-Out Programs Worth It?

If the reality is that there will be limited funding for gifted education programs in the foreseeable future, then we need to look carefully at how we are spending the money that is available. Although pull-out programs are popular at the elementary level, they allow only a few hours a week of instruction for moderately gifted students. Typically, these classes offer little continuity, rarely allow students to study something

> **The educational benefits of part-time pull-out programs for gifted students are modest at best.**

in depth, and usually offer just one kind of curriculum to all gifted children, no matter where their gifts lie. Research on these programs has shown them to be of modest benefit. In actuality, these classes are not much different from good classes for ordinary children. Students of any ability level would probably benefit from the kinds of open-ended, project-based learning that goes on in the best enrichment classes. So, is this the best way to be spending the limited funds for gifted education?

Are Full-Time Gifted Classes Better?

A few school districts have established full-time gifted classes that include moderate grade skipping. Because the entrance requirement for these classes is typically a score of 130 or higher on an IQ test, these programs serve moderately gifted students. Research studies show that students in these classes do achieve more than equally gifted children who remain in a mixed-ability classroom; the benefits are modest, but better than the part-time pull-out programs. As for grade skipping, studies of moderate skipping show that this kind of acceleration has beneficial effects for students and is not harmful socially or emotionally.

Raising Standards for All

The needs of moderately gifted children can be met not only by the various special programs I have mentioned in this book but also by raising the standards for all children. Numerous research studies have shown that when standards are raised in classrooms, achievement rises for all levels of students, including the brightest. Thus, the ongoing nationwide movement to raise standards for all students may be the single most effective beginning step for improving the educational experience for those who are moderately gifted, provided they also have access to other educationally challenging opportunities.

Winner (1996) believes that another strong piece of evidence that raising standards results in higher achievement levels for all students comes from international comparisons of student achievement. It is well known that American children fare poorly on achievement tests compared with children in most other developed countries in Western Europe and Asia. The only plausible explanation for the higher performance of average students in other countries is that these students are held to higher expectations.

What Do We Do for the Profoundly Gifted?

Programs for gifted students, as currently formatted, do not address the needs of the profoundly gifted. First, these students need to be evaluated in terms of their specific talents rather than by a composite IQ score, which often reveals nothing about a student's unique abilities. Second, school districts should develop fast-paced and intensive courses for these students, either during the school year or in the summer. Many of the talent search programs sponsored by universities suggest model programs to address the needs of these extremely gifted students (see the section on **Resources**). Allocating resources and devising courses for the profoundly gifted need not mean sacrificing the needs of the moderately gifted. For, if we elevate our standards, the moderately gifted also would be appropriately challenged.

> **Schools need to do more to address the needs of profoundly gifted students.**

Teacher Training

Teacher training institutions must recognize that gifted education is the responsibility of all teachers, not just the few who specialize in that particular area. At least some training in gifted education should be provided to undergraduates and graduate students who plan to become professional educators. School administrators, too, must endeavor to ensure that policies on meeting the needs of gifted students are developed and translated into practice within each classroom. Only through our concerted efforts will we be certain that our schools are doing their best to meet the needs of our brightest students.

CONCLUSION ■

Neuroscientists are continually probing the human brain to discover the mechanisms and networks that allow it to carry out its many functions. They are exploring concepts as diverse as intuition, psychic phenomena, mind-body connections, and how the brain manages the information that creates consciousness. Surely the revelations that are to come will offer a deeper understanding of how the brain learns so that we can be more successful in helping all our children reach their fullest potential.

APPLICATIONS

THE CHARACTERISTICS OF GIFTEDNESS SCALE

The following scale may help the teacher make a more valid preliminary judgment about a specific student's abilities. Research studies conducted in the 1980s identified 25 characteristics of gifted individuals (Silverman, Chitwood, and Waters, 1986). More recent experimental and clinical studies continue to support these characteristics.

Guidelines:

- On this scale, the teacher should rate each characteristic by circling a number from 1 to 5 that best describes how often that characteristic is evident. The scale is just a guide and is by no means a definitive measure of giftedness. However, if the teacher scores the student at the 4 or 5 end of the scale on more than half of the characteristics, further assessment is warranted.

- Students gifted in the performing arts usually display many of the characteristics of giftedness on this scale in addition to their advanced skills in the main area of competence. Thus, the scale can be used to identify students who are talented in different domains.

- Although these characteristics can distinguish between gifted and average students, they have not been shown to distinguish different levels of giftedness.

- Students who score high on the characteristics scale but who do not get high scores on tests of achievement may have other problems, such as hearing and vision deficits that impair their classroom participation and depress scores on standardized tests. In this case, look at the subtest scores to determine areas of strength and weakness.

THE CHARACTERISTICS OF GIFTEDNESS SCALE—Continued

CHARACTERISTICS OF GIFTEDNESS (Adapted from Silverman, Chitwood, and Waters, 1986)	
Compared to other students in the class, this student...	Seldom Occasionally Often
1. Has a longer attention span.	1 ----- 2 ----- 3 ----- 4 ----- 5
2. Displays an excellent memory.	1 ----- 2 ----- 3 ----- 4 ----- 5
3. Has keen powers of observation.	1 ----- 2 ----- 3 ----- 4 ----- 5
4. Displays ability with numbers.	1 ----- 2 ----- 3 ----- 4 ----- 5
5. Perseveres, when interested.	1 ----- 2- ---- 3 ----- 4 ----- 5
6. Is concerned with justice and fairness.	1 ----- 2 ----- 3 ----- 4 ----- 5
7. Shows high intensity in studies.	1 ----- 2 ----- 3 ----- 4 ----- 5
8. Has a wide range of interests.	1 ----- 2 ----- 3 ----- 4 ----- 5
9. Uses an extensive vocabulary.	1 ----- 2 ----- 3 ----- 4 ----- 5
10. Displays personal sensitivity.	1 ----- 2 ----- 3 ----- 4 ----- 5
11. Shows a high degree of creativity.	1 ----- 2 ----- 3 ----- 4 ----- 5
12. Tends to be a perfectionist.	1 ----- 2 ----- 3 ----- 4 ----- 5
13. Has a preference for older companions.	1 ----- 2 ----- 3 ----- 4 ----- 5
14. Is good at jigsaw puzzles.	1 ----- 2 ----- 3 ----- 4 ----- 5
15. Has good problem solving and reasoning abilities.	1 ----- 2 ----- 3 ----- 4 ----- 5
16. Displays a vivid imagination.	1 ----- 2 ----- 3 ----- 4 ----- 5
17. Shows compassion for others.	1 ----- 2 ----- 3 ----- 4 ----- 5
18. Makes judgments mature for age.	1 ----- 2 ----- 3 ----- 4 ----- 5
19. Has an excellent sense of humor.	1 ----- 2 ----- 3 ----- 4 ----- 5
20. Demonstrates unusual curiosity.	1 ----- 2 ----- 3 ----- 4 ----- 5
21. Has high degree of energy.	1 ----- 2 ----- 3 ----- 4 ----- 5
22. Shows early or avid reading ability.	1 ----- 2 ----- 3 ----- 4 ----- 5
23. Tends to question authority.	1 ----- 2 ----- 3 ----- 4 ----- 5
24. Demonstrates moral sensitivity.	1 ----- 2 ----- 3 ----- 4 ----- 5
25. Appears to learn rapidly.	1 ----- 2 ----- 3 ----- 4 ----- 5

Glossary

Acceleration. Presenting information at a fast pace that corresponds more closely to the pace at which gifted students learn.

Adaptive decision making. The process of solving a problem that has multiple solutions depending on the context and priorities of the moment, as in, "What gift should I buy for my nephew's birthday?"

Alphabetic principle. The notion that written words are composed of letters of the alphabet that intentionally and systematically represent segments of spoken words.

Amygdala. The almond-shaped structure in the brain's limbic system that encodes emotional messages to long-term storage.

Angular gyrus. A brain structure that decodes visual information about words so they can be matched to their meanings.

Asperger's syndrome. A developmental disorder also known as high functioning autism because people with the disorder generally display higher mental performance.

Attention-deficit hyperactivity disorder (ADHD). A syndrome that interferes with an individual's capacity to regulate activity level, inhibit behavior, and attend to tasks in developmentally appropriate ways.

Autism. A spectrum disorder that affects an individual's ability to communicate, form relationships with others, and relate appropriately to the environment.

Axon. The neuron's long and unbranched fiber that carries impulses away from the cell to the next neuron.

Bloom's Taxonomy of the Cognitive Domain. A model developed by Benjamin Bloom in the 1950s for classifying the complexity of human thought into six levels.

Brain stem. One of the major parts of the brain, it receives sensory input and monitors vital functions such as heartbeat, body temperature, and digestion.

Broca's area. A region in the left frontal lobe of the brain believed responsible for generating the vocabulary and syntax of an individual's native language.

Cerebellum. One of the major parts of the brain, it coordinates muscle movement.

Cerebrum. The largest of the major parts of the brain, it controls sensory interpretation, thinking, and memory.

Chunking. The ability of the brain to perceive a coherent group of items as a single item or chunk.

Compacting. Eliminating drill and repetitious material from the curriculum so that gifted students can move on to more challenging material.

Computerized tomography (CT, formerly CAT) scanner. An instrument that uses X-rays and computer processing to produce a detailed cross-section of brain structure.

Constructivism. This theory of learning states that active learners use past experiences and chunking to construct sense and meaning from new learning, thereby building larger conceptual schemes.

Corpus callosum. The bridge of nerve fibers that connects the left and right cerebral hemispheres and allows communication between them.

Cortex. The thin but tough layer of cells covering the cerebrum that contains all the neurons used for cognitive and motor processing.

Dendrite. The branched extension from the cell body of a neuron that receives impulses from nearby neurons through synaptic contacts.

Electroencephalograph (EEG). An instrument that charts fluctuations in the brain's electrical activity via electrodes attached to the scalp.

Frontal lobe. The front part of the brain that monitors higher-order thinking, directs problem solving, and regulates the excesses of the emotional (limbic) system.

Functional magnetic resonance imaging (fMRI). An instrument that measures blood flow to the brain to record areas of high and low neuronal activity.

Glial cells. Special "glue" cells in the brain that surround each neuron providing support, protection, and nourishment.

Gray matter. The thin but tough covering of the brain's cerebrum also known as the cerebral cortex.

Hemisphericity. The notion that the two cerebral hemispheres are specialized and process information differently.

Hippocampus. A brain structure that compares new learning to past learning and encodes information from working memory to long-term storage.

Hyperlexia. A term describing children who have precocious reading skills but who also have significant problems with learning and language.

Imagery. The mental visualization of objects, events, and arrays.

Immediate memory. A temporary memory where information is processed briefly (in seconds) and subconsciously, then either blocked or passed on to working memory.

Inclusion. Grouping students into a regular classroom without regard to ability.

Limbic system. The structures at the base of the cerebrum that control emotions.

Long-term storage. The areas of the cerebrum where memories are stored permanently.

Magnetic resonance imaging (MRI). An instrument that uses radio waves to disturb the alignment of the body's atoms in a magnetic field to produce computer-processed, high-contrast images of internal structures.

Motor cortex. The narrow band across the top of the brain from ear to ear that controls movement.

Myelin. A fatty substance that surrounds and insulates a neuron's axon.

Neuron. The basic cell making up the brain and nervous system, consisting of a globular cell body, a long fiber called an axon which transmits impulses, and many shorter fibers called dendrites which receive them.

Neurotransmitter. One of nearly 100 chemicals stored in axon sacs that transmit impulses from neuron to neuron across the synaptic gap.

Phonemes. The smallest units of sound in a language that combine to make syllables.

Positron emission tomography (PET) scanner. An instrument that traces the metabolism of radioactively tagged sugar in brain tissue producing a color image of cell activity.

Prefrontal cortex. The foremost part of the brain's frontal lobes, responsible for coordinating all cognitive and executive functions.

Prodigy. A child of high intelligence who is able to perform a specific skill at an adult level of competence, and is aware of thinking strategies.

Rehearsal. The reprocessing of information in working memory.

Retention. The preservation of a learning in long-term storage in such a way that it can be identified and recalled quickly and accurately.

Reticular activating system (RAS). The dense formation of neurons in the brain stem that controls major body functions and maintains the brain's alertness.

Savant. An individual with an exception ability to perform a specific skill, usually artistic, musical, or mathematical, but who often displays flat emotions and is unaware of thinking strategies.

Self-concept. Our perception of who we are and how we fit into the world.

Synapse. The microscopic gap between the axon of one neuron and the dendrite of another.

Thalamus. A part of the limbic system that receives all incoming sensory information, except smell, and shunts it to other areas of the cortex for additional processing.

Twice-Exceptional. A term used to describe gifted individuals who also have a learning disability.

Underachievement. A significant difference between an individual's ability and performance.

Veridical decision making. The process of solving a problem that has only one correct answer, as in, "What is my dentist's telephone number?"

Wernicke's area. A section in the left temporal lobe of the brain believed responsible for generating sense and meaning in an individual's native language.

White matter. The support tissue that lies beneath the cerebrum's gray matter (cortex).

Working memory. The temporary memory wherein information is processed consciously.

References

Achor, T., and Tarr, A. (1996, Spring). *Underachieving gifted students*. Arlington, VA: ERIC Clearinghouse on Disabilities and Gifted Children.

Adams, K. (1990). *Examining black underrepresentation in gifted programs*. Arlington, VA: ERIC Clearinghouse on Disabilities and Gifted Children.

Alexander, J., Carr, M., and Schwanenflugel, P. (1995). Development of metacognition in gifted children. *Developmental Review, 15*, 1-37.

Alexander, J. E., O'Boyle, M. W., and Benbow, C. P. (1996, August-September). Developmentally advanced EEG alpha power in gifted male and female adolescents. *International Journal of Psychophysiology, 23*, 25-31.

Amend, E. R. (2000). *Misdiagnosis of Asperger's disorder in gifted youth*. In Webb, J. T. (2000, August 7) *Mis-diagnosis and dual diagnosis of gifted children: Gifted and LD, ADHD, OCD, Oppositional Defiant Disorder*. Paper presented at the annual convention of the American Psychological Association, Washington, DC, August 7, 2000.

American Psychiatric Association (APA). (2000). *Diagnostic and Statistical Manual of Mental Disorders*, Fourth Edition, Text Revision (DSM-IV). Washington, DC: American Psychiatric Publishing Group.

Barnhill, C. (2001, May). What's new in AS research: A synthesis of research conducted by the Asperger syndrome project. *Intervention in School and Clinic, 36*, 300-305.

Baron-Cohen, S., and Hammer, J. (1997). Parents of children with Asperger's syndrome: What is the cognitive phenotype? *Journal of Cognitive Neuroscience, 9*, 548-554.

Baum, S. (1994). Meeting the needs of gifted/learning disabled students. *The Journal of Secondary Gifted Education, 5*, 6-16.

Bauer, S. (1996). Asperger syndrome. *Online Asperger Syndrome Information and Support* [Online]. Available at http://www.udel.edu/bkirby/asperger.

Beatty, J. (2001). *The human brain: Essentials of behavioral neuroscience.* Thousand Oaks, CA: Sage Publications.

Benbow, C. P., and Stanley, J. C. (1983). Sex differences in mathematical reasoning ability: More facts. *Science, 222*, 1029-31.

Bernal, E. M. (2002). Three ways to achieve a more equitable representation of culturally and linguistically different students in GT programs. *Roeper Review, 24*, 82-88.

Berns, G. S., Cohen, J. D., and Mintun, M. A. (1997). Brain regions responsive to novelty in the absence of awareness. *Science, 276*, 1272-1275.

Bischoff-Grethe, A., Proper, S. M., Mao, H., Daniels, K. A., and Berns, G. S. (2000). Conscious and unconscious processing of nonverbal predictability in Wernicke's area. *Journal of Neuroscience, 20*, 1975-81.

Blanton, R. E., Levitt, J. G., Thompson, P. M., Narr, K. L., Capetillo-Cunliffe, L., Nobel, A., Singerman, J. D., McCracken, J. T., and Toga, A. W. (2001, July). Mapping cortical asymmetry and complexity patterns in normal children. *Psychiatry Research, 107*, 29-43.

Bloom, B. S. (1956). *Taxonomy of educational objectives (cognitive domain).* New York: Longman.

Bock, M. (2001, May). SODA strategy: Enhancing the social interaction skills of youngsters with Asperger's syndrome. *Intervention in School and Clinic, 36*, 272-278.

Buckner, R. L., Kelley, W. M., and Petersen, S. E. (1999, April). Frontal cortex contributions to human memory formation. *Nature Neuroscience, 2*, 311-314.

Buescher, T. M., and Higham, S. (1990). *Helping adolescents adjust to giftedness.* Arlington, VA: ERIC Clearinghouse on Disabilities and Gifted Education.

Burruss, J. D. (1999). Problem-based learning. *Science Scope, 22*, 46-49.

Cappelletti, M., Waley-Cohen, H., Butterworth, B., and Kopelman, M. (2000). A selective loss of the ability to read and write music. *Neurocase, 6*, 332-341.

Carr, M., Alexander, J., Schwanenflugel, P. (1996). Where gifted children do and do not excel on metacognitive tasks. *Roeper Review, 18*, 212-217.

Carter, R. (1999, September 10). Tune in turn off. *New Scientist, 164*, 30-35.

Cash, A. B. (1999, September). A profile of gifted individuals with autism: The twice-exceptional learner. *Roeper Review, 22*, 22-27.

Ceci, S. (2001, July/August). Intelligence: The surprising truth. *Psychology Today,* 46-53.

Chiang, W. C., and Wynn, K. (2000) Infants' tracking of objects and collections. *Cognition, 77*, 169-195.

Chochon, F., Cohen, L., van der Moortele, P. F., and Dehaene, S. (1999). Differential contributions of the left and right inferior parietal lobules to number processing. *Journal of Cognitive Neuroscience, 11*, 617-630.

Clark, G., and Zimmerman, E. (1998). Nurturing the arts in programs for gifted and talented students. *Phi Delta Kappan, 79*, 747-751.

Cline, S., and Hegeman, K. (2001, Summer). Gifted children with disabilities. *Gifted Child Today, 24*, 16-24.

Cobine, G. (1995). *Effective use of student journal writing.* Bloomington, IN: Indiana University, ERIC Clearing House on Reading, English, and Communication.

Cunningham, C. M., Callahan, C. M., Plucker, J. A., Roberson, S. C., and Rapkin, A. (1998). Identifying Hispanic students of outstanding talent: Psychometric integrity of a peer nomination form. *Exceptional Children, 64*, 197-209.

Dapretto, M., and Bookheimer, S. Y. (1999). Form and content: Dissociating syntax and semantics in sentence comprehension. *Neuron, 2*, 427.

Dehaene, S., Spelke, E., Pinel, P., Stanescu, R., and Tsivkin, S. (1999, May 7). Sources of mathematical thinking: Behavioral and brain-imaging evidence. *Science, 284*, 970-974.

Dehaene-Lambertz, G. (2000). Cerebral specialization for speech and non-speech stimuli in infants. *Journal of Cognitive Neuroscience, 12*, 449-460.

Delisle, I. (1996). Multiple intelligences: Convenient, simple, wrong. *Gifted Child Today Magazine, 19*, 12-13.

Delisle, J. R., and Berger, S. L. (1990). *Underachieving gifted students.* Arlington, VA: ERIC Clearinghouse on Disabilities and Gifted Education.

Dix, J., and Schafer, S. (1996). From paradox to performance: Practical strategies for identifying and teaching GT/LD students. *Gifted Child Today, 19*, 22-25, 28-31.

Elbert, T., Pantev, C., Weinbruch, C., Rockstrub, B., and Taub, E. (1995). Increased cortical representation of the fingers of the left hand in string players. *Science, 270*, 305-307.

Engle, R. W., Laughlin, J. E., Tuholski, S. W., and Conway, R. A. (1999, September). Working memory, short-term memory, and general fluid intelligence: a latent-variable approach. *Journal of Experimental Psychology, 128*, 309-331.

Field, T., Harding, J., Yando, R., Gonzales, K., Lasko, D., Bendell, D., and Marks, C. (1998, Summer). Feelings and attitudes of gifted students. *Adolescence, 33*, 331-342.

Ford, D. Y. (1995). *A study of achievement and underachievement among gifted, potentially gifted, and average African-American students* (Research Monograph 95128). Storrs, CT: University of Connecticut, The National Research Center on the Gifted and Talented.

Ford, D. Y. (1996). *Reversing underachievement among gifted black students: Promising practices and programs*. New York: Teachers College Press.

Ford, D. Y., and Thomas, A. (1997, June). *Underachievement among gifted minority students: Problems and promises*. Arlington, VA: ERIC Clearinghouse on Disabilities and Gifted Children.

Francis, R., and Underhill, R. G. (1996). A procedure for integrating math and science. *School Science and Mathematics, 96*, 114-119.

Frasier, M. and Passow, A. H. (1994) *Toward a new paradigm for identifying talent potential*. Storrs, CT: University of Connecticut, National Research Center on the Gifted and Talented.

Frederikse, M. E., Lu, A., Aylward, E., Barta, P., and Pearlson, G. (1999, December). Sex differences in the inferior parietal lobule. *Cerebral Cortex, 9*, 896-901.

Gagne, F. (1985). Giftedness and talent: Reexamining a reexamination of the definitions. *Gifted Child Quarterly, 29*, 103-112.

Galuske, R. A. W., Schlote, W., Bratzke, H., and Singer, W. (2000). Interhemispheric asymmetries of the modular structure in human temporal cortex. *Science, 289*, 1946-1949.

Gamoran, A., Nystrand, M., Berends, M., and LePore, P. C. (1995, Winter). An organizational analysis of the effects of ability grouping. *American Educational Research Journal, 32*, 687-715.

Gardner, H. (1983). *Frames of mind: The theory of multiple intelligences.* New York: Basic Books.

Gentry, M, and Kettle, K. (1998, Winter). Distinguishing myths from realities: NRC/GT research. *National Research Center on the Gifted and Talented Newsletter.*

Gilger, J. W., Ho, H., Whipple, A. D., and Spitz, R. (2001). Genotype-environment correlations for language-related abilities. *Journal of Learning Disabilities, 34*, 492-502.

Glass, G. V., McGaw, B., and Smith, M.L. (1981). *Meta-analysis in social research.* Beverly Hills, CA: Sage.

Glassman, R. B. (1999). Hypothesized neural dynamics of working memory: Several   chunks might be marked simultaneously by harmonic frequencies within an octave band of brain waves. *Brain Research Bulletin, 50*, 77-93.

Gohm, C. L., Humphreys, L. G., and Yao, G. (1998, Fall). Underachievement among spatially gifted students. *American Educational Research Journal, 35*, 515-531.

Goldberg, E. (2001). *The executive brain: Frontal lobes and the civilized mind.* New York: Oxford University Press.

Goleman, D. (1995). *Emotional intelligence: Why it can matter more than I.Q.* New York: Bantam Books.

Gollub, J. P., Bertenthal, M. W., Labov, J. B., and Curtis, P. C. (Eds.). (2002). *Learning and understanding: Improving advanced study of mathematics and science in U.S. high schools.* Washington, DC: National Academy Press.

González, M. A., Campos, A., and Pérez, M. J. (1997). Mental imagery and creative thinking. *Journal of Psychology, 13*, 357-364.

Gregersen, P. K., (1998). Instant recognition: The genetics of pitch perception. *American Journal of Human Genetics, 62*, 221-223.

Grigorenko, E. L. and Sternberg, R. J. (1997, Spring). Styles of thinking, abilities, and academic performance. *Exceptional Children, 63*, 295-312.

Gur, R. C., Turetsky, B. I., Matsui, M., Yan, M., Bilker, W., Hughett, P., and Gur, R. E. (1999, May 15). Sex differences in brain gray matter and white matter in healthy young adults: Correlations with cognitive performance. *Journal of Neuroscience, 19*, 4065-4072.

Halsted, J. W. (1990). *Guiding the gifted reader.* Arlington, VA: ERIC Clearinghouse on Disabilities and Gifted Education.

Haroutounian, J. (2000). The delights and dilemmas of the musically talented teenager. *Journal of Secondary Gifted Education, 12*, 3-14.

Henderson, L. M. (2001, Summer). Asperger's syndrome in gifted individuals. *Gifted Child Today, 24*, 28-35.

Henson, R., Shallice, T., and Dolan, R. (2000). Neuroimaging evidence for dissociable forms of repetition priming. *Science, 287*, 1269-1272.

Hittmair-Delazer, M., Semenza, C., and Denes, G. (1994). Concepts and facts in calculation. *Brain, 117*, 715-728.

Hoeflinger, M. (1998, May-June). Mathematics and science in gifted education: Developing mathematically promising students. *Roeper Review, 20*, 224-227.

Howe, R., Davidson, J., and Sloboda, J. (1998). Innate talents: Reality or myth? *The Behavioral and Brain Sciences, 21*, 399-407.

Itoh, K., Fujii, Y., Suzuki, K., and Nakada, T. (2001). Asymmetry of parietal lobe activation during piano performance: A high field functional magnetic resonance imaging study. *Neuroscience Letters, 309*, 41-44.

Jausovec, N. (2000, September). Differences in cognitive processes between gifted, intelligent, creative, and average individuals while solving complex problems: An EEG study. *Intelligence, 28*, 213-240.

Johnsen, S. K., and Ryser, G. R. (1996). An overview of effective practices with gifted students in general-education settings. *Journal of Education for the Gifted, 19*, 379-404.

Johnson, D. T. (2000, April). *Teaching mathematics to gifted students in a mixed-ability classroom.* Arlington, VA: ERIC Clearinghouse on Disabilities and Gifted Education.

Kalchman, M., and Case, R. (1999). Diversifying the curriculum in a mathematics classroom streamed for high-ability learners: A necessity unassumed. *School Science and Mathematics, 99*, 320-329.

Kenny, D. A., Archambault, F. X., and Hallmark, B. W. (1994). *The effects of group composition on gifted and non-gifted elementary students in cooperative learning groups.* Storrs, CT: University of Connecticut, the National Research Center on the Gifted and Talented.

Koelsch, S., Gunter, T., and Friederici, A. D. (2000). Brain indices of music processing: "Nonmusicians" are musical. *Journal of Cognitive Neuroscience, 12*, 520-541.

Kupperman, P., Bligh, S., Barouski, K. (2002). Hyperlexia. *Center for Speech and Language Disorders* [Online]. Available at http://www.csld.org.

Lando, B. Z., and Schneider, B. H. (1997). Intellectual contributions and mutual support among developmentally advanced children in homogeneous and heterogeneous work discussion groups. *Gifted Child Quarterly, 41*, 44-57.

Leahey, E., and Guo, G. (2001). Gender differences in mathematical trajectories. *Social Forces, 80*, 713-732.

LeDoux, J. E. (2002). Emotions, memory and the brain. *Scientific American, 12*, 62-71.

Lovecky, D. V. (1999, October). *Gifted children with AD/HD*. Arlington, VA: ERIC Clearinghouse on Disabilities and Gifted Children.

Martin, A., Wiggs, C. L., and Weisberg, J. (1997). Modulation of human medial temporal lobe activity by form, meaning, and experience. *Hippocampus, 7*, 587-593.

Masataka, N. (1999). Preference for infant-directed singing in 2-year-old hearing infants of deaf parents. *Developmental Psychology, 35*, 1001-1005.

Mayseless, O. (1993). Gifted adolescents and intimacy in close same-sex relationships. *Journal of Youth and Adolescence, 22*, 135-46.

McEachern, A. G., and Bornot, J. (2001, October). Gifted students with learning disabilities: Implications and strategies for school counselors. *Professional School Counseling, 3*, 34-41.

M.I.N.D. Institute. (2002, January). Major strides toward math literacy. *M.I.N.D. Newsletter, 1*, 1-11.

Milius, S. (2001). Face the music: Why are we such a musical species—and does it matter? *Natural History, 110*, 48-58.

Mingus, T. T. Y., and Grassi, R. M. (1999). What constitutes a nurturing environment for the growth of mathematically gifted students? *School Science and Mathematics, 99*, 286-293.

Miyake, A., Friedman, N. P., Rettinger, D. A., Shah, P., and Hegarty, M. (2001, December). How are visuospatial working memory, executive functioning, and spatial abilities related? A latent-variable analysis. *Journal of Experimental Psychology, 130*, 621-640.

Mueller, C. M., and Dweck, C. S. (1998). Praise for intelligence can undermine children's motivation and performance. *Journal of Personality and Social Psychology, 75*.

National Association for Gifted Children (NAGC). (1998). *Pre-K-Grade 12 gifted program standards*. Washington, DC: Author.

National Center for Education Statistics (NCES). (1999). *Highlights from the Third International Mathematics and Science Study (TIMSS): Overview and key findings across grade levels*. Washington, DC: Author.

National Center for Education Statistics (NCES). (2001). *Highlights from the Third International Mathematics and Science Study-Repeat (TIMSS-R)*. Washington, DC: Author.

Nielsen, M. E., and Morton-Albert, S. (1989). The effects of special education on the self-concept and school attitude of learning-disabled/gifted students. *Roeper Review, 12,*29-36.

Ohnishi, T., Matsuda, H., Asada, T., Aruga, M., Hirakata, M., Nishikawa, M., Katoh, A., and Imabayashi, E. (2001). Functional anatomy of musical perception in musicians. *Cerebral Cortex, 11*, 754-760.

Oktem, F., Diren, B., Karaagaoglu, E., and Anlar, B. (2001, April). Functional magnetic resonance imaging in children with Asperger's syndrome. *Journal of Child Neurology, 16*, 253-256.

Olszewski-Kubilius, P. (1998). Talent search: Purposes, rational, and role in gifted education. *Journal of Secondary Gifted Education, 9*, 106-113.

Pallas, A. M., Entwisle, D. R., Alexander, K. L., and Stluka, M. F. (1994, January). Ability-group effects: Instructional, social, or institutional? *Sociology of Education, 67*, 27-46.

Pantev, C., Oostenveld, R., Engelien, A., Ross, B., Roberts, L. E., and Hoke, M. (1998, April 23). Increased auditory cortical representation. *Nature, 392*, 811-813.

Pascual-Leone, A., Dang, N., Cohen, L., Brasil-Neto, J., Cammarota, A., and Hallett, M. (1995). Modulation of muscle responses evoked by transcranial magnetic stimulation during the acquisition of new fine motor skills. *Journal of Neurophysiology, 74*, 1037-1045.

Persky, H. R., Sandene, B. A., and Askew, J. M. (1999). *The NAEP 1997 Arts Report Card*. Washington, DC: National Center for Education Statistics.

Powell, T., and Siegle, D. (2000, Spring). Teacher bias in identifying gifted and talented students. *National Research Center on the Gifted and Talented Newsletter*, 13-15.

Purves, D. (Ed.). (2001). *Neuroscience,* (2nd ed.). Sunderland, MA: Sinauer.

Reis, S. M., Burns, D. E., and Renzulli, J. S. (1992a). *Curriculum compacting: The complete guide to modifying the regular curriculum for high ability students*. Mansfield Center, CT: Creative Learning Press.

Reis, S. M., Burns, D. E., and Renzulli, J. S. (1992b). *A facilitator's guide to help teachers compact curriculum*. Storrs, CT: University of Connecticut, The National Research Center on the Gifted and Talented.

Reis, S. M., Hébert, T. P., Díaz, E. I., Maxfield, L. R., and Ratley, M. E. (1995). *Case studies of talented students who achieve and underachieve in an urban high school* (Research Monograph 95120). Storrs, CT: University of Connecticut, The National Research Center on the Gifted and Talented.

Reis, S. M., Westberg, K. L., Kulikowich, J. M., and Purcell, J. H. (1998, Spring). Curriculum compacting and achievement test scores: What does the research say? *Gifted Child Quarterly, 42*, 123-129.

Renzulli, J. (1978). What makes giftedness? Reexamining a definition. *Phi Beta Kappan, 60*, 180-184, 261.

Renzulli, J. (1986). The three-ring conception of giftedness: A developmental model for creative productivity. In Sternberg, R. J., and Davidson, E. (Eds.), *Conceptions of giftedness* (53-92). New York: Cambridge University Press.

Restak, R. M. (2001). *The secret life of the brain*. Washington, DC: John Henry Press.

Rhodes, L. (1992). Focusing attention on the individual in identification of gifted black students. *Roeper Review, 14*, 108-110.

Rimm, S. B. (1996). *Dr. Sylvia Rimm's smart parenting: How to raise a happy achieving child*. New York: Crown Publishers.

Rittle-Johnson, B., and Alibali, M. W. (1999). Conceptual and procedural knowledge of mathematics: Does one lead to the other? *Journal of Educational Psychology, 91*, 175.

Rivera, D. B., Murdock, J., and Sexton, D. (1995). Serving the gifted/learning disabled. *Gifted Child Today, 18*, 34-37.

Robinson, A. and Clinkenbeard, P. R. (1998, August). Giftedness: An exceptionality examines. *Annual Review of Psychology, 49*, 117-139.

Rodgers, J. L., Cleveland, H. H., van den Oord, E., and Rowe, D. C. (2000, June). Resolving the debate over birth order, family size, and intelligence. *American Psychologist, 55*, 599-612.

Rogers, K. B. (1998). Using current research to make "good" decisions about grouping. *NASSP Bulletin, 82,* 38-46. Research data is also available online at http://www.educ.state.mn.us/gifted.

Rotigel, J. V., and Lupkowski-Shoplik, A. (1999). Using talent searches to identify and meet the educational needs of mathematically gifted youngsters. *School Science and Mathematics, 99,* 330-337.

Scarr, S., and McCartney, K. (1983). How people make their own environments. *Child Development, 54,* 424-435.

Schacter, D. L. (2001). *The seven sins of memory: How the mind forgets and remembers.* New York: Houghton Mifflin.

Schlaug, G., Jancke, L., Huang, Y., and Steinmetz, H. (1995). In vivo evidence of structural brain asymmetry in musicians. *Science, 267,* 699-701.

Schlaug, G., and Christian, G. (2001, May 8). *Musical training during childhood may influence regional brain growth.* Paper presented at the 53rd Annual Meeting of the American Academy of Neurology, Philadelphia.

Schwartz, W. (1997, May). Strategies for identifying the talents of diverse students. *ERIC Clearinghouse on Urban Education Digest, 122,* 1-6.

Shadmehr, R. and Holcomb, H. H. (1997). Neural correlates of motor memory consolidation. *Science, 277,* 821-825.

Shaywitz, B. A., Shaywitz, S. E., and Gore, J. (1995). Sex differences in the functional organization of the brain for language. *Nature, 373,* 607-609.

Shaywitz, S. E., Holahan, J. M., Fletcher, J. M., Freudenheim, D. A., Makuch, R. W., and Shaywitz, B. A. (2001, Winter). Heterogeneity within the gifted: Higher IQ boys exhibit behaviors resembling boys with learning disabilities. *Gifted Child Quarterly, 45,* 16-23.

Shore, B. M., and Delcourt, M. A. B. (1996). Effective curricular and program practices in gifted education and the interface with general education. *Journal of Education for the Gifted, 20,* 138-154.

Silverman, L. K. (1989a). Invisible gifts, invisible handicaps. *Roeper Review, 12,* 37-42.

Silverman, L. K. (1989b). The visual-spatial learner. *Preventing School Failure, 34,* 15-20.

Silverman, L. K. (1993). *Counseling the gifted and talented.* Denver: Love Publishing.

Silverman, L. K., Chitwood, D. G., and Waters, J. L. (1986). Young gifted children: Can parents identify giftedness? *Topics in Early Childhood Education, 6*, 23-38.

Sloboda, J. A., Davidson, J. W., Howe, M. J. A., and Moore, D. G. (1996). The role of practice in the development of performing musicians. *British Journal of Psychology, 87*, 287-309.

Smutny, J. F. (2000, May). *Teaching young gifted children in the regular classroom*. Arlington, VA: ERIC Clearinghouse on Disabilities and Gifted Children.

Smutny, J. F. (2001, June). *Creative strategies for teaching language arts to gifted students (K-8)*. Arlington, VA: ERIC Clearinghouse on Disabilities and Gifted Children.

Sousa, D. A. (2001a). *How the brain learns*, (2nd ed.). Thousand Oaks, CA: Corwin Press.

Sousa, D. A. (2001b). *How the special needs brain learns*. Thousand Oaks, CA: Corwin Press.

Southern, W. T., Jones, E. D., and Stanley, J. C. (1993). Acceleration and enrichment: The context and development of program options. In Heller, K. A., Monks, F. J., and Passow, A. H. (Eds.), *International handbook of research and development of giftedness and talent* (387-409). Oxford: Pergamon.

Sowell, E. R., Thompson, P. M., Holmes, C. J., Jernigan, T. L., and Toga, A. W. (1999). In-vivo evidence for post-adolescent brain maturation in frontal and striatal regions. *Nature: Neuroscience, 2*, 859–861.

Squire, L. R. and Kandel, E. R. (1999). *Memory: From mind to molecules*. New York: W. H. Freeman.

Sternberg, R. J. (1985). *Beyond IQ: A triarchic theory of human intelligence*. New York: Cambridge University Press.

Sternberg, R. J. (2000, December). Identifying and developing creative giftedness. *Roeper Review, 23*, 60-64.

Sternberg, R. J. and Zhang, L. (1995, September). What do we mean by giftedness? A pentagonal implicit theory. *Gifted Child Quarterly, 39*, 88-94

Sternberg, R. J., Ferrari, M., Clinkenbeard, P. R., and Grigorenko, E. L. (1996). Identification, instruction, and assessment of gifted children: A construct validation of a triarchic model. *Gifted Child Quarterly, 40*, 129-137.

Sternberg, R. J., Grigorenko, E. L., Jarvin, L., Clinkenbeard, P., Ferrari, M., and Torfi, B. (2000, Spring). The effectiveness of triarchic teaching and assessment. *National Research Center on the Gifted and Talented Newsletter,* 3-8.

Stewart, L., and Walsh, V. (2001). Music of the hemispheres. *Current Biology, 11,* R125- R127.

Swiatek, M. A. (1995). An empirical investigation of the social coping strategies used by gifted adolescents. *Gifted Child Quarterly, 39,* 154-160.

Sytsma, R. E. (2001, November). *Gifted education in America's high schools: National survey results.* Paper presented at the meeting of the National Association for Gifted Children, Cincinnati, OH.

Thompson, M. (1999). Developing verbal talent. *Center for Talent Development* [Online]. See http://www.ctd.northwestern.edu/.

Thompson, P. M., Cannon, T.D., Narr, K. L., van Erp, T., Poutanen, V., Huttanen, M., Lönnqvist, J., Standertskjöld-Nordenstam, C., Kaprio, J., Khaledy, M., Dail, R., Zoumalen, C., and Toga, A. (2001, December 1). Genetic influences on brain structure. *Nature Neuroscience, 4,* 1253-1258.

Tomlinson, C. A. (1995). *How to differentiate instruction in mixed-ability classrooms.* Alexandria, VA: Association for Supervision and Curriculum Development.

Tomlinson, C. A. (1999). *The differentiated classroom: Responding to the needs of all learners.* Alexandria, VA: Association for Supervision and Curriculum Development.

Toll, M. F. (1993). Gifted learning disabled: A kaleidoscope of needs. *Gifted Child Today, 16,* 34-35.

Treffert, D. A. (2000a). *Extraordinary people: Understanding savant syndrome.* Lincoln, NE: iUniverse Press.

Treffert, D. A. (2000b). The savant syndrome in autism. In Accardo, P., Magnusen, C., and Capute, A. (Eds.). *Autism: Clinical and research issues.* Baltimore: York Press.

Tremblay, T., and Gagné, F. (2001). Beliefs of students talented in academics, music, and dance concerning the heritability of human abilities in these fields. *Roeper Review,23,* 173-177.

Tuholski, S. W., Engle, R. W., and Baylis, G. C. (2001, April). Individual differences in working memory capacity and enumeration. *Memory and Cognition, 29,* 484-492.

Tyler-Wood, T. L., Mortenson, M., Putney, D., and Cass, M. A. (2000). An effective mathematics and science curriculum option for secondary gifted education. *Roeper Review, 22*, 266-269.

Udall, A. J. (1987). *Peer referral as a process for locating Hispanic students who may be gifted.* Unpublished doctoral dissertation, University of Arizona.

Udall, A. J. and Passe, M. (1993). Gardner-based performance-based assessment notebook. Charlotte, NC: Charlotte-Mechlenburg Schools.

Van Rooy, C., Stough, C., Pipingas, A., Hocking, C., and Silberstein, R. B. (2001, October). Spatial working memory and intelligence biological correlates. *Intelligence, 29*, 275-292.

VanTassel-Baska, J., Johnson, D. T., Hughes, C. E., and Boyce, L. N. (1996). A study of language arts curriculum effectiveness with gifted learners. *Journal of Education for the Gifted, 19*, 461-480.

Wagner, A. D., Schacter, D. L., Rotte, M., Koutstaal, W., Maril, A., Dale, A. M., Rosen, B. R., and Buckner, R. L. (1998, August 21). Building memories: Remembering and forgetting of verbal experiences as predicted by brain activity. *Science, 281*, 1188–1191.

Wakeley, A., Rivera, S., and Langer, J. (2000). Can young infants add or subtract? *Child Development, 71*, 1525-1534.

Webb, J. T. (2000, August 7). *Mis-diagnosis and dual diagnosis of gifted children: Gifted and LD, ADHD, OCD, Oppositional Defiant Disorder.* Paper presented at the annual convention of the American Psychological Association, Washington, DC.

Webster, P. (2000). Reforming secondary music teaching in the new century. *Journal of Secondary Gifted Education, 12*, 17-24.

Westberg, K. L., and Archambault, F. X., Jr. (1997). A multi-site case study of successful classroom practices for high ability students. *Gifted Child Quarterly, 41*, 42-51.

Whalen, J., McCloskey, M., Lesser, R. P., and Gordon, B. (1997). Localizing arithmetic processes in the brain: Evidence from a transient deficit during cortical stimulation. *Journal of Cognitive Neuroscience, 9*, 409-417.

White, D. A. and Breen, M. (1998). Edutainment: Gifted education and the perils of misusing multiple intelligences. *Gifted Child Today, 21,* 12-14, 16-17.

Willard-Holt, C. (1999, May). *Dual exceptionalities.* Arlington, VA: ERIC Clearinghouse on Disabilities and Gifted Education.

Winebrenner, S. (2000, September). Gifted students need an education, too. *Educational Leadership, 58*, 52-55.

Winebrenner, S., and Devlin, B. (2001, March). *Cluster grouping of gifted students: How to provide full-time services on a part-time budget: Update 2001*. Arlington, VA: ERIC Clearinghouse on Disabilities and Gifted Children.

Winner, E. (1996). *Gifted children: Myths and realities*. New York: Basic Books.

Winner, E. (2000). The origins and ends of giftedness. *American Psychologist, 55*, 159-169.

Witelson, S. F., Kigar, D. L., and Harvey, T. (1999, June 19). The exceptional brain of Albert Einstein. *The Lancet, 353*, 2149-2153.

Wynn, K. (1992). Addition and subtraction in human infants. *Nature, 358*, 749-750.

Wynn, K. (1998). Psychological foundations of number: Numerical competence in human infants. *Trends in Cognitive Sciences, 2*, 296-303.

Resources

TEXTS

Assouline, S., Colangelo, N., Lupkowski-Shoplik, A., and Lipscomb, J. (1999). *Iowa acceleration scale manual: A guide for whole-grade acceleration (K-8)*. Scottsdale, AZ: Great Potential Press.

Bireley, M. (1995). *Crossover children: A sourcebook for helping children who are gifted and learning disabled*. Reston, VA: Council for Exceptional Children.

Cline, S., and Schwartz, D. (1999). *Diverse populations of gifted children: Meeting their needs in the regular classroom and beyond*. Upper Saddle River, NJ: Prentice Hall.

Colangelo, N., and Davis, G. A. (Eds.) (1997). *Handbook of gifted education*. Boston: Allyn and Bacon.

Kay, K. (Ed.) (2000). Uniquely gifted: Identifying and meeting the needs of the twice exceptional student. Gilsum, NH: Avocus Publishing.

Rogers, K. B. (2002). Re-forming gifted education: Matching the program to the child. Scottsdale, AZ: Great Potential Press.

Smutny, J. F., Walker, S. Y., and Meckstroth, E. A. (1997). *Teaching young gifted children in the regular classroom: Identifying, nurturing, and challenging ages 4-9*. Minneapolis, MN: Free Spirit Publishing.

Sousa, D. A. (2001a). How the brain learns, (2nd ed.). Thousand Oaks, CA: Corwin Press.

Sternberg, R. J. (1997). *Successful intelligence*. New York: Plume.

Strip, C. A., and Hirsch, G. (2000). Helping gifted children soar: A practical guide for parents and teachers. Scottsdale, AZ: Great Potential Press.

Tomlinson, C. A. (1999). The differentiated classroom: Responding to the needs of all learners. Alexandria, VA: Association for Supervision and Curriculum Development.

Tomlinson, C. A., Kaplan, S. N., Renzulli, J. S., Purcell, J., Leppien, J., and Burns, D. (2002). *The parallel curriculum*. Thousand Oaks, CA: Corwin Press.

Winner, E. (1996). Gifted children: Myths and realities. New York: Basic Books.

ORGANIZATIONS

American Hyperlexia Association
195 West Spangler, Suite B
Elmhurst, Illinois 60126
Tel. (630) 415-2212
Web: www.hyperlexia.org

The Association for the Gifted
Indiana Academy for Science, Mathematics, and Humanities
Ball State University
Muncie, IN 47306-0580
Tel. (765) 285-7455
Web: www.cectag.org

Center for Excellence in Education (Applications of Technology)
Indiana University
201 North Rose Avenue
Bloomington, IN 47405-1006
Tel. (812) 856-8210
Web: http://cee.indiana.edu

Council for Exceptional Children
1110 North Glebe Road, Suite 300
Arlington, VA 22201-5407
Tel. (888) CEC-SPED (888-232-7733)
Web: www.cec.sped.org

Davidson Institute for Talent Development (Resources for Profoundly Gifted Youth)
9665 Gateway Drive, Suite B
Reno, Nevada 89521
Tel. (775) 852-3483
Web: www.davidson-institute.org

ERIC Clearinghouse on Disabilities and Gifted Education
1110 North Glebe Road
Arlington, VA 22201-5704
Tel. 1-800-328-0272
Web: www.ericec.org

The Gifted Child Society
190 Rock Road
Glen Rock, NJ 07452-1736
Tel. (201) 444-6530
Web: www.gifted.org

Gifted Development Center
1452 Marion Street
Denver, CO 80218
Tel. (303) 837-8378
Web: www.gifteddevelopment.com

National Association for Gifted Children
1707 L Street NW, Suite 550
Washington, DC 20036
Tel. (202) 785-4268
Web: www.nagc.org

National Research Center on the Gifted and Talented
University of Connecticut
2131 Hillside Road, Unit 3007
Storrs, CT 06269-3007
Tel. (860) 486-4826
Web: www.gifted.uconn.edu/nrcgt.html

Supporting Emotional Needs of the Gifted
P.O. Box 6550
Scottsdale, AZ 85261
Tel. (206) 498-6744
Web: www.sengifted.org

World Council for Gifted and Talented Children, Inc.
18401 Hiawatha Street
Northridge, CA 91326
Tel. (818) 368-7501
Web: www.worldgifted.org

TALENT SEARCH PROGRAMS

Program	Address and Web Site	Type of Talent Search
Academic Talent Search	California State University 6000 J Street Sacramento, CA 95819-6098 http://edweb.csus.edu/projects/ats	Elementary and middle school students in northern California
Rocky Mountain Talent Search	University of Denver Office of Academic Youth Programs 1981 South University Boulevard Denver, CO 80208 www.du.edu/education/ces/rmts.html	For 6th through 9th graders in Colorado, Nevada, Idaho, Montana, New Mexico, Utah, and Wyoming
Center for Talent Development	Northwestern University 617 Dartmouth Place Evanston, IL 60208-4175 http://ctdnet.acns.nwu.edu	For 3rd to 8th graders in surrounding states
Iowa Talent Search	Iowa State University (OPPTAG) 310 Pearson Hall Ames, IA 50011 www.public.iastate.edu/~opptag_info	For 7th graders in and around Iowa
The Belin-Blank Center for Gifted Education and Talent Development	University of Iowa 210 Lindquist Center Iowa City, IA 52242 www.uiowa.edu/~belinctr	For 4th through 9th graders nationwide

Program	Address and Web Site	Type of Talent Search
Center for Talented Youth	Johns Hopkins University 3400 North Charles Street Baltimore, MD 21218 www.cty.jhu.edu	For 2nd through 8th graders nationwide
Talent Identification Program	Duke University (TIP) Box 90747 Durham, NC 27708 www.tip.duke.edu	Elementary and middle school students nationwide
Carnegie Mellon Institute for Talented Elementary Students	Carnegie Mellon University (C-MITES) 4902 Forbes Avenue, #6261 Pittsburgh, PA 15213-3890 http://www.cmu.edu/cmites	For 3rd through 6th graders in Pennsylvania
Halbert and Nancy Robinson Center for Young Scholars	University of Washington Box 351630 Seattle, WA 98195 http://depts.washington.edu/cscy	For 5th through 8th graders in Washington
Canada: Center for Gifted Education	University of Calgary 170 Education Block 2500 University Drive NW Calgary, Alberta, T2N 1N4, Canada http://www.acs.ucalgary.ca/~gifteduc/talent.html	For 4th, 5th, and 6th graders in Calgary and Edmonton

WEBSITES

This list of websites is just a sampling of the various resources that are available for obtaining information about gifted programs. Some sites offer puzzles, problems, and games for challenging gifted children. The list is by no means complete, but it will serve as a useful starting point for exploring the vast number of resources that are available on the Internet. Nearly all of the websites have hyperlinks to other sites. The website addresses were accurate as of time of publication.

Center for the Improvement of Early Reading Achievement (CIERA)
www.ciera.org

Creative Learning Press
www.creativelearningpress.com

Edward deBono's Official Website
Provides information about his teaching materials and games as well as other resources to enhance creativity and lateral thinking ability. If you are familiar with de Bono's work, you'll find all those resources described here. There are also pre-seminar materials at the deBono Institute. Finding your way around the site is an interesting lateral thinking puzzle in itself.
Web: www.edwdebono.com/

Future Problem Solving Program
www.fpsp.org

HighIQWorld,
Articles and links related to gifted education.
www.s-2000.com/hi-iq/intelligence/gifted_kids.html

Hoagie's Gifted Education Page,
Includes the latest research on parenting and education (including academic acceleration or enrichment, home schooling, traditional programs, the highly gifted, etc.)
Web: www.hoagiesgifted.org

Hollingworth Center for Highly Gifted Children
Web: www.hollingworth.org

International Baccalaureate Organization
Web: www.ibo.org

Mensa Foundation for Gifted Children (MFGC)
Resources for Very Able and Gifted Children
Includes links to:
Support Groups for Very Able and Gifted Children
Advice for Parents and Teachers
Educational Resource Links
Distance Learning and Educational Materials
Web: www.mfgc.org.uk/mfgc/links.html

Mindspring.Com
Includes the latest research on academic acceleration or enrichment, home schooling, traditional programs, the highly gifted.
Web: www.mindspring.com/~mensa/pages

National Conference of Governors' Schools
Web: www.ncogs.org

Odyssey of the Mind
Web: www.odyssey.org

Online Asperger Syndrome Information and Support (O.A.S.I.S.)
Web: www.udel.edu/bkirby/asperger

Portfolio usage suggestions from ERIC
The portfolio and its use: Developmentally appropriate assessment of young children.
Web: www.ed.gov/databases/ERIC_Digests/ed351150.html

Smarter Kids.com
An array of educational books, software and games; fill out the free Learning Style Survey to find out how your child learns best; explore the Parent Resource Center, which includes activities, tips and a collection of SmarterSites, providing materials for Advanced Students.
Web: www.smarterkids.com

Index

Page numbers in **boldface** are **Applications**.

Order These Best-Selling Titles in Brain-Compatible Learning from David A. Sousa

ORDER FORM

riority code: D2815

BILL TO (if different) *Please attach original purchase order.*

☐ Purchase Order #_____

Name:_____

Title:_____

Organization:_____

Address:_____

City:_____State:_____

Zip Code:_____

Telephone
Required: ☐☐☐-☐☐☐-☐☐☐☐

Four EASY WAYS to order!

SHIP TO

Name:_____

Title:_____

Organization:_____

Address:_____

City:_____State:_____

Zip Code:_____

Qty.	Book#	Title	Unit Price	Total Price
	D2815-0-7619-3829-X	How the Gifted Brain Learns	$34.95	
	D2815-0-7619-7851-8	How the Special Needs Brain Learns	$34.95	
	D2815-0-7619-4668-3	How the Special Needs Brain Learns, Video	$99.95	
	D2815-0-7619-7765-1	How the Brain Learns	$39.95	
	D2815-0-7619-4666-7	Como Aprende el Cerebro	$29.95	
	D2815-0-7619-7522-5	Brain-Based Learning, Video	$99.95	

Attach a sheet of paper for additional books ordered. ☐ Please send your latest catalog | **FREE** | **FREE** |

Total Book Order

DISCOUNTS ARE AVAILABLE
for large quantity orders —
CALL (800) 818-7243
and ask for a sales manager.

Prices subject to change without notice.
Professional books may be tax-deductible
Federal ID Number 77-0260369

Sales Tax
Add appropriate sales tax in CA, IL, MA, MD
Add appropriate GST & HST in Canada

Shipping and Handling
$3.50 for first book, $1.00 for each additional book
Canada: $10.00 for first book, $2.00 each additional book

Total Amount Due $
Remit in US dollars

All orders are shipped Ground Parcel.
For other shipping methods and cost, **call (800) 818-7243**

Payment Method

☐ Check #_____ Payable to Corwin Press

CREDIT CARD
☐ VISA   ☐ MasterCard   ☐ DISCOVER   ☐ AMERICAN EXPRESS

Credit Card #:
☐☐☐☐-☐☐☐☐-☐☐☐☐-☐☐☐☐
☐☐/☐☐
month/year
Signature:_____

In case we have questions...

Telephone:☐☐☐-☐☐☐-☐☐☐☐

Fax:☐☐☐-☐☐☐-☐☐☐☐

E-mail:_____

☐ Yes, you may e-mail other Corwin Press offers to me.
Your email address will NOT be released to any third party.